Japan, a Model and a Partner

International Studies in Sociology and Social Anthropology

Editors

Tukumbi Lumumba-Kasongo
Rubin Patterson
Masamichi Sasaki

VOLUME 98

Japan, a Model and a Partner

Views and Issues in African Development

edited by

Seifudein Adem

BRILL
LEIDEN • BOSTON
2006

Formerly published in journal 'African and Asian Studies' AAS Vol. 4, no. 4, 2005.
Special issue: Africa and the Japanese Experience. Guest Editor: Seifudein Adem.

This book is printed on acid-free paper.

Library of Congress Cataloging-in-Publication Data

A C.I.P. record for this book is available from the Library of Congress.

ISSN 0074-8684
ISBN 90 04 15270 9

PRINTED IN THE NETHERLANDS

Contents

Foreword

TUKUMBI LUMUMBA-KASONGO*

I am very grateful that Professor Seifudein Adem of the University of Tsukuba in Japan, (and also at Binghamton University, State University of New York in 2006) enthusiastically and kindly accepted my invitation to be the Guest Editor of the Special Issue of African and Asian Studies of 2005. This is an excellent work that should be used as the foundation for provoking further debates about what specific lessons Africa could learn from the Japanese experience.

Indeed, this is a very valuable publication that deals with specific African and Japanese educational, economic, cultural, social and political experiences in their comprehensiveness in the post-Cold War era, using interdisciplinary and multidisciplinary methodologies and intellectual and analytical perspectives. Taken collectively, this work not only transcends the logic and the principles of Hobbesian classical African-Japanese international relations as articulated by the new realism school of thought in political science, but it also, to a large extent, challenges them. The authors project different meanings of geography, cultures, economic partnerships, and international relations in an era of liberal globalization with its old and new contradictions. While Africa is in search of new paradigms for explaining itself in the world, the theories that should be used as the foundation of its socio-economic and political development, Japan also is gradually diversifying its economic and political relations in a world that embodies many elements of uniformity and universalism within liberal globalization and also particularism and dissimilarity within the quest for multipolarity-based kinds of resistance movements against liberal globalization.

* Wells College; Center for the Study of International Cooperation in Education (CICE), Hiroshima University, Japan; CEPARRED (Pan-African Studies and Research Center in International Relations and Education for Development; *and* Department of City and Regional Planning, Cornell University; and the Editor of African and Asian Studies, Brill.

The arguments developed by many contributors in this book can be appreciated with the logic of Paulo Freire's concept of dialogical relationship. Both Africa and Japan have a lot to learn from one another. They have to foster that consciousness through concrete projects and realizations. They have also a lot to gain from one another, as Africa located ideologically and economically in the Global South needs Japan, and Japan as a nation-state located economically and politically in the Global North and geo-culturally located in Global South needs Africa. The dualism that characterizes Japan as being part of the Global North and also sharing many elements with the Global South is an important factor that should be taken into account in making an assessment of the theories of collective benefits within African and Japanese experiences. This dialogical relationship is founded neither on the forces of nature nor on principles of metaphysics. Thus, the authors are coming from a multiplicity of perspectives such as diplomacy, sociology, political science, history, economics, and public policy to examine their subject matter with critical approaches.

One of my goals in 2005 as part of my responsibility as the Editor of African and Asian Studies was to set up a program through which social scientists could study the achievements, or lack of, in the relationship between Africa and Asia since the Bandung Conference in 1955. Thus, in inviting Professor Adem I wanted to explore the possibility for celebrating the 45th year anniversary of the Bandung Conference through an intellectual event or research project. Although this project focuses on Africa and Japan, the book is part of this celebratory program. It provides a Japanese perspective in projecting the complexity of the relationship between Africa and Asia. The role of Japan in this Afro-Asian coalition is central.

From 18 to 25 April 1955, the Prime Ministers of the group, called five Colombo powers, (namely Burma (Myanmar), Ceylon (Srilanka), Indonesia, India, and Pakistan) organized a meeting in Bandung to discuss the themes and problems of economic cooperation, human rights, and self-determination, the problems of dependent people, and the promotion of peace. The foreign ministers and many delegates from the colonies from Africa and other parts of Asia joined the conference. The conference was well popularized and publicized. It should be noted that in 1955, all the African countries, with the exception of Egypt, Ethiopia, and Liberia were still under the yoke of the European colonialism. Ethiopia was invaded by Italy in 1930. Mussolini's invasion was supported by Japan although Japan had previously good relations with the Ethiopian imperial power. But the Northern Province of Ethiopia, Eritrea was colonized by Italy.

The ideas, spirit, and debates associated with, or originated from, the Bandung conference in 1955 in Indonesia where imperialism was strongly condemned, became actualized in the nonalignment movement (NAM). This is the beginning of Afro-Asian coalition, which led to the articulation of South-South relations. Although the Japanese government was reluctant to send a delegation, finally based on its own interests and persuaded by the United States, Japan sent a representative to this conference not by a foreign minister but by Takasaki Tatsunosuke, Minister of State and Director-General of the Economic Counsel Board. Economic dimension of this Bandung conference became a strong issue in the development of the non-alignment. The non-alignment movement, which was articulated since the 1950s and promoted by the group of 77 in the United Nations by the Afro-Asian bloc, is being revived with the rise of the activism of the World Social Forum.

Japan became a powerful economic entity in the 1960s at a time when most African countries had just gained their political independence. Despite internal contradictions and ambiguous national agenda (or total lack of it at all), most of these African states enveloped their policies with some nationalistic languages and politics and Japan as a new emerging power started to challenge, without much tambours *à la Japonaise* the existing global power relations. As Jun Morikawa stated:

> During this period (1960-75), Japan actualized its dual diplomacy towards White and Black Africa in the context of the intensification of the East-West confrontation in Africa and the rapid economic growth of Japan. The increase in Japan's economic power was confirmed on 28 April 1964, when Japan achieved membership in the 'advanced nations club' when it was admitted as a full member to the Organization for Economic Co-operation and Development (OECD). Only four years later, Japan's gross national product had reached a level surpassed only by the United States and the Soviet Union (1997, p. 55).

As Morikawa continued to argue:

> The Post-Cold War and the post-apartheid era have made African economic development problems and democratization even more important issues, and African expectations of Japan (now the largest aid donor among all the countries of the world) have increased dramatically since the disintegration of the Soviet Union and the emergence of the 'aid fatigue' phenomenon in the United States and Western Europe (1997, p. 3).

As is well known, since the end of the 1970s, Japan has increased its assistance to Sub-Saharan African countries ten times over as it became the top bilateral donor in many African countries. In the 1990s, it also became the second contributor to the African Development Bank from outside the region and the number one contributor to the African Development Fund.

We are now in the era of global negotiations at the end of Cold War politics. Thus, for instance, through the Tokyo International Conference on Africa's Development (TICAD), Japan has formulated a development agenda for Africa, a different kind of partnership. What are its main objectives? What is the content of TICAD? What are its implications in the long run, and who will benefit from it politically, economically, and socially? How is Japan addressing the issues related to the demands for democracy in Africa by both social movements and political parties? How are the African actors perceiving and re-defining Japan's role in the post-Apartheid and post-Cold War Africa?

As I stated early, this is not a book of classical international relations; rather, it is the book on the search for new paradigms. I invite different audiences with various concerns and agendas to read this book critically and comprehensively, and to project the issues raised and the answers suggested by the authors within the global challenges of the call for progressive changes in Africa and rethinking development. The authors have paid attention to small details while giving due consideration to the broad picture. This is the beginning of a broad debate based on empirical research projects that may help us think critically about what Japan can offer to Africa and what Africa can offer to Japan in a pragmatically and historically defined policy framework, and how these offers would shape the national social, political and economic experiences of each milieu. This is an important step in which I sincerely congratulate the Guest Editor, Professor Seifudein Adem and the contributors, for undertaking such a monumental work, which provides a major analytical framework for further policy inquiries in the 21 century.

References

Drifte, Reinhard. *Japan's Foreign Policy for the 21st Century: From Economic Superpower to What Power?* Second Edition, St. Anthony's College, Oxford and New York: St. Martin's Press, 1998.

Morikawa, Jun. *Japan and Africa: Big Business and Diplomacy*, Trenton, NJ and Asmara, Eritrea, Africa World Press, Inc., 1997.

Editor's Introduction

In the summer of 2004 I challenged a score of Japanese, African and American scholars to re-assess why Japan succeeded and Africa failed to modernize. The response was overwhelmingly positive, with those who had the capacity and willingness to say something coming forth with original contributions. We published the collection of the essays in the Special Issue of African and Asian Studies under the theme of 'Africa and the Japanese Experience'. Due to the wider relevance of the issues raised for contemporary Africa as well as the interest already generated, the essays are appearing here in an edited volume in order to stimulate further discussions about African renaissance.

Africa and Japan are seas apart geographically as well as in terms of the level of success in taming nature and organizing their societies. And yet, as the chapters in this book demonstrate, scholars and policy-makers need to grasp and relate the experiences of Japan and Africa not despite such marked separation between the two, but, in fact, because of this very reason. Each chapter scrutinizes Japan's experience in this spirit to deepen our understanding of Africa's developmental challenges, and in the process, stimulate intellectual discussions and policy debates about Africa, and about Africa and Japan.

Past and contemporary experiences of the Western world are frequently summoned by scholars and policy makers, explicitly or implicitly, to highlight what Africa should and shouldn't do to overcome the challenges of modernization. The liberal-capitalist and socialist experiments in post-colonial Africa, both of which failed to bear fruit, could only be seen as a reflection of this fact. While Africa's experiments with the capitalistic model are far from complete, the viability of the model has proved questionable. On the other hand, those who doubted the relevance of the Western experience for Africa's development or disliked it for one reason or another, insisted Africa should go indigenous and look inward rather than outward. In short, the prevailing approach has been either imitative or rejective of the Western model.

Like other societies, Japan was also faced with a common dilemma – the dilemma of whether to imitate the experience of the West or to reject it altogether. While interpretations may vary depending on the level of abstraction employed, it can be argued that the approach the Japanese pursued was neither entirely rejective nor totally imitative of the Western experience. The Japanese used a third path which involved a measure of imitation and rejection of the Western model. Building upon its own, Japan domesticated what it borrowed from outside. It is also arguable that Japan is culturally nearer to Africa more than it is to the West. If so, and if Japan could selectively borrow ideas and institutions from the West and successfully use them in its pursuit of modernization, then, the question is, could Africa also borrow from the Japanese experience for the same purpose? To be sure, this way of looking at the experience of Japan is rather rare in much of the discussions about the challenges Africa has faced. In fact there are only a handful of works to date which closely examine the relevance of Japan's experience to the African condition. This book seeks to make a modest contribution to the filling up of this gap.

However, Africa being what it is, a continent with rich diversity and complex history, no single approach can adequately capture contemporary realities in the continent. Reflecting this fact, Africa and the Japanese experience are analyzed in this book from a variety of angles, a fact also mirrored in the diversity of the background of the contributors. Our purpose is, of course, to provoke discussions rather than to try to offer a definitive solution to the problem.

It is gratifying thus to announce, first and foremost, that the team of contributors to this book include aspiring young scholars as well as experienced academics and analysts: a historian, a diplomat, economists, and political scientists; by place of origin, they are based in or hail from Africa, North America, Asia and Europe. The approaches used to offer insights into the various issues affecting Africa and Japan are informed by the disciplines of history, economics, area studies, comparative politics and international relations. Methodologically, some of the papers are explicitly comparative, others are less so; some tackle specific issues, others are general.

The themes covered range from education, culture, investment, technology policies, TICAD to bilateral relations and the teaching of African history in Japan. Viewed in light of our broader goal, these seemingly discrete issues are interconnected in a mutually supportive way. Even though each contribution highlights different aspects of the same phenomenon, Africa and the Japanese experience in the context of the contending views about and issues in African development, sometimes introducing a new dimension to the discussion, each chapter also reinforces or further clarifies the core arguments in one or another. For the reader's convenience, the chapters have been arranged in such a way that those concerned with Africa and Japan in general will come before those dealing with specific countries or bilateral issues; developmental issues have been placed before somewhat technical and more academic matters. What unites all of them is that each starts from a fresh reassessment of Japan and the African condition and then suggests, implicitly or explicitly, what ought to be done about it.

As indicated above, there have been sometimes excessive preoccupation in Africa and other parts of what used to be the Third World with the Western model, preoccupation which was expressed either by embracing the model or dismissing it altogether. There are, of course, a host of reasons for that. But it is not that there haven't been scholarly works which appeared periodically about the Japanese experience, specially by Western scholars. To me, however, many of these works were limited in scope and aspiration as their authors (understandably) sought to define Japan to their own (Western) audience and dwelt narrowly on what the West could learn from one or another aspect of the Japanese experience. Only a handful of them dealt with issues pertaining to the relevance of the Japanese experience to the modernization effort underway in the developing world.

There were exceptions, of course. One such exceptional scholar is the distinguished economist E. Wayne Nafziger, whose 1995 book, *Learning from the Japanese*, was an inspiration and eye-opener for many of us. We are fortunate to have a chapter in this book by Nafziger himself in which he squeezes out from his many years of research on Japan what he thinks are some of the useful lessons for Africa. Nafziger focuses on Meiji Japan's capital formation and technology practices and addresses whether the model used by Meiji modernizers is useful for contemporary Africa or the circumstances in Africa today necessitate a modification of the model. Nafziger's analysis elucidates what Africa ought to learn and unlearn from the development experience of Meiji Japan.

Following that, Shinsuke Horiuchi offers insights about arguably one of the major post Cold-War foreign policy initiatives of Japan – the Tokyo International Conference on Africa's Development (TICAD) process in relation to the overall features, functions and limitations of such conferences. He also examines how distinct each TICAD conference has been from one another and assesses what have come out of them. Deeply involved as Horiuchi himself is in the TICAD project, his analysis provides important factual information and analytic reflection about the process in addition to his views on how to make more effective use of such arrangements.

There were and still are less than a handful African students and scholars as well as other Africanists who had the privilege to observe the Japanese society and study its experience from a close-range. One explanation for this is the linguistic barrier, the Japanese language, a tool without which it is nearly impossible to systematically observe the Japanese society, let alone scrutinize the extensive written records of Japanese intellectuals and observers. Geographic distance, if not necessarily cultural distance, between Japan and Africa also reduced the close interactions between the two peoples.

Geographic bias, as some people put it, also exist in Japan which is generally unfavorable to Africa and the Africans, and is reflected both in the realm of Japan's diplomacy and academia. Of course, there are all kinds of biases in Japan, as elsewhere, regarding people from other lands. Even so, rightly or wrongly, it seems Japanese see a set of hierarchy virtually in everything, including the degree of prejudice to which foreigners should be subjected to, a degree which is largely a function of the extent, in their eyes, to which those people have or have not achieved material progress. Although all foreigners are unequal (to the Japanese) some are more unequal than others. Having not achieved much in material terms, Africa and Africans are placed in the lowest echelon of hierarchy in the Japanese worldview, and as such Africa has not commanded the intellectual interest and diplomatic attention of the Japanese in comparison to the other regions. This is in spite of all the worthy things Japan does for Africa in the spirit of international cooperation.

In his informed and constructive critique of Japan's foreign policy towards Africa after the Cold War, Jun Morikawa draws upon his extensive and intimate knowledge of Japan' foreign policy and on his profound understanding of African issues to outline for us some of these biases as reflected in Japan's diplomacy in recent years. Morikawa prefaces his analysis with a concise review of the history of Japan-Africa relations in the Cold War period. With a particular emphasis on the interactions between Japan and Apartheid South Africa, Morikawa also contends that just as with Japan's history in Asia, there is within Japan a syndrome of not facing Japan's history in Africa. In addition, Morikawa focuses on TICAD and delves deeper into what it is and what it is not and then offers some specific, if tentative, suggestions for fixing what he regards as the major structural problems in Japan's diplomacy towards Africa.

While Nafziger draws upon his wide-ranging knowledge about economic history of Japan and of issues of economic development and relate it to Africa in general, Getachew Felleke zooms on one specific place and issue area to investigate the matter more closely. From his unique position as a Western-educated, African-born educator in Japan, Getachew singles out Ethiopia, which, like Japan, has a long history and was also never colonized – except for a brief occupation by Italy. Going beyond these similarities, important as they are, he then focuses on the educational strategies pursued by both countries in the early 19th century and examines the variable outcomes of these strategies which were rewarding in the case of Japan's modernization but were of little consequence, in the long term, in the case of Ethiopia. Getachew asks why this was so, why early investment in education in Japan was able to pay off whereas it failed to deliver on its promise of progress in Ethiopia. Getachew suspects that the crucial difference lies in the educational strategies used, and, to see if historical evidence bears him out, he comparatively examines the evolution of educational strategies in the two countries, also in light of the role played in the process by such factors as geography and level of receptivity to imported system of education in both societies.

Kweku Ampiah, one of the leading experts on Japan's bilateral relations with major countries in Africa, examines what he sees as a fledgling relationship between Nigeria and Japan. Ampiah assesses the bilateral relations between the two countries over the recent years, seeks to detect outstanding patterns, and suggests directions the relations are likely to take in the future. Ampiah underscores that there have been marked improvements in the bilateral relations between Japan and Nigeria, especially after Olusegon Obasanjo was elected president of Nigeria. After empirically supporting his argument and examining the factors which enabled the improvements and their expressions, Ampiah speculates on the nature of issues which would likely affect how the 'special' relationship is likely to develop in the future.

Toyomu Masaki, a young Japanese scholar and the only female contributor to this volume, begins by asking why Malaysia and Cote d'Ivore, two countries that were at a roughly similar level of economic development until 1980, are so different today. Focusing on the role of Japanese investment in Malaysia's industrialization, she argues that the difference can be accounted for, in part, by Japan's huge investment in Malaysia, a move which was driven by self-interest. The effect of the investment was positive both for Japan and Malaysia. Masaki goes on to suggest that it will be of mutual benefit likewise for Africa and Japan to increase the volume of FDI in Africa, given an improved investment climate for doing so in the latter.

The general absence or obscurity of Africa in the Japanese academia is another reflection of the so-called geographic bias against Africa in Japan. Not that there are no Japanese Africanists in Japan; there are many of them indeed who are passionately involved in African issues, and a long-standing academic society too, which is concerned solely with African issues. But few Japanese Africanists specialize in issues which are really consequential to Africa's political and economic development. Rare indeed are studies by Japanese scholars which focus on modernization of Africa, or its failure to modernize. The question thus becomes, why do Japanese scholars shy away from such subjects?

It is not that Japanese-Africanist scholars are unconcerned about the African condition. Neither is it that Japanese scholars have no views about what went wrong in Africa. One reason seems to pertain to the fact that many, or perhaps even most, of Japanese Africanists are not well versed with the major European or African languages, a situation which seems to have induced a general lack of interest in getting deeply involved in matters which they learn only through second hand translations. This is not to deny that some important works do appear about Africa in Japanese and for the Japanese. But whatever the original merits of these works, they are rarely discussed outside the narrow circle of the specialists.

Another reason why Africa does not feature as much as one would wish and expect in the Japanese academia might have to do with the tendency of the Japanese scholar to avoid thorny issues, those which may involve the taking of sides sometimes in opposition to Japan's mainstream scholarship or the policies of the government. The extent of the compatibility of academic outputs with official policies is sometimes specially taken seriously because of the government's significant influence over education and research institutions of higher education in the country. It remains to be seen if the recent reform of Japanese national universities, which transformed them effectively to semi-private corporations, would have a significant effect. But the signs are not very promising. In any case, many Japanese Africanists are either completely detached from issues which really matter to Africa or are merely policy intellectuals, restricting their task primarily to a *post facto* explanation or rationalization of the policies of the Japanese government.

John Edward Philips probes into what he sees as one form of academic bias in Japan, a bias based on misconceptions about African history in the mainstream scholarship about Africa. John Philips argues the teaching of African history is underdeveloped, even distorted; and then he explores possible explanations for this state of affairs. As a long-term participant observer and partial insider of Japan, Philips's analysis and observations provide a rare glance at one segment of Africanist scholarship in Japan. Philips concludes that quantitative and qualitative improvement in the teaching of African history is beneficial for a better understanding of Africa's past and for a more meaningful and lasting friendship between Africa and Japan in the future.

Analysts are divided to this date as to the main catalyst of Japan's successful modernization. Or to put it more precisely, different observers see different factors as having played more or less prominent role in Japan's rapid modernization. Some see domestic factors as having played more decisive role in the transformation; others consider external factors in a similar light. When we break down the internal factors, analysts are further divided on which elements of domestic variables were more important, some saying that enduring cultural attributes of the society were more crucial. For others, it was the relatively more transient variables such as the role of government and policy-makers that were more important. And so forth. Seifudein Adem subscribes to the view that culture was more important, for the governmental policies themselves were able to bear fruit, and indeed they were initiated, not in a vacuum but within a specific cultural context. A related issue is of course the question of whether and to what extent Japanese culture had changed in the process. On this, two major schools of thought can be identified. One claims Japan's culture has significantly changed as a result of the nation's modernization; for another school, it hasn't changed much or the change was only superficial. After closely examining both suppositions and the assumptions on which they are based, Adem argues that Japanese culture has not changed much and that Japan was able to modernize because of its culture and not in spite of it. Based on such interpretation, the author formulates some broad ideas such as that Africa ought to consider indigenizing modernity just like Japan had done, rather than dismantling indigenous values in the name of accommodating the putative pre-requisites of modernity.

Seifudein Adem

Meiji Japan as a Model for Africa's Economic Development

E. WAYNE NAFZIGER

ABSTRACT

This paper examines the major ways in which the economic development model of Meiji Japan, 1868-1912, applies to contemporary Africa. The focus is on capital formation and technology policies that contributed to Meiji Japan's rapid industrial capitalist growth: self-directed strategies, technological borrowing, taking advantage of shifts in comparative advantage from the product cycle, educational policy, business assistance, financial institutions, transfer of agricultural savings to industry, low wages policy, industrial dualistic complementarity, and foreign-exchange rate policies conducive to export expansion. For each of these policies, the author analyzes the extent to which African countries can emulate Meiji Japan's approaches or whether changing circumstances require modification of the Japanese model.

Japan, whose 1868 level of economic development was only slightly more than other Afro-Asian countries, has had the world's fastest growth in real GDP per capita since then. Japan restored the Meiji emperor during its early modern period, 1868-1912. During this period, among 33 countries for which we have estimates, Japan ranked among the top one-fourth in per-capita income growth (Maddison 2001, who uses 1870-1913 figures).

Africa's GDP per capita was lower in the 1990s than it was at the end of the 1960s (World Bank 2000: 1). Africa's per-capita GDP ($PPP) is the lowest in the world. Moreover, reversing the global trend, life expectancy in Africa has recently declined to the level of 1975, 46 years (Japan's 44 in 1895), primarily because of the high adult prevalence of HIV/AIDS.

Although the Tokugawa shoguns isolated Japan from foreign influence from 1638 to the 1860s, they provided a more favorable legacy for capitalist development than Africa's today. Mid-19th-century feudal Japan had a literacy rate as high as England's, well developed transport and tax systems, a commercialized agriculture whose productivity per hectare exceeded Africa today, and guild and clan-monopoly workshops producing silk textiles, *sake*, cotton cloth, and processed products for Edo (Tokyo), Osaka, and Kyoto (Nakamura 1983; Lockwood 1954: 4).

According to Maddison (2000: 264), Africa's GDP per capita ($PPP) is comparable to that of 1912 Japan. I examine lessons from the Meiji Development Model (MDM) for contemporary Africa. The focus is on capital formation and technology policies that contributed to Meiji's rapid industrial capitalist growth. I consider the extent to which African countries can emulate Meiji's approaches or whether changing circumstances require modification of the MDM.

I. Self-Directed Development

Despite unequal treaties with the West from 1858 to 1899, Japan had substantial economic autonomy compared to Africa, either colonized or subject to informal imperial economic controls. Japan partially circumvented the West's 5-percent limit for tariff protection through tax rebates, subsidies, government purchase contracts, and state enterprises. Furthermore, Meiji was committed to economic and military development, promulgating joint-stock organization and freedom of enterprise. The Act of 1872 established a national emphasis on scientific and technological education, rather than skills for the junior civil service like schools in the late-19th- and early 20th-century European colonies in Africa. Unlike colonial Africa, Japan virtually banned foreign investment between 1868 and 1899 (except coal mining and shipbuilding, 1870-72), hiring thousands of foreigners to adapt and improve technology under ministry (or local business) direction. The Meiji government invested in infrastructure – telegraphs, postal service, water supply, coastal shipping, ports, harbors, bridges, lighthouses, river improvements, railways, electricity, gas, and technical research. In the last quarter of the 19th century, Japan organized a banking system (the Bank of Japan, semiofficial development banks, and locally run private banks), expanded bank credit for government or private investment, regulated banks, and stabilized the currency. In contrast, even as late as the 1950s, the British and French colonial governments in Africa interfered little in private-dominated banks, whose power was only slowly eroded after independence. Nor did Meiji thwart industrial exports and import substitution, as in early 20th-century Nigeria.

Meiji, in contrast, helped domestic business find export opportunities, exhibit products, borrow abroad, establish trading companies, and set marketing standards.

Meiji's experience indicates the advantage of domestic political and economic control, which contrasts to Africa, subject to European domination from the late 19th century through independence, and neocolonial dependence subsequently. Since 1980, OECD countries, the major shareholders of the international financial institutions (IFIs), the World Bank and the International Monetary Fund, have found new ways to retain its economic suzerainty in Africa. Commercial banks, OECD governments, and the World Bank rely on an IMF "seal of approval" for stabilization programs (usually contingent on the borrower's reducing demand) before arranging adjustment loans and debt writeoffs for Africa. Requiring this approval leaves Africa's stagnant economies little room to maneuver. In reality international policy enforcement is cartelized, with OECD governments, especially the U.S., the European Union, and Japan, largely determining policy through their control of the IFIs. Moreover, Africa is highly dependent on OECD countries for inputs, markets, aid, and capital.

II. Borrowing and Modifying Foreign Technology

Does the MDM provide lessons for borrowing by contemporary Africa? To maintain political independence, Meiji adopted "enriching the nation to strengthen the army," a goal requiring adopting Western technology. But since Meiji could not rely on foreign aid, government and private firms paid the full cost of foreign technical expertise. This cost, together with introducing universal primary education and compulsory adult male military service, caused a financial strain. From 1868 to 1892, the central government directed technological transfer by spending 1.5 percent of its expenditures for foreign employees, and 0.4 percent to send more than 4,000 students and government officials for training and education abroad. The Ministry of Industry, which invested in heavy and chemical industries, mining, and infrastructure, employed 1,000 foreign experts, advisors, and teachers from 1870 to 1885. The Ministry of Home Affairs hired 250 foreigners from 1873 to 1895 to establish agricultural experiment stations to introduce Western farming methods and model factories transferring technology to industry. Also the Ministry of Finance used 125 foreign experts to help establish a modern monetary system and corporate business organization. Other ministries and public enterprises hired 5,000 and the private sector 12,500 foreigners during 1870-99 (Inukai 1981: 79-85).

Japan learned a lesson in the 1870s that Africa has still not learned or learned only recently: that importing Western replicas may fail if the local country lacks capital, foreign exchange, and skills. Meiji modified foreign techniques – substituting hand-powered machines in silk reeling and wood for iron in Jacquard weaving machines – to save capital. Japan's 1884 (*Kogyo Iken*) Ten-year Plan advocated projects conforming to local conditions and capital, urging improvement engineering by upgrading artisan production rather than importing Western replicas (*ibid.*, pp. 85-95; Nakamura 1983: 70).

In agriculture, in the early 1880s, two Germans at the Komaba School of Agriculture advised that the small Japanese farms should rely on biological and chemical, not Western mechanical, innovations. In 1885, the Ministry of Agriculture and Commerce used foreign farm scientists to develop technology for small farms and local soil, and sent veteran farmers and Japanese agricultural graduates to diffuse the best seed varieties then used locally. For most of Africa, with high worker-land ratios, the Meiji biochemical emphasis is more sensible than the capital-intensive approaches of the U.S. and Canada.

Meiji introduced agricultural innovations, such as better seed varieties (a rice Green Revolution in 1911), improved irrigation and seedling beds, and plowing deeper to increase labor per hectare (Inukai 1981: 86-87; Hayami 1975; Ishikawa 1981: 18, 32). Africa's agriculture crisis, declining food output per person in the last 40 years, resulted from the neglect of agriculture and exploitation of peasants by governing elites, whose policies included the disincentives of price ceilings, the socialist ideology (Ghana, Tanzania, Mozambique, Zimbabwe collective or statist policies ensuing from holding peasants in contempt), an emphasis on mechanized large-scale farming, and an incompetent political leadership and bureaucracy (Ayittey 2005).

In government training schools and private industrial firms, foreign experts were often unsuitable, importing techniques regardless of their relevance to Japan. In the raw silk industry, imported equipment was too costly, too mechanically sophisticated, and inconsistent with inadequate storage facilities for the perishable cocoon. In flood control, Dutch experts introduced a system used in Holland where floodwater rises from sea level, overlooking Japan's floodwater coming down the mountains. Repeated failures of Dutch technology convinced the Japanese government to change control measures. By the last two decades of the 19th century, the Japanese questioned foreign industrial and flood control experts in light of differing local conditions (Inukai 1981: 85-88).

Meiji hired foreign experts directly and restricted foreign direct investment (FDI). Although the immediate cost of limiting investment was substantial, Japan avoided restrictions on the transfer of technology, continuing technical dependence on foreign sources, and foreign concentration, that much of Africa faces today. Meiji learned by the 1880s that foreign technology had to be adapted and modified.

During Meiji, labor was relatively more abundant in Japan than in the developed countries (DCs). Accordingly, Japan frequently substituted more appropriate labor-intensive technology for the "best-practice" techniques available from the West.

Following are major patterns of Meiji's appropriate technology:

(1) Emphasizing the production of more labor-intensive goods such as raw silk, silk, and cotton textiles.
(2) Labor-intensive adaptation to simplify production. Silk-reeling equipment in 1875 consisted of a blacksmith-made steam boiler, ceramic cocoon boiling and silk-reeling kettles, and a locally built frame. Additionally, many Japanese manufacturers bought used machinery in good condition from the West. The cotton textile industry used two shifts, and substituted labor in peripheral processes. Furthermore, ancillary activities, such as transport and machine repair, were done cheaply by small firms using simple, labor-intensive processes.
(3) Using manual labor instead of Western ancillary equipment in coal and mineral mines.
(4) Adoption of technology used earlier in the West.
(5) Adaptation of foreign technology to industries catering to the indigenous market, including traditional soybean sauce and indigenous dyeing houses. As these enterprises learned through experience, many learned the technology needed to export.
(6) Substituting labor-intensive techniques to produce goods of lower quality and performance than imports, such as bicycles (Ishikawa 1981: 355-87. Nafziger 2005: Ch. 11).

Meiji Japan imitated, borrowed from, and modified approaches from the West. A question today is: Can Africa be as successful emulating and adapting DC innovations?

Contemporary Africa has to be more cautious than Meiji in importing capital and technology. Since Africa is even more technologically backward relative to DCs than Meiji was to the West, it may be more difficult for Africa to adapt technology to indigenous production. For example, foreign textile technologies available to Meiji were labor-using while most technologies for Africa today are labor-saving.

Africa is less likely to directly control experts transferring technology than Meiji did. Finally, contemporary Africa is more likely to face unalterable capital-labor ratios and pursue factor-price distortions than Meiji (Nafziger 2005).

African planning officers should rely more on government ministries, local research institutions, and chambers of commerce and industry for technological analysis. Nationals need to prepare adjustment programs. Africa must, as Meiji, direct its development to capture technological learning gains.

III. Product Cycle and Global Production Networks

Comparative advantage may be based on a technological advantage, perhaps an innovation such as a new product or production process that gives the country a temporary monopoly in the world market until other countries imitate (Schumpeter 1961). The product-cycle model states that a good that requires highly skilled labor later, with standardization, can be mass-produced by LDCs with less skilled labor. Britain and the U.S., 1868-1939, had a comparative advantage in non-standardized goods, while Meiji and less-advanced economies had a comparative advantage in standardized goods (Vernon 1966: 190-207).

England specialized in cotton textiles from the mid-18th to late 19th centuries. In the 1880s and 1890s, Japan substituted indigenous production with British machines for imports from Britain. By 1921-39, Japan's had a comparative advantage in textiles, invading English and Western markets. In the 1960s, Japan imported cotton textiles from South Korea, Taiwan, Hong Kong, and Singapore, many of which used Japanese investment and technology to compete even in Japan. While China combined existing technology and cheap labor to expand textile exports for the last 40 years, Africa has gained little from this phase.

Contemporary Africa cannot compete as Meiji did, with imitation and low-level innovation. As real aid to less-developed countries (LDCs) fell during the 1990s and 21st century, FDI shares increased, comprising 74 percent of 2002 resource flows to LDCs (UNCTAD 2003: 4). The World Bank (1997: 2) states: "Participation in the global production networks [GPN] established by multinational enterprises provides developing countries with new means to enhance their economic performance by accessing global know-how and expanding their integration into world markets."

A major explanation for LDC manufacturing export expansion is reduced protection on GPN-industry inputs and resources, allowing LDCs to climb the value-added ladder. Low-income countries (LICs) expand low technology exports and middle-income countries' (MICs') technology-intensive exports (World Bank 2004: 65-73).

Might LDCs' increased manufacturing exports reflect only the increasing value-added steps?. No. Indeed, each LICs and MICs groupings have a higher percentage of value added in industry than DCs do (World Bank 2003: 41-47, 189-92).

Much international trade and FDI has shifted from the exchange of consumer goods to the production and exchange of parts and components, blurring the nationality of products. In 1998, the U.S. comprised only 37 percent of its car's value added (World Bank 2003: 55; World Bank 2004: 66-69), in contrast to Henry Ford's 1921 assembly-line produced Model T and the U.S. factory of the 1950s. GPNs, organized by multinational corporations (MNCs), with LDCs participating in lower value-added steps, expanded rapidly the last quarter of the 20th century. The share of imported to total intermediate inputs in manufacturing in DCs and their value added from imported inputs as a share of exports increased substantially from the 1970s to the 1990s (World Bank 2003: 56).

Technological progress in transport, communications, electronics, and data processing has increased GPNs and FDI. Cheaper and faster telephone, fax, internet, cargo connections, and improved data analysis, using electronic interchange, have facilitated GPNs. Lower tariffs also contributed to increased imported intermediate inputs to total sales of U.S. affiliates (World Bank 2003: 57-58).

Since the late 1980s and early 1990s, MNCs increased international outsourcing, offshoring services (especially in information and communications technology or ICT), importing components from low-cost sources abroad, and exporting to overseas processors. In 1998, almost half of ICT imports by OECD countries were from non-OECD countries, primarily in Asia (OECD 2000; Nafziger 2005: Chapter 11). U.S., Japanese, other OECD, and even South African firms have organized GPNs utilizing LICs in a new division of labor. Trans-Pacific or Asian borderless economies may be organized like flying-geese, with technically advanced economies in the lead; newly industrializing countries (NICs) specializing in sophisticated R&D- and technology-intensive industries; and LICs undertaking less sophisticated, labor-intensive, low value-added assembly. However, recently countries such as India and China have climbed the ladder toward providing the skills and organization for late-stage processing in global ICT.

Tropical Africa, with its poor investment climate, has not participated in these GPNs. Although FDI is not a panacea, improved institutions and infrastructure, good governance, sound macroeconomic policies, and investment incentives would increase Africa's benefit from globalized production.

IV. Education

Africa's 2002 literacy rate was 46 percent, a rate Japan reached during the late 19th century. Japan's primary enrollment rate, 28.1 percent in 1873, reached virtually 100 percent by 1911. Furthermore, the state expanded primary and vocational education and stressed scientific and technical education during Meiji, when Europeans in Africa were educating elites mostly for government service (Yasuba and Dhiravegin 1985: 26-27). Starting with a common language, Meiji developed uniform primary education that fostered national unity and sped acquiring Western ideas and technologies. Today Africa's primary enrollment rate is 60 percent (UNDP 2003: 121).

The emphasis on "Japanese spirit and western technology" meant that Meiji education stressed subservience to superiors and the state, superiority to other Asians, and acquiring Western technologies but not human dignity or learning the method for developing science (Munakata 1965: 540-59). The Meiji experience reinforces studies indicating a high rate of return to African investment in primary, science, and vocational education but provides no model for countries using education to promote democracy, human rights, and female equality.

V. An Indigenous Capitalist Class

Political revolutions in Western Europe in the 17th and 18th centuries reduced the power of the church and landed aristocracy so that industrial and commercial capitalists took much of this power. Since most African countries, like Meiji, do not have strong capitalist-class leadership, can they look to Meiji's "guided capitalism" as a model?

Following the fall of the shogun, 1860 to 1868, Meiji was controlled primarily by lower-ranking samurai, not merchants and industrial capitalists. From 1870 to 1885, this government owned and operated factories and mines, many expropriated from the shogunate and feudal lords (Shishido 1983: 259). Throughout the late 19th century, the Meiji regime comprised half the investment outside agriculture, including mines, construction, engineering, cement, soap, and chemical industries, as well as infrastructure, shipbuilding, iron and steel, other heavy industries, and arms factories to strengthen the military. After private-sector skills improved, government profits proved meager, and the state needed funds for armaments, it sold most industrial properties, often at bargain prices, to private businessmen, many samurai. Additionally, in 1876, the state strained public credit to commute the pensions of 400,000 feudal lords and samurai to cash and bonds, and to pay off debts owed to relatively privileged merchants and moneylenders (such as the House of Mitsui) who had financed the 1867-68 coup. The more enterprising recipients used these funds for new industrial enterprise. Moreover, the state aided private industry through a laissez-faire labor policy (low wages and child labor), low taxes on business enterprise and high incomes, a favorable legal climate, destruction of economic barriers between fiefs, lucrative purchase contracts, tax rebates, loans, and subsidies. For example, the government imported spindle-spinning machines, 1878-79, to sell on lenient credit terms to private enterprise in textiles. From these state-assisted entrepreneurs came the zaibatsu, frugal and able financial combines that dominated industry and banking and contributed to high income inequality.

Both Meiji and contemporary Africa have favored existing elites in privatization. The IFIs and bilateral donors insisted on abrupt privatization, which created a concentrated business, similar to early Japan. However, in other ways, Meiji's policies differed substantially from that of contemporary privatization. Meiji Japan provided more aid to small industrialists. Moreover, Japan's privatization was initiated by the state whereas privatization in much of Africa was thrust on it by IFI- and creditor-initiated adjustment programs. Thus, emerging private enterprise in Meiji was virtually all indigenous, whereas the World Bank insisted that Africa open investment to foreign private enterprise. For example, Nigeria, under two World Bank structural adjustment programs (SALs), 1986-88 and 1989-91, not only sold equity in public enterprises to private investors but allowed foreign investors in most manufacturing, large trade, and petroleum sectors. Foreign investors are major contributors to high industrial concentration and factor-price distortions.

Perhaps as many as one-fourth of the farmers in the late Tokugawa and early Meiji managed second businesses such as small bars, rapeseed oil selling, lumber vending, eating-house management, bean curd making, confection making, tobacco selling, sundry shopkeeping, carpentry, and plastering. Landlords were fertilizer merchants, pawnbrokers, moneylenders, doctors, dry goods merchants, and brewers of *sake*, soy sauce, and bean paste. Furthermore, many merchants became landlords (Nakamura 1983: 51). By contrast, African landowners and wealthy farmers rarely invest in industry. African landlords value consumption and real estate expenditure highly, and lack experience in coordinating a production process with specialized work tasks and machinery and in overseeing secondary labor relations.

Many economists, noting the disproportionate samurai representation among early Meiji businesses, stress the spirit of the community-centered samurai entrepreneur, sacrificing for national economic progress (Hirschmeier 1964; Ranis 1955: 80-98). But Yamamura's evidence (1968: 148-58) indicates that samurai status in early Meiji was blurred, as many from peasant and merchant families purchased this status during the late Tokugawa period. The major force to establish banks and factories came from merchants and landlords motivated by profit, not longstanding samurai motivated by nationalism.

The MDM provides an alternative to the Soviet approach for accumulating capital where there is no strong bourgeoisie. Yet Meiji's selling state-owned industrial properties to private firms contributed to high industrial concentration, high income inequalities, and slow growth of an independent middle class. Moreover, today populist pressures prevent most African political elites from pursuing the low-wage policies, unrestricted labor rules, low welfare spending, and large subsidies that Meiji used to foster capitalist development. Furthermore, few African societies have the Japanese community reciprocal obligation that reduces the destructive power of capitalism.

Yet Meiji's bourgeoisie, though weaker than that the West's, were more experienced in large commercial ventures, and were not as far behind DCs as Africa today. The Japanese capitalist class was capable of responding to government policies to encourage private industry. Furthermore, Meiji's bureaucracy had the vision to plan programs to abet entrepreneurs. Ironically, while the weakness of the African bourgeoisie indicates the need for skilled government intervention and planning to spur entrepreneurship and capital accumulation in industry, few African bureaucracies have the capability and probity to facilitate these in the private sector or manage these in the public sector.

In contrast to Meiji, most African states are soft states, in which the authorities that decide policies rarely enforce them and reluctantly place obligations on people. These states are dependent on buying political support through concessions to powerful interest groups. Regime survival in Africa requires the support of business people, professionals, executives, high-ranking military officers, civil servants, and commercial farmers through policies that frequently sacrifice growth, income distribution, external balance, and the development of indigenous skills.

VI. Financial Institutions

Meiji created Japan's financial system through conscious selective adaptation of features of the American, British, French, and German systems but virtually no foreign ownership or management. In comparison, European colonials, through foreign ownership and management, owned and organized tropical Africa's financial system.

In contrast to Africa, Meiji's currency and credit institutions through the mid-1890s were "supply-leading," created in advance of demands for industrial loans and financial services, and private savings deposits. In 1872, the government set up national banks, and in 1876 allowed commercial banks. Throughout the rest of the century, Meiji undertook financial reforms and provided banks and funding for industrial development.

The private banks' high ratio of currency issues to specie and the government banks' liberal lending contributed to rapid inflation, 1876-81, reducing peasant and former military real incomes, and increasing capitalist speculative profits, thus forming capital accumulation for industrialists.

Still Finance Minister Matsukata Masayoshi created a central Bank of Japan in 1882 to limit paper currency, levied new consumption taxes, restrained lending except to export industries accumulating specie, and balanced the government budget, bringing about more stable expectations among investors (Takeda 1965: 432-36).

All in all, the new financial institutions standardized the currency, integrated the national market, and channeled savings into industry. By 1897, Japan's credit standing had improved so it could borrow in foreign capital markets. With few exceptions, the money supply grew rapidly from 1880 to 1940, accommodating rapid though fluctuating growth rates, but virtually avoiding recessions with negative growth (Lockwood 1954: 14; Nakamura 1983: 8-9, 60-61).

The rapid growth of Japan's banking and credit institutions indicates the advantage of self-directed financial development. However, Meiji, in her drive for national economic and military power, tolerated growing financial concentration, a growth pathology that Africa has not avoided.

VII. Transfer of Agricultural Surplus

Many economists advocate relying on an agricultural surplus for industrial capital for a NIC since, as in Meiji and today's Africa, agriculture usually contributes more to an LDC's GDP than any other sector. Agricultural surplus refers to an excess of savings over investment, an amount transferred (through taxes and private savings) to industry.

Meiji's centralized government replaced the feudal landed gentry (*daimyo*) with smaller, village landlords who had purchased their land. The village landlords, who were often farmers themselves during early Meiji, frequently improved productive methods (Dore 1965: 487-93).

The Meiji bureaucrats imposed an 1873 land tax to squeeze capital from agriculture, partly through moderate inflation redistributing resources to finance state and private industries. In 1873, the land tax comprised 94 percent of central government revenue, appropriating one-third of the total crop, nearly as much as the feudal lord under the shogun (Lockwood 1954). The land tax provided more than 80 percent of government revenue through 1882 and contributed to net resource outflows from agriculture to government through 1922 (Ohkawa, Shimizu, and Takamatsu 1982: 10). Landlords used tenant rents to accumulate capital for industries such as brewing, pawnbroking, retail shops, and village moneylending (*ibid.*, pp. 11-12). Meiji Japan has probably relied more on using agricultural savings for initial industrial capital formation than any other present DC, unless you include the Soviet Union, where the collectivization of the 1930s accumulated capital from agriculture.

The land tax had little effect on farm output. The owner, unable to shift the tax to middlemen or consumers, could only shift the incidence to a tenant without alternative employment. The high and regressive land taxes, required in cash, the growing burden of other taxes (1890-1910), and high rents reduced farm disposable income, especially among tenants and peasants, who faced heavy debts, frequent bankruptcies, and abject poverty.

Other countries may find it difficult politically to extract agricultural surplus through land taxes. Few African states have enough rural political tolerance to squeeze agriculture in excess of existing agriculture-industry transfers.

Japan's agricultural growth relied heavily on research by local scientists (assisted by foreign experts), biochemical innovations, and extension by veteran farmers and Japanese agricultural graduates to diffuse the best seed varieties used to highly literate farmers. Despite the land tax, farm technical progress was fast, contributing to the rapid annual percentage growths of 1.8 in agriculture and 2.0 in farm productivity per worker, 1880-1920, that facilitated substantial transfer to industry (Ohkawa and Shinohara 1979: 86; Hayami 1975: 228). The agricultural surplus in most African countries is too small and growing too slowly for industry to exploit without severe political costs.

Africa needs a thriving agriculture to produce food and raw materials for other sectors. Should we not discourage the following African policies to transfer the agricultural surplus to industry: (1) food price ceilings and industrial price floors to raise industry/farm prices, (2) concentration of government investment in industry, (3) tax incentives and subsidies to pioneering firms only in industry, (4) setting below-market prices for foreign currency, reducing domestic currency from agricultural exports but lowering the price of foreign capital and inputs to large industry, (5) tariff and quota protection for industry, raising prices to farmers, and (6) spending for education, training, housing, plumbing, nutrition, medical care, and transport in urban rather than rural areas. These urban-bias policies have contributed to agricultural disincentives and high rates of rural poverty and undernourishment in Africa (Nafziger 2005: Chapter 7).

These disincentives are perhaps as great as those that threatened rural rebellion in Meiji Japan. African rural poverty is probably no less than those in Meiji. Additionally, rural populist pressures in Africa today are politically more destabilizing than peasant pressures in 1870s' Meiji Japan.

While this analysis, similar to the IMF's, indicates that price controls and exchange-rate misalignments have contributed to external crises in Africa, I reject the IMF policy of immediately freeing markets and contracting spending to resolve the disequilibrium. After 1981, the IMF emphasized shock treatment for demand restraint in LICs, rarely provided financing for external adjustments, and cut programs from three years to one year, applying Reaganomics internationally. One year is not enough for adjustment. Demand restrictions, inflation deceleration, and currency depreciation do not switch expenditures to exports and import substitutes or expand primary production quickly enough to reduce inflation and trade deficits much. Studies indicate that even in DCs (such as the U.S., 1985-88), the current-account improvement from devaluation takes about two to five years, usually beginning with a worsening trade balance in the first year. The time for adjustment results from lags between changes in relative international prices and responses in quantities traded. Lags include time for decision, delivery, replacement, and production (Grubel 1981: 349-88). Even after 1988, despite increased emphasis on SALs and long-term sectoral change, Africa still faces unrealistically short adjustment times, resulting in severe economic disruption and excessive hardship for the poor.

The IMF has stressed devaluation and foreign-exchange decontrols to improve the trade balance, increase domestic agricultural prices, and reduce shortages of foreign inputs, along with market interest rates to improve capital allocation. African states complain that IFI adjustment programs fail to consider market imperfections. However, government frequently creates market imperfections through financial repression, interest-rate ceilings, foreign exchange controls, high reserve requirements, and restrictions on private capital markets to increase resource flow to the public sector without higher taxes, inflation, or interest rates. Yet although government helped to create these market imperfections, the state cannot immediately decontrol all prices and liberalize foreign exchange and capital markets. Although devaluation raises import prices, the demand for foreign exchange may not be restrained, as relaxing foreign-exchange restrictions spurs foreign input use and may increases short-run capital flight. Indeed, substantial devaluation may generate hyperinflation, as the domestic currency experiences an irreversible free fall (Zambia in 1985-87).

The effect of devaluation (say, from C90 = $1 to C228 = $1) on the trade balance depends on demand and supply elasticities, low in African agriculture, especially for one to two years. The elasticity of demand for primary products like beverages and sugar is so low that increasing agricultural exports to undertake IFI-sponsored adjustment might result in reduced revenues. On the supply side, African farmers have little short-run (one year or less) but substantial long-run elasticity (0.3-0.9) for cash crops, as farmers allocate labor and land to commercial output, subsistence, black markets, nonfarm work, or leisure. In Tanzania, supply response would be at least a year or two for cotton and tobacco and 5-6 years for tree crops such as coffee, tea, cashews, and sisal. Cost-induced inflation from devaluation (from economic interests fighting to maintain consumption shares) should reduce output expansion. Inadequate infrastructure, such as poor transport for Ghanaian cocoa, limits supply increases, slowing export response to higher cedi prices per dollar price of cocoa. Indeed, most African countries remove balance-of-payments deficits quickly not from expenditure switching from exchange-rate changes but from reduced import demand from a fall in real income. Still, Africa no longer opposes devaluation but wants more control on its size, timing, structure, and accompanying policies (*ibid.*; Godfrey 1985: 32; Chhibber 1989: 56; Campbell and Stein 1992: 20-22).

VIII. Low Industrial Wages

During Meiji, agricultural unskilled *real* wages remained at subsistence. Unlike LFR models, the marginal productivity of labor (MP_L) was positive, though less than the wage (Minami 1973: 200), since the village supplied subsistence to those with a MP_L below it. As in LFR, employers in the formal industrial sector paid a premium (say 30 percent) to compensate for such as migration and psychological costs of city life. This premium remained low partly because much of industry's wage labor – female, second and third sons, or off-farm part-time – merely supplemented household income (Shinohara 1970: 342-44). But subsistence rose over time as the minimum maintenance level expected by society increased. The relatively stable agricultural (and thus industrial) real wages can be attributed partly to increased productivity in agriculture (and cheap food from colonies after 1911) which enabled the industrial sector to buy food without declining terms of trade. These low real industrial wages increased industrial profits, business savings, and labor-intensive manufacturing export competitiveness.

Over a normal range, where product and labor demand increases gradually, labor supply elasticities were high (though not infinite as in LFR), benefiting from vast reserves in the rural and informal sectors (Minami 1973). But the 1915-19 war-induced increase in demand for industrial products and labor was too much to be satisfied by the elastic portion of the labor supply curve.

Developing Japan's labor supply grew slower than contemporary Africa's. Late 19th-century Japan's birth rate, 22 per 1,000, kept down by farmland shortages, extended-family dissolution, and high literacy, was lower than Africa's 38 per 1,000 (2004), while Meiji's death rate, 18 per 1,000, was higher than Africa's 14 per 1,000, lowered, despite the recent AIDS pandemic, by access to the nutritional, medical, health, and production techniques of the past century. Meiji's annual labor growth never exceeded 1 percent. In contrast, Africa's yearly labor force growth was 1.9 percent in the 1960s, 3.0 percent in the 1970s, 3.2 percent in both 1980s and 1990s, and 3.0 percent in the early 21st century. Yet Meiji's density of farm population per cultivated hectare of land (higher than India and Africa today) put pressure on the nonagricultural sector. But Japan's annual industrial employment growth rate, 1878-1914, was 3.9 percent of the total labor force, compared to contemporary Africa's 0.4 to 0.7 percent. While contemporary Africa absorbs only 13-23 percent of the increased labor force, Japanese industry at the turn of the 20th century absorbed 4.5-5.0 times the labor increase. Crucial in Japan's absorption was slower population growth and labor-intensive industrialization, spurred by government's low-wage and appropriate technology policies, but *not* a faster annual industrial growth rate than Africa (Tachi and Okazaki 1965: 497-515; Nafziger 2005, chapters 8 and 9).

While Africa faces labor surpluses today from rapid population growth and slow industrial employment demand growth, these surpluses are more likely to be reflected in urban unemployment instead of low wages, because of political pressures for minimum wages, labor union strength, factor-price distortions, unsuitable capital-intensive technologies, unrealistic job aspirations by graduates, bias toward urban amenities, and wage pressures from food price rises.

Meiji had faster food output growth and more stable food prices than contemporary Africa, mainly because of rapid farm technical progress. African food supply problems often result from urban bias in investment and amenities, agricultural price disincentives, and bureaucratic mismanagement in supplying farm inputs. African food demand has risen fast, because of high income elasticities of demand for food from rapid population growth.

Amid a large urban wage premium, the flood of urban immigrants is restrained only by high open urban unemployment rates, which keep down *expected* urban wages (wages times the probability of employment as in Harris-Todaro 1970: 126-42) but not actual urban wages. The LFR model's unlimited long-run supply of labor to the industrial sector, roughly valid in Meiji Japan, is replaced by relatively high wages in Africa today, reducing industrial profits and savings.

IX. Industrial Dualism

In this section, I do not focus on peasant agriculture-modern industry dualism but on dualism within industry. Meiji did not stress large leaps to advanced industrial technology but step by step improvements in technology and capital as ministries, regions, industries, firms, and work units learn by doing. In early Meiji, this meant technical and management assistance and credit facilities to improve and increase the scale of small workshops, handicraft producers, and cottage industry left from before 1868, causing less social disruption, as small industry's environment was not alien. The 1884 plan emphasized improving traditional technology through applied science and favored postponing massive foreign large-scale factory transplantation until traditional enterprises could utilize new techniques (Inukai 1979: 5). Meiji's factory enterprises developed faster but were less destructive of cottage and workshop industry than Africa's.

Large industry evolved, after state assistance and two wars (1894-95 and 1904-05), into zaibatsu concentration by 1910, but small industry, encouraged by government to take cooperative action, was retained, even in the leading manufacturing industry, textiles.

Many African countries use training, extension, credit, and industrial-estate programs to encourage small-scale manufacturing. But few contemporary African countries have had a small-scale manufacturing sector as well developed as Meiji. Many African states, trying to modernize, have emphasized capital-intensive technology representing the most advanced state of arts in DCs, allowing small industry to decline (see Nafziger 2005: Chapter 11 on appropriate technology). Africa has not stressed gradual technical improvement and learning from experience among existing ministries and industries, together with dissemination of technology consistent with local factor endowment and culture. Creating small industry from scratch is not as effective as maintaining and upgrading small industry from earlier development. Once small industry has been disrupted or destroyed, it is difficult to reconstruct.

To be sure, the technological gap between LDCs and DCs is greater today than during Meiji. But contemporary Africa still has many alternatives to best-practice capital-intensive techniques.

X. Export Expansion and Import Substitution

From 1868 to World War II, the Japanese had a policy (first forced and later chosen) of multilateral, nondiscriminatory foreign trade outside their empire (1904-1945). This trade policy contributed to rapid growth, although it would be a mistake to regard Japan's drive for foreign markets as the motor force of her industrialization.

Meiji was more open to international trade than contemporary Africa. Although foreign trade was modest by Western standards during Meiji's first 25 years, its influences stimulated technological learning. The large domestic market usually absorbed most products of this new technology. Subsequently, as the Japanese mastered and modified innovations, they began exporting, as with textiles, the leading export, 1874 to 1940; and other light manufactures such as consumer goods and simple machines that replaced primary-product exports in second place at the turn of the 20th century.

Unlike contemporary Africa, Meiji did not discriminate against exports. Increased tariff protection in the first quarter of the 20th century reduced the price of foreign exchange, but government export promotion through a bank to finance trade, exhibiting Japanese products overseas, sales bureaus abroad, chambers of commerce and commodity guilds for cooperative export activity, merchant-marine subsidies, and business privilege in the new empire (Lockwood 1954: 531) brought export inducements near that of an equilibrium exchange rate through 1913. Japan's annual real average growth rate in exports was 8.4 percent from 1880 to 1913 (compared to 3.2 percent for the world as a whole, 2.6 percent for Britain, and 4.2 percent for the U.S.), a comparatively faster rate that continued from 1913 and 1937. Today many African LDCs overvalue their domestic currency relative to foreign currency, discouraging domestic producers from exporting and substituting imports unless protected by massive subsidies.

Meiji's exports also benefited from favorable international economic conditions. In 1868-97, the yen chronically depreciated vis-à-vis the U.S. dollar. In 1882-1897 the yen was on a de facto silver standard, as silver declined relative to gold, enabling Meiji to avoid a substantial trade deficit despite military expenses during wars in the late period.

Given Africa's lack of GPN participation, today's international economic conditions are not as favorable to African export expansion. The most rapidly expanding African manufactured exports during the last 30 to 40 years have been textiles, clothing, footwear, and simple consumer goods requiring labor-intensive technology widely available. But the competition from other aspiring newly industrial exporting countries, especially China, is more severe than it was for Meiji Japan.

A single country, such as Meiji Japan, exporting agricultural and light manufacturing goods, would often be a price taker with substantial scope in expanding export receipts alongside a long-run elastic supply curve. However, today a single-country analysis suffers from a fallacy of composition: What is true of the individual case is not necessarily true of numerous African LICs under pressure from IFI adjustment programs to expand primary-product exports. Africa is caught in an export trap, since as it expands export supply, the terms of trade fall, reducing export purchasing power during most of the last quarter of the 20th century. DCs' high effective rate of protection also blocks technologically feasible primary-product processing and light industry, tightening the export noose that blocks export expansion as an engine of growth for Africa. Widespread currency devaluation under IFI adjustment also spurs export expansion in primary products, suggesting that the export trap may be the impulse supporting African resistance to devaluation (Nafziger 2005).

XI. Conclusion

How applicable is the MDM to present-day Africa? First, although Meiji indicates the advantages of self-directed development, many small African countries are limited in reducing dependence on DC trade and capital movements. But the MDM does underline the importance of African governments controlling the employment of DC personnel introducing technology. This is especially important since the technological distance between today's DCs and Africa is large, making it less likely that foreign experts will adapt technology to local conditions and indigenous production without African direction. Second, as goods become more standardized and as value-added steps are outsourced, Africa has the opportunity to increase its specialization at the bottom of the product cycle, with reduced protection, improved macroeconomic policy and institutions, and incentives for investment. Third, Meiji Japan's emphasis on primary, vocational, and scientific education provides a model for contemporary African countries except in the promotion of democracy and human rights. Fourth Meiji-type "guided capitalism" is limited in Africa today, because of a rent-seeking political elite, inadequate government capability to spur private business, populist opposition to pro-business policies, and high income inequality between business people and others. Fifth, Japanese economic history demonstrates the importance of a government role in creating and regulating financial institutions, without tolerating growing concentration of private financial institutions. Sixth, many African countries, like Meiji Japan, have tried to transfer large amounts of agricultural income to industry for investment capital but, like Japan, some have sacrificed rural incomes and nutritional levels, and spurred agrarian discontent. Seventh, high labor supply elasticities resulting from vast reserves from the agricultural and informal industrial sectors, together with low industrial wage premiums, kept Meiji (but not African) unskilled industrial wage rates relatively low, increasing business profits and reducing urban unemployment. Eighth, Meiji exemplifies the importance of improving capital and technology step by step, utilizing existing small industry, rather than making substantial leaps to the most advanced technologies available. Ninth, although today's international economic conditions are less favorable to Africa than those of Meiji, Africa could still benefit from the Japanese approach of using international competition and market-clearing exchange rates to spur rapid export expansion.

While contemporary Africa can learn useful lessons from the MDM, these lessons are limited because of Meiji Japan's historically specific conditions, and because some aspects of the Meiji approach that spurred rapid economic growth contributed to pathologies, such as zaibatsu concentration, income inequality, labor union repression, militarism, and imperialism. In the seven decades before the end of World War II, the indenturing of young workers by parents, the increased tenancy rates and greater tenure insecurity, the slums in major cities, the serious environmental noise and pollution problems, the cost of soldiers and civilians killed, crippled, and disabled under imperialism, the torture and imprisonment of opponents to the regime, the suffering of colonial peoples in Taiwan and Korea, the suffering of adversaries during World War II, the independence of the military command from cabinet control, the rampant militarism in the 1930s, and authoritarianism were connected to an economic strategy emphasizing low wages, a stronger military, samurai subsidies, zaibatsu facilitation, capital transfer from agriculture, little spending on social welfare, and the neglect of human rights (Halliday 1975; and Dower 1975). These pathologies were not reduced until military defeat was followed by the democratic reforms of an occupational government, a series of events not to be recommended, nor likely to improve income equality, accelerate economic growth, and democratize the political economy in Africa as it did in Japan. Today's Africa cannot wholly adopt the Meiji model but must select components piecemeal, such as self-directed development planning, technological adaptation, scientific and practical education, state role in infrastructure and human capital investment, labor-intensive industrial export expansion, improving capital and engineering step by step, and learning by doing.

References

AYITTEY, GEORGE B.N.
2005 *Africa Unchained: The Blueprint for Africa's Future.* New York: Palgrave Macmillan.

CAMPBELL, HORACE AND HOWARD STEIN, eds.
1992 *Tanzania and the IMF: The Dynamics of Liberalization.* Boulder, Colo.: Westview.

CHHIBBER, AJAY
1989 "The Aggregate Supply Response: A Survey." In Simon Commander, ed. *Structural Adjustment and Agriculture: Theory and Practice in Africa and Latin America.* London: Overseas Development Institute, pp. 48-62.

DORE, RONALD P.
1959 *Land Reform in Japan.* London: Oxford University Press.

DOWER, JOHN W., ed.
1975 *Origins of the Modern Japanese State: Selected Writings of E.H. Norman.* New York: Pantheon.

GODFREY, MARTIN
1985 "Trade and Exchange Rate Policy in Sub-Saharan Africa." *IDS Bulletin* 16(3): 31-38.

GRUBEL, HERBERT G.
1981 *International Economics.* Homewood, Ill.: Irwin.

HALLIDAY, JON
1975 *A Political History of Japanese Capitalism.* New York: Pantheon.

HARRIS, JOHN R. AND MICHAEL P. TODARO
1970 "Migration, Unemployment, and Development: A Two-sector Analysis." *American Economic Review* 60(1): 126-42.

HAYAMI, YUJIRO
1975 *A Century of Agricultural Growth in Japan: Its Relevance to Asian Development.* Tokyo: University of Tokyo Press.

HIRSCHMEIER, JOHANNES
1964 *The Origins of Entrepreneurship in Meiji Japan.* Cambridge, Mass.: Harvard University Press.

INUKAI, ICHIROU
1979 "The Kogyo Iken: Japan's Ten Year Plan, 1884." *Kyoto Sangyo University Economic and Business Review* (May): pp. 1-100.
1981 "Experience in Transfer of Technology from the West: Lessons from False Starts." In Haruo Nagamine, ed. *Nation-building and Regional Development: The Japanese Experience.* Hong Kong: Maruzen Asia.

ISHIKAWA, SHIGERU
1981 *Essays on Technology, Employment, and Institutions in Economic Development: Comparative Asian Experience.* Tokyo: Kinokuniya.

LOCKWOOD, WILLIAM W.
1954 *The Economic Development of Japan: Growth and Structural Change, 1868-1938.* Princeton: Princeton University Press.

MADDISON, ANGUS
1970, 2001 *The World Economy: A Millennial Perspective.* Paris: Development Centre of the OECD.

MINAMI, RYOSHIN
1973 *The Turning Point in Economic Development: Japan's Experience.* Tokyo: Kinokuniya.

MUNAKATA, SEIYA
1965 "The Course and Problems of National Education." *Developing Economies* 3 (December): 540-59.
NAFZIGER, E. WAYNE
1995 *Learning from the Japanese: Japan's Pre-War Development and the Third World.* Armonk, NY: M.E. Sharpe.
2005 *Economic Development.* 4th ed. New York: Cambridge University Press.
TAKAFUSA, NAKAMURA
1983 *Economic Growth in Prewar Japan.* Trans. Robert A. Feldman. New Haven: Yale University Press.
ORGANIZATION FOR ECONOMIC COOPERATION AND DEVELOPMENT (OECD)
2000 *OECD Information Technology Outlook 2000.* Paris: OECD.
OHKAWA, KAZUSHI, YUTAKA SHIMIZU, AND NOBUKIYO TAKAMATSU
1982 "'Agricultural Surplus' in Japan's Case: Implication for Various Possible Patterns in the Initial Phase of Development." International Development Center of Japan Working Paper No. 19, March.
OHKAWA, KAZUSHI AND MIYOHEI SHINOHARA, eds
1979 *Patterns of Japanese Economic Development: A Quantitative Appraisal.* New Haven, CT: Yale University Press.
RANIS, GUSTAV
1955 "The Community-centered Entrepreneur in Japanese Development." *Explorations in Entrepreneurial History*, 8(2) 80-98.
SCHUMPETER, JOSEPH A.
1961 *The Theory of Economic Development.* Cambridge, Mass.: Harvard University Press.
SHINOHARA, MIYOHEI
1970 *Structural Changes in Japan's Economic Development.* Tokyo: Kinokuniya.
SHISHIDO, TOSHIO
1983 "Japanese Industrial Development and Policies for Science and Technology." *Science* 219 (January 21): 259-64.
TACHI, MINORU TACHI AND YOICHI OKAZAKI
1965 "Economic Development and Population Growth – with Special Reference to Southeast Asia." *Developing Economies* 3(4) (December): 497-515.
TAKEDA, TAKAO
1965 "The Financial Policy of the Meiji Government." *Developing Economies* 3 (December): 427-49.
UNITED NATIONS CONFERENCE ON TRADE AND DEVELOPMENT (UNCTAD)
2003 *World Investment Report 2003.* New York: United Nations.
UNITED NATIONS DEVELOPMENT PROGRAM (UNDP)
2003 *The Human Development Report 2003.* Oxford: Oxford University Press.
VERNON, RAYMOND
1966 "International Investment and International Trade in the Product Cycle." *Quarterly Journal of Economics* 2(2): 190-207.
WORLD BANK
1997 *Global Economic Prospects and the Developing Countries 1997.* Washington, D.C.: World Bank.
2000 *Can Africa Claim the 21st Century?* Washington, D.C.: World Bank.
2003 *Global Economic Prospects and the Developing Countries 2003.* Washington, D.C.: World Bank.

2004 *Global Economic Prospects and the Developing Countries 2004*. Washington, D.C.: World Bank.

YAMAMURA, KOZO

1968 "A Re-examination of Entrepreneurship in Meiji Japan (1868-1912)." *Economic History Review* 21 (February): 148-58.

YASUBA, YASUKICHI AND LIKHIT DHIRAVEGIN

1985 "Initial Conditions, Institutional Changes, Policy and their Consequences: Siam and Japan, 1850-1914." In Kazushi Ohkawa and Gustav Ranis, eds. *Japan and the Developing Countries: A Comparative Analysis*. (Oxford: Basil Blackwell), pp. 19-34.

TICAD after 10 Years: A Preliminary Assessment and Proposals for the Future*

SHINSUKE HORIUCHI

ABSTRACT

Ten years have passed since the first Tokyo International Conference on African Development (TICAD) was held in 1993. Since then, TICAD II, III, and Ministerial Level Meetings followed with each meeting producing either internationally agreed upon documents or action plans. There are many similar initiatives for development of African countries. In fact, cynics in and out of Africa castigate TICAD and other international initiatives as waste of time and energy because they have not been associated with any useful and concrete projects and the overall growth of Africa. This paper sets out to assess positive contributions that have been made by international initiatives including TICAD. The premise of this paper is that we are all in the game of globalization and development of Africa is a sub-game of globalization. Any game is played by the rules. Functions of international conferences for development could be defined in terms of setting development rules, guiding strategies and providing opportunities to build capacity for development. The paper examines what TICAD has offered to African countries as well as international community over ten years within this simple framework of analysis.

* Based on a paper presented at the United Nations University Workshop, Tokyo, Japan, 2004.

Framework of Analysis

TICAD I (the first Tokyo Conference for African Development) was held in 1993 and, commemorating its 10th anniversary, four co-organizers – Japan, the United Nations (UNDP, UNSAA), the Global Coalition for Africa and the World Bank – held TICAD III in 2003. This paper is intended to assess the role of TICAD in African development. Various approaches could be devised to assess the contribution of the TICAD process. For example, it could be evaluated in terms of the results of the projects or funds pledged at the TICAD meetings. TICAD II set a number of numerical goals in many areas such as education and literacy; achievements in these areas could be compared to the numerical goals. At the outset of TICAD I and throughout the TICAD-related meetings it was made clear that TICAD was not a pledging conference but a developmental framework or a catalyst for African development. What does that mean?

There are many international conferences related to African development, including TICAD, and the issues on the agenda are often quite similar. What are the purposes of these international conferences? What role do these international conferences play in international relations?

Sovereign countries or groups of countries such as the EU employ varied diplomatic means in order to realize their visions, values, ideals, and national interests or to maximize the interests of the ruling power, enterprises and other interest groups. Each country carries its own constraints, namely complex domestic political and economic issues. Let us call these continuing activities to achieve certain objectives a "game". We are all familiar with the fact that at the diplomatic as well as the domestic level, various games are being simultaneously played. A game can be a "plus sum", "minus sum" or "zero sum" game. War might be the ultimate minus sum game, but even in war there are rules of the game to be followed. Whether they are faithfully observed or not is beside the point. An international conference is one scene in the games among countries. All issues on the table are examined and discussed many times within and outside a country.

As long as it is a game, there is a winner and a loser. In a simplified scheme, the probability of being a winner is high for the one who invented the rules of the game to his advantage. The history of trade disputes demonstrates clearly this supposition. (1) In other words, the one who has power or influence over setting rules probably wins. A country that has the "power" to decide the rules will be the winner with a high probability. (2) Under the same rules, however, the side who devises the better game strategy may win. A country that develops better strategies or plans for development, i.e., a country that has ample ability to formulate creative policies may succeed. (3) In addition, the side having the better capacity to play the game could win. A country that has the better ability to fight, i.e., a country with three branches of government efficiently functioning, may win.

Let me hasten to add that there are many international conferences with only participants from the private sector. In fact, many international rules or standards related to electronics, ICT and others are decided by the private sector. In this paper, though, let me refer only to officially sponsored conferences. Furthermore, the players do not always decide on rules, and an international norm prevailing at any given time could be the rule.

Let me compare the functions of international conferences to the first three elements of games.

The first function is to formulate rules or to adjust rules to changing conditions. At international conferences, the participating countries negotiate rules to gain advantages. This may include reassurance or reaffirmation of existing rules. Promising or pledging certain actions according to rules could be included in this function.

The second function is to provide information and knowledge for formulating strategies and priority sequences of actions. Let us take a set of economic policies as an example. Even if the economic policies are well thought out, the expected results cannot be attained if the sequence of their implementation is not right. An international conference can be a forum where participants are able to obtain necessary information.

The third function is to learn or to empower institutional capacity. Although the strategy for economic development could be excellent, success is unlikely if a country does not have the institutional capacity to effectively implement it. If a central bank has a shortage of competent staff and organization, monetary policy cannot be effectively executed. International conferences, especially those designed for learning and exchanging technical knowledge and experiences, serve as fora that can contribute to raising the institutional capacity of participating organizations.

The fourth function is to build up environments or conditions for alternative rules. One may call this the function of advocacy. There are many conferences where information is exchanged that lead eventually to changes in the rules. During the 70's and 80's, many conferences were held on debt issues, for example. No single conference changed the rules on debt issues, but they all help create the international environment for subsequent changes in debt management.

Globalization and the African "Development Game"

During the Cold War, the West and the East decided the rules of the game of African development. (1) They used military and economic assistance in order to bring as many countries as possible under their political influence. The super-powers were little concerned about the internal politics in African countries. Assistance was given on the basis of political support, regardless of the legitimacy of the governments, even to dictatorships that neglected human rights and kleptocracies featuring rampant corruption. (2) Africans did not decide these rules, i.e., there was no participation by Africa. (3) A handful of African political elites took advantage of these rules to maximize their personal gains and to maintain their political power. The consequences of such political choices were political confusion and economic deterioration in many African countries.

After the Cold War the name of the game became globalization, and no country can escape its influence. A few powerful developed countries dominate international politics and economics. The development game in Africa is a sub-game of globalization. What are the rules of globalization? President Bush put it very clearly in the National Security Strategy of the United States of America, September 2002. They are freedom, democracy and free market economics. The central interests of the game for developed countries are economic prosperity and the maintenance of peace. The major rules are democratization, liberal market economics, respect for human rights, and the rule of law; there are many more specific rules, but the developed countries predominantly determine all of them. African countries have a very limited voice in deciding even the rules of the sub-game of African development. As for economic reform in Africa, the broad rules are demonstrated in the Policy Framework Paper (PFP), Structural Adjustment Policies (SAP), Poverty Reduction Strategy Paper (PRSP); the more specific rules are loan conditionalities by the World Bank and the IMF. Simplifying somewhat, the Washington Consensus or the Post Washington Consensus have provided main frameworks for the rules, which are based on the neo-classical economics of the developed countries and on the protection of the interests of large corporations and various vested interest groups in developed countries.

Neglected African Initiatives

Africans and African intellectuals did not lack initiatives to navigate their own developmental path. From the early part of the 70s, efforts were made by Africans to formulate their own framework for development based on their own analysis. In 1976 the ECA (Economic Commission for Africa) prepared a Revised Framework of Principles for Implementation of a New International Order. It revolved around four principles: self-help efforts, independent sustainability, democratization of the development process, and the reduction of poverty and unemployment. This provided a theoretical background for successive initiatives. Five important initiatives were released: 1) The Lagos Plan of Action for the Economic Development of Africa, 1980-2000 and the Final Act of Lagos (1980), 2) Africa's Priority Programme for Economic Recovery 1986-1990 (APPER), which later became the United Nations Programme of Action for Africa's Economic Recovery and Development (UN-PAAERD) (1986), 3) The African Alternative Framework to Structural Adjustment Programme for Socio-Economic Recovery and Transformation (AAF-SAP) (1989), 4) The African Charter for Popular Participation for Development (1990), and 5) The United Nations New Agenda for the Development of Africa in the 1990s (UN-NADAF. 1991). However, these failed to become focal points for the international community. Donors, the World Bank and IMF did not support them. In other words, donors rejected the rules for the African development game formulated by Africans. Political leaders in Africa who held power also did not want to change the system because it allows them to maintain power, which equates to wealth.

TICAD I: African Ownership and Asia-Africa cooperation

TICAD I was held in 1993. Let us call to mind the situation the world was in at that time, shortly after the end of the Cold War. Military confrontations were disappearing from view, and a wave of optimism swept the world as expectations of a "peace dividend" grew. The attention of the donor nations of the West was focused on Eastern Europe and the former Soviet Union. Africa's "lost decade" of the 1980s had caused these donors to feel a sort of despairing aid fatigue, and their concern was further reduced by the fact that the geopolitical interests in Africa created by the East-West confrontation were no longer operative. Responding to press interviews, the heads of both the UK and the US delegations to TICAD I stated that their countries were not contemplating any increases in assistance to Africa. The conference succeeded in refocusing international attention on African development and reached a broad consensus on the direction of this development, as expressed in the Tokyo Declaration on African Development. In short TICAD I was able to demonstrate the fourth function of international conferences: reintroducing the African development game, which might have lost its relative importance within the process of globalization.

The Tokyo Declaration on African Development is a rather short document consisting of 35 paragraphs. On political reform it focuses especially on democratization, the respect of human rights, and good governance. On economic reform it emphasizes diversification and liberalization of economic activities, poverty reduction and improved general welfare by means of increased employment opportunities and expanded social services. In short, continuation of structural adjustment policies is the main strategy. The priority areas are the private sector, foreign direct investment and infrastructure. ODA is given a secondary role to private investment, and private foreign investment in Africa is encouraged to diversify exports and to expand access to the world market. Developed countries are requested to formulate a comprehensive strategy incorporating ODA, trade and debt reduction. So far as the development strategy was concerned, it did not go beyond the Washington Consensus.

There were two distinctive features in TICAD I. The first was the introduction of expression and the concept of development partners and African ownership in the development process. Paragraph 5 of the Tokyo Declaration states that "political, economic and social reforms must be initiated and carried out by African countries themselves, based on their visions, values and individual socio-economic background." The specific term "ownership" is not used in the Tokyo Declaration, but "self-reliance" is urged in African development. Development partners are requested "to support African initiatives in political and economic reforms". In his speech Mr. Matsuura, Assistant Foreign Minister used the term "ownership" in the sense of "the attitude of taking charge of one's affairs and assuming responsibility for the consequences". Both democratization and free market economies are rules imposed on Africans by donors. Let me hasten to add that there is nothing wrong with these rules and Africans share their values, but they are not rules formulated by Africans. African development must be undertaken in accordance with rules formulated by Africans, and developed countries should support those efforts as development partners. The concept of "ownership" is a new one for the international community, and it has raised a significant issue on the rules of African development. This is a forceful suggestion of change in the rules of the sub-game of African development. TICAD I displayed the fourth function here.

The second feature was the promotion of cooperation that applies the experience of Asian countries to Africa's development. Paragraph 24 of the Tokyo Declaration specifically lists seven policy measures that Asian countries have followed. The rapid development experienced in East and Southeast Asia could provide some lessons for Africans to apply. This could be taken an additional strategy. This, then, is the second function of international conferences.

In concluding the discussion on TICAD I, I would like to raise four points that were not touched on adequately in the Tokyo Declaration. First, agricultural development was only mentioned in connection with environmental and population issues. In spite of the facts that the majority of Africa's population resides in rural areas and that agriculture is the backbone of the economy, measures for promotion of agriculture have not been undertaken. It seems that a specific strategy for agricultural development should have been suggested in TICAD I.

Second, there is the basic issue of the economic dependency of the African economy on developed economies; little effort has been shown by developed countries to correct the situation. One aspect of dependency is the idea that the larger the ODA or inputs, the larger the output or growth. The experiences of the 80s and the 90s witnessed no linear relation between inputs and outputs. Developed economies find that the present economic structure of African countries as exporters of primary goods suits them. Officials, multi-national enterprises, and interest groups in developed countries have made no single policy decision to that effect, but the accumulation of hundreds of decisions by them maintain the present economic structure, which has failed to reduce poverty in Africa. Nevertheless, political leaders on both sides seem to find benefit in it.

Third, it is not enough to encourage political reforms. The power structure that distributes resources arbitrarily is the root cause of corruption, poor governance and slow progress in reforms. A new set of rules that tackles the power structure itself must be proposed. Conferences like TICAD do not carry any legally binding force and consequently can present proposals that all participants cannot agree on. The fourth function of advocacy for a change of rules can play a useful role in a case like this.

Fourth, Africa is urged to diversify exports, but African countries remain suppliers of primary goods. Under the structural adjustment policies, the liberalization of trade and the repeal of various regulations were undertaken. Cheap goods from Asia chased domestic producers out of their own markets, and African manufactured goods are not able to penetrate the markets of developed countries, which are protected by tariffs, non-tariff barriers and subsidies. The trade rules of developed countries are impediments to what they advocate: free trade. This point should be presented more forcefully.

TICAD II: Proactive role of the state

TICAD II was held in 1998. The year 1994 offered a bright hope but also revealed the dark side of Africa. That year saw the start of a new government headed by President Nelson Mandela in South Africa and the genocide in Rwanda. Unlike TICAD I, global interest in aid and development for Africa was by then on the rise. In Asia, meanwhile, the currency and financial crises of 1997 dealt a devastating blow to the region's emerging economies. Massive packages of financial assistance for hard-hit Asian countries created in some quarters the fear that they would have to cut back on funding for Africa. Such fears were put to rest, however, by Tokyo's commitments at TICAD II. Unintentionally TICAD II played out the fourth function of international conferences.

After three preparatory meetings in Africa and long and intensive discussions at TICAD II, the Tokyo Agenda for Action (TAA) was adopted. The co-chairs statement says, "The Tokyo Agenda for Action is intended to guide concrete policy implementation by African countries and their partners for African development toward the 21st century". Paragraph 9 of the TAA states that "the 1995 Cairo Agenda for Action defines the economic and social development priorities for Africa as determined by Africa itself and the TICAD II initiative supports these priorities. Ownership is derived when development priorities, as set by Africa, are pursued." TICAD II had the overriding goals of economic growth and poverty reduction. The agreed goals and priority actions are in the areas of 1) social development (education, health and population, measures to assist the poor), 2) economic development (private sector development, industrial development, agricultural development, external debts), and 3) foundations for development (good governance, conflict prevention and post-conflict development). For each subject, actions for African countries and their developmental partners are spelled out. In other words, TAA proposes rules and strategies for African development under the African ownership. This is the point of departure of TICAD II from other initiatives. Although TAA proposes that the private sector should be allowed to do what it does better, this is not defined and the emphasis is placed on the role of the state in economic growth.

The state is asked to take more positive actions in every area of activities. TAA recommends, among other measures, mobilization of resources that can be obtained by the rationalization of public investments, the creation of employment opportunities, improvements in income distribution, the revitalization of rural communities, the improvement of public expenditures, and the expansion of social services, especially safety nets. This is a significant departure from the rules advocated by the liberal economics. These proposals are exact enumerations of Asian experiences and represent shifts from the standardized structural adjustment policies. The fourth function and also the second function of international conferences are demonstrated.

In TAA, unlike at TICAD I, agricultural development is discussed in detail as an important policy priority in the reduction of poverty. It is proper to pay attention to small holders and agricultural households headed by women rather than large-scale commercial agriculture. Efforts in support of small irrigation facilities, access to rural markets, rural infrastructure, extension services, and improved quality of rural life are emphasized. These are not new proposals and have been recommended many times by FAO and IFAD, but they were not converted into working measures by African governments. Continued attention on agriculture in TICAD II may induce more attention by African governments; if so, it will be a demonstration of the fourth function.

Democratization, good governance, and conflict resolution were the rules repeated at many international conferences. At the time of TICAD II some improvements in political conditions were observed, but political reforms were not able yet to correct the concentration of power in the hands of a few, weak legislatures, a lack of checks and balances in governments, and widespread corruption. TAA requested strongly that governments reaffirm their commitment to improvements in democratic elections, strengthen the capacity of the legislature and judiciary, prevent corruption, devolve power, and restructure the civil service. It also recommended that development partners support the efforts by African governments to enhance capacity building in the administration, legislature and judiciary. Here clearly TICAD II reaffirmed the rules recommended in various forums, that is, the first function. It is regrettable that the support in the area of good governance and democratization is not the main thrust of Japanese ODA as a co-organizer of TICAD.

Among the many issues in conflict resolution, special attention was called to the illicit possession and transfer of small arms and light weapons, their illegal sales and accumulation, and monitoring. This was a proposal for a change of rules based on the well-known fact that small arms are flooding into Africa and a large percentage of them are produced and sold by the permanent members of the Security Council. On Asia-Africa cooperation at TICAD I, the proposal was followed by the Asia-Africa Forum held in Bandon in 1994 and Bangkok in 1997. New contacts have been developed between the two continents that disappeared 500 years ago, according to the Co-Chairs statement. By sharing developmental experiences among Asian and African countries new potentials have emerged. The proposal at TICAD I for the addition of a rule became a useful fixture of the TICAD process.

TICAD II provided a unique feature: a list of more than 350 ongoing and pipeline programs and projects. They were selected as examples for follow-ups of TAA objectives and actions. They were taken as TICAD projects, inviting some misunderstanding, but the list was prepared to demonstrate projects and programs that were in line with TAA strategy. This fulfills the third function. In addition, TICAD II gave clear instructions for follow-ups over a wide range of issues. This also relates to the third function of international conferences. In conclusion, it is safe to state that TICAD II facilitated all four functions.

TAA presented a comprehensive strategy but it did not grapple with the issues of the dependency of Africa on developed economies and the diversification of exports. Only three paragraphs are related to the subject: regional cooperation for liberalizing trade arrangements (paragraph 12), promotion of the transfer of technologies to African countries (paragraph 25), and enhancement of international competitiveness in tradable goods and services through the expanded application of appropriate technologies, including labor-intensive technology, to improve skills and productivity and provide essential services more efficiently (paragraph 23). Africa does not stand on a level playing ground with developed countries, but stands on the lower end of a lopsided ground. It is essential to demonstrate Africa's efforts to diversify exports and to graduate from the status of primary goods exporters, but at the same time it is essential for developed countries to offer comprehensive assistance embracing trade measures, technology transfer and investments. TICAD II was not able to supply or suggest any such strategy or rules.

TICAD II reaffirmed the rules on democratization. No one expects liberal democracy to take root in Africa overnight. The reality seems to be a formal democracy being maintained to a degree acceptable by donors, but political leaders with power are on top of the neo-patrimonial system and the rules of domestic politics have not changed to a significant degree. Poor governance is an impediment for economic growth and social development. A new generation of young political leaders appears on the horizon now, and it is time for TICAD and other initiatives to actively support them. A new rule of political reform is in order.

TICAD Ministerial-level Meeting: Support of NEPAD

The TICAD ministerial-level meeting was held in December 2001. A preparatory meeting was held in October in Dakar. Both meetings produced a Chair's summary and these documents were finally adopted at the end of the Ministerial Meeting. The Okinawa G8 Summit was held in 2000 and the presidents of Algeria, Nigeria and South Africa were invited to meet the heads of state of the G8. This meeting contributed to formulating a continent-wide development vision and plan based on a number of initiatives being prepared by South Africa, Senegal and

ECA that later became the NAI (New African Initiative) and the NEPAD (New Partnership for African Development).

Around the same time the EU and the OAU concluded the "Cairo Plan of Action", and the US Congress passed the AGOA (African Growth and Opportunity Act). China also held a conference on Africa and has shown keen interest in the continent. In addition to the traditional support of the U.K. and France, these initiatives from other donors and African efforts culminating in NEPAD helped to focus attention on Africa in spite of the 9-11 terrorism attack in the US. Prime Minister Koizumi in his opening statement said, "The circumstances facing the international community are very severe because of the political and economical impact of the recent terrorist attacks in the United States. Even in this situation, though, it is essential that the international community strengthen its joint efforts to address the issues Africa is facing." This TICAD meeting did not fail to call the attention of the international community to Africa.

The Chair's summary report (Dakar Preparatory Meeting) lists the following priority areas: 1) governance, 2) peace, 3) investment in people, 4) health (HIV/AIDS and other infectious diseases), 5) agricultural development (including food security), 6) infrastructure, 7) the private sector, and 8) ICT development. Following the Okinawa Summit initiatives on the digital divide and infectious diseases, these two sectors were given special attention. Incidentally they were the ones not covered well at TICAD II; however, they have gathered increasing attention from the international community since then.

The Chair's statement noted the digital gaps between Africa and developed countries and within Africa. Governments were asked to prepare the necessary policies, institutions, and environments, including basic communications infrastructure. There was no proposal of a new rule for the development of this sector. As in developed countries, the private sector is supposed to be the main actor for its development. However, in many African countries so far the communications industry has been managed by the public sector. Privatization has been promoted but the shortage of sufficient capacity in terms of capital, human resources and technology in the private sector and the fact that the communications sector has been a rich hunting ground for the patronage system mean that it will not be easily privatized. It seems that a new rule must be introduced involving governments, the African private sector and foreign companies so that the digital divide can be closed quickly and so that the state does not lose the control of the industry to foreign capital.

On HIV/AIDS and other infectious diseases, many measures were introduced and recommended for adoption but they were not new proposals. If some new rule is to be found in the statement, it is the one concerning the provision on supplying anti-HIV drugs cheaper. In 2001 this was a contentious issue.

The value of the Ministerial-level meeting is found in its commitment to the support of NEPAD. NEPAD is a vision and strategy formulated by Africans. It is the expression of the political will of African leaders. As mentioned earlier, developed countries neglected many African initiatives, but the UN, G8 and many other developed countries and international organizations have indicated their support of NEPAD. NEPAD is a set of development rules formulated by Africans that is literally under African ownership. Will African development be pursued according to NEPAD from now on? No; more than three years have passed since NEPAD was introduced, but conditionalities by the World Bank and the IMF dominate development policies in Africa.

NEPAD offers a set of rules by Africans but the principal rules are democratization and liberal market economics, which are no different from other initiatives advanced by developed countries. Political leaders in Africa have experienced confusion and hardship as the result of wholesale introduction of liberal economic measures, but they formulated NEPAD as if there are no alternatives. The visions in NEPAD seem to express the sentiments and ideas of African people, but the strategy follows the free market system. On the one hand it vehemently advocates self-reliance, but on the other hand a huge amount of resource flow is expected from developed countries. One gets glimpses of a dependency syndrome.

In NEPAD one recognizes "the ownership" of African visions and "the Washington Consensus" strategy being intermingled. TAA by TICAD II advocated an active role for the state in African development strategy partly because the market system does not function in Africa as well as in developed market economies. It does not mean to preclude activities by the private sector. The roles of development partners should be limited to gently prodding on self-reliance efforts, not taking leadership. Conceptually NEPAD and TAA will find areas where their strategies may not agree each other, but at the project or program levels there will be little possibility of conflict, and at any rate cooperation means that both programs would be coordinated where possible.

In conclusion, the TICAD Ministerial-level Meeting displayed efficiently the fourth function of advocacy on HIV/AIDS and other infectious diseases as well as ICT development, most importantly the support of NEPAD.

TICAD III: Human security and other critical issues

TICAD III was held in 2003 and 23 heads of state participated. The number of heads of state increased from 5 at TICAD I and 15 at TICAD II to 23 at TICAD III. Attendance at TICAD must have offered some benefits.

TICAD III could be summarized by saying that it provided a useful forum where new and old issues were raised for reexamination. In other words, it demonstrated amply the fourth function of international conferences. Prime Minister Koizumi listed three pillars of the Japanese support program: "human centered development," "poverty reduction through economic growth," and "consolidation of peace." The major premises of "poverty reduction through economic growth" are "consolidation of peace," "peace and security," and "democratization and good governance." African leaders recognize candidly that internal factors such as civil wars, conflicts, and poor governance are causes of the vicious cycle of poverty in Africa. Oversight functions by the AU and the "peer review" mechanism of NEPAD that may speak on internal affairs are expected to build democratic systems with transparency and accountability in Africa. When peace is maintained, "poverty reduction through economic growth" moves up to the starting line.

Economic reforms that started in the mid-80s have so far registered successes only for a limited number of countries or certain time periods. There are no bright prospects for continuing problems such as poverty reduction, income gap reduction and slow growth. Discussions took place on domestic as well as foreign impediments such as decreasing ODA, small GDI, a mounting debt burden, and a lack of infrastructure such as ICT facilities and services. Reflecting on the aftereffects of the failure of the Cancun meeting, African participants emphasized the removal of restrictions on access to the markets of developed countries for African manufactured goods using wheet, suger, beef, dairy products, maize, cotton and other raw materials. Also, subsidies by developed countries for agricultural products are in effect preventing industrialization and an increase in exports of primary goods from Africa. This is the old issue of Africa's dependency on developed economies. The issue was again raised because it cannot be resolved by internal policy measures such as SAP and PRSP; action by developed countries is the key to the solution.

As one impediment to "poverty reduction through economic growth," the capacity of people and of organizations was extensively discussed in connection with the rapid spread of HIV/AIDS, the slow progress of primary education, and inadequate medical services. The question was simple: why were so many institutions not operating effectively and efficiently?

TICAD III raised a new and very important issue which has not been extensively discussed yet in international fora in the context of African development: "human security". In his opening remarks at the start of the conference, Chairperson Mori drew particular attention to human security. Today, he said, human security "is one of the key visions of Japanese diplomacy, and it provides a new perspective to the TICAD process." The concept of human security is not well understood in the international community yet. It seems that this concept and its implications were buried under the overwhelming attention on other agenda items. Nevertheless, I believe that the concept will become a major rule of the sub-game of African development. It proposes human-centered development, not state security-oriented development. While TICAD II put forward the proposition that the state can play a positive role, TICAD III placed human security before the international community as a possible rule of the game. I believe that the broad philosophical framework of human security covers what Prime Minister Koizumi gave as his three pillars, namely, "human centered development", "poverty reduction through economic growth" and "consolidation of peace."

Mrs. Ogata, the Co-Chair of the Commission on Human Security, stated in her remarks that the human security concept proposes a two-pronged strategy focusing on the protection and empowerment of people. Protection refers to the norms, processes and institutions that shield people from critical and pervasive threats. It implies a "top-down" approach such as building accountable and transparent institutions and democratic governance processes. Empowerment emphasizes people as actors and participants in defining their security and rights. It implies a "bottom-up" approach. I fully concur that, through the empowerment of people, the ownership of development processes by people and by communities is established; otherwise no effort to grapple with the chronic insecurity of the people of Africa will be sustainable.

Furthermore, Mrs. Ogata raised a very important and fundamental issue on the implementation of assistance. Pointing out that it is impossible to separate the issues of development, poverty eradication, social equality, conflict resolution, and peace building, she cast doubt on the adequacy of the existing international cooperation machinery: "I seriously question whether the assumptions underlying the existing international machinery, such as the primacy of states and national sovereignty, are still adequate today." The implications of the issue she raised are so enormous that the TICAD process as well as all donors and all recipients must review past experiences and the reality of Africa, that is in short, dilapidated cities and poverty-stricken rural villages after more than thirty years of assistance. What she raised is a serious proposition for changing the rules of assistance.

Another concept that runs through TICAD III can be recognized. It is the development approach based on African communities. It is a proposal for rural development under the ownership of communities. Health and sanitation services as well as potable water supply are supposed to be undertaken by the bottom-up method. The emphasis is on infrastructure that connects communities rather than large-scale construction. The priority is set on IT facilities to improve the living conditions of the community. The consolidation of peace proposes the reconstruction of traditional communities. This is recognition of the importance and usefulness of a comprehensive strategy involving African communities that has been the basis of African life. Needless to say, this is another proposal for a change of rules.

A number of other important issues were raised during the conference.

1) While donors make free use of the words ownership and partnership, the aid policies they implement are still "supply driven," not "demand driven" on the African side. NEPAD was initiated as an attempt to break through this impasse and return African development to the hands of the continent's people. Participants called for donors to provide support for this political commitment made by Africa's leaders by reconsidering the methods and priorities of their aid programs and to build a new partnership based on mutual respect and trust. This was the major proposition made at the TICAD Ministerial-level Meeting.

2) International organizations reported that Africa is facing crisis with respect to agriculture and food, and indeed the world's media have given prominent play to droughts, food imports, and emergency food aid. The delegates at the conference demonstrated a common understanding that agriculture, which is a core sector in the African economy, has been plagued by a plethora of problems. While participants shared the recognition that agriculture is of vital importance to African development, opinion was divided on the question of why so many problems remain unresolved. One hard-hitting remark made from the donors' side was that African governments have not directed sufficient long-term investment into agriculture, with the result that this sector has developed deep-seated structural problems.

3) One of the barriers to investment in Africa, whether by domestic or foreign companies, is a general lack of information, especially regarding investment conditions and opportunities. Comprehensive measures are needed to foster the information industry in general, which must be able to prepare and assemble information in an organized fashion and

have the means to convey this information. Tackling this challenge should be seen as a matter of crucial significance to African economies.

4) South-South cooperation, particularly that drawing on the Asian experience, has been a feature of the TICAD process from its inception. One of the fruits of this collaboration is NERICA, the "new rice for Africa," which is a superior variety of rice combining the strengths of African and Asian species. A proposal was put forward at TICAD III for the formation of a network to facilitate cooperation between Asian and African countries in areas such as agriculture, capacity building, technology transfer, trade, and investment, and Asian countries expressed their commitment to active cooperation. Such a network will add a strategy to African development if more Asian countries respond to this call.

TICAD Process and Follow-up

1) It would be more productive if preparations for an international conference would focus on its specific functions. Documents on the same subject may be prepared from different perspectives, depending on the organizers' intent, and appropriateness of the conference. It would be no use to prepare for the change of the rules, if the conference does not have any mandate to change them. But the preparation can plan to maximize the effect of advocacy.

2) So far TICAD is not a forum where agreements have been reached to change the rules. But after three TICAD conferences and in view of the fact that so many important propositions have been made in the first three TICAD conferences, the next TICAD conference could focus on the promotion of human security and its implications for development strategies in Africa.

3) The TICAD process has advocated from the beginning African ownership. NEPAD is supposed to be the embodiment of African vision and strategy, but its strategy is closer to "the Washington Consensus". It will be extremely difficult for Africa to get rid of its dependency on the developed economies, but globalization without Africa is out of the question. The TICAD process should place more emphasis on good governance and the empowerment of people.

4) Respect for the ownership of Africa means supporting programs and projects started by Africans using their own resources and initiatives. It is not useful to supply assistance on account of the "lack of materials," "shortage of technical people", "shortage of resources" and so forth. The objective of development partners is to support self-help efforts by Africans. As it is, there is keen competition to grant "supply-driven" assistance among donors, government agencies, international organizations and numerous NGOs. This only helps to deepen the depen-

dency syndrome. Future TICAD meetings should make this issue very clear for both donors and Africans.

5) Poverty reduction requires sustainable economic growth for an extended period of time. Given the facts that more than half of the population is under the poverty line in Africa, market mechanisms will not lead to the best possible growth path. In other words, People in poverty are "uncaptured by market". It is clear the market cannot adequately address the poverty issue. Weak states in Africa cannot be replaced by market. The TICAD process should chart actions for the state once again in addition to the role defined in TAA. But the overall role of the state could be reexamined and redefined in the TICAD process. The modern concept of the nation states includes the capability of imposing and maintaining a certain kind of social order, that is the capacity to "govern" people, – "govern-ment". But, in the context of human security and contemporary Africa, what is expected of the nation-state is to "deliver" services to people. "Govern-ment" must transform itself to "deliver-ment". Future TICAD could go beyond TAA on the role of the state and the strong state is necessary to deliver adequate services and environment for the reduction of poverty as well as for a significant lift of production capacity.

6) The first step in poverty reduction must be the reconstruction of rural communities. Rural communities sustain the life of African society in times of difficulty. The initiatives and vitality of people can be brought together if many restrictions are removed and appropriate incentives are given. These communities do not comprise the civil society in the Western sense and do not appear to be well organized and institutionalized. However, they are informal organizations formulated over several hundred years. The TICAD process should propose rules to vitalize and mobilize rural communities.

7) The consolidation of peace is the key for the success of TICAD and NEPAD. Many causes for conflicts are well known and can be listed. At the same time many measures can also be drawn up. There is not much room for foreign countries to effectively intervene, but the TICAD process should introduce checks and balances in government as rules of good governance. Also the co-organizers of TICAD can develop a program separately to support young political and civil leaders who share with us the same values.

8) The TICAD process has been advocating the South-South cooperation, especially between Asia-Africa. In the light of developments in India and China, it looks potentials for mutual benefits of Asia – Africa cooperation could not be emphasized more. In the areas of private investments in development of SMEs and technical cooperation in community development, the South-South cooperation seems to offer a plethora

of productive opportunities. As one of main strategies of African development, future TICAD cannot miss these opportunities.

References

Gaimusho, Dai 1 kai Africa Kaihatukaigi (TICAD I) kouhyou bunnsho, October 1993.
Gaimusho, Dai 2 kai Africa Kaihatukaigi (TICAD II) kouhyou bunnsho, October 1998.
Gaimusho, Dai 2 kai Africa Kaihatukaigi (TICAD II) kouhyou bunnsho, Bessatu Houdoukijishu, January 1999.
TICAD Ministerial-Level Meeting, Speech by Prime Minister Koizumi, December 3, 2001.
TICAD Ministerial-Level Meeting, Speech by Foreign Minister Tanaka, December 3, 2001.
Chair's Statement of the Ministerial-level Meeting of TICAD, December 4, 2001.
Chairman's Summary Report of Dakar Preparatory Meeting for TICAD Ministerial-level Meeting, October 31, 2001.
TICAD Tenth Anniversary Declaration, October 1, 2003.
SUMMARY by the Chair of TICAD III, October 1, 2003.
Opening Remarks by Mr. Yoshiro Mori, Chairperson of TICAD III, September 29, 2003.
Keynote Speech by Prime Minister Junichiro Koizumi at TICAD III, September 29, 2003.
Speech by Mrs. Sadako Ogata, Co-Chair, Commission on Human Security, September 29, 2003.
Speech by H.E. Joaquim Alberto Chissano, President of the Republic of Mozambique, Chairman of the African Union, September 29, 2003.
Speech by H.E. Ato Meles Zenawi, Prime Minister of Ethiopia, Co-Chairperson of the Global Coalition for Africa, September 29, 2003.
Statement by H.E. Yoweri Kaguta Museveni, President of the Republic of Uganda, September 29, 2003.
Ministry of Foreign Affairs, Draft Reference Paper for TICAD III Discussion, September 2003.
Special Unit/TICAD, UNDP, Review of Implementation of Tokyo Agenda for Action (TAA): Achievements of Goals and Objectives: Actions by Africa and Its Partners, September 2003.
Global Coalition for Africa (GCA), Review of TICAD, September 2003.
Adebayo Adedeji, "From the Lagos Plan of Action to the New Partnership for African Development and from the Final Act of Lagos to the Constitutive Act: Wither Africa? in NEPAD: New Path?," edited by Anyang' Nyong'o and others, Heinrichi Boell Foundation, Nairobi, 2002.
Peter Anyang'Nyong'o, 'Democracy and Political Leadership in Africa in the Context of NEPAD,' paper presented at Symposium on Sustainable Development and Governance in Africa; Governance for Africa by Africans, supported by Ministry of Foreign Affairs and JIIA, August 31, 2002.
Patrick Bond ed, "Fanon's Warning, A Civil Society Reader on the New Partnership for Africa's Development," Africa World Press, 2002.
Patrick Chabal, "The quest for good governance and development in Africa: is NEPAD the answer?" International Affairs, 2002, 7, pp. 447-62.
G8 African Action Plan, 2001.
Global Coalition for Africa, Policy Forum: NEPAD and Security, GCA Document /01/22-23/2003.
Government of South Africa, The Millennium Partnership for the African Recovery Programme (MAP), 2001.
Government of Senegal, OMEGA PLAN FOR AFRICA, 2001.

The Japan Institute of International Affairs, Policy Recommendations for the Third Tokyo International Conference on African Development (TICAD), June 2003.
M. Jazairy, el, The State of World Rural Poverty, IFAD 1992.
NEPAD Secretariat, The New Partnership for Africa's Development (NEPAD), 2001.
NEPAD Secretariat, The African Peer Review Mechanism (APRM), 2003.
Nippon Keizai Shinbun, October 9, 1998 and Yomiuri Shinbun October 7, 1998.
UNECA, Compact for African Recovery, Operationalising the Millennium Partnership for the African Recovery Programme, 2001.
United Nations Millennium Declaration.
The National Security Strategy of the United States of America, Office of President, United States of America, Sept, 2002.
United Nations University, TICAD III: United Nations University's Policy Brief, 2003.
United Nations, Report of the Secretary-General, "The causes of conflict and the promotion of durable peace and sustainable development in Africa," 1998.
United Nations, Implementation of the United Nations New Agenda for the Development of Africa in the 1990s, A/55/350, September 2000.
United Nations, Resolution; Final Review and appraisal of the United Nations New Agenda for the Development of Africa in the 1990s and support for the New Partnership for Africa's Development, 57/7, 20 November 2002.
United Nations, Final review and appraisal of the implementation of the United Nations Programme of Action for African Economic Recovery Development A/RES/46/151, 18 December 1991.
Wiseman Nkuhlu, New Partnership for Africa's Development: "the Principle, the Goals and the Expectations," paper presented at African Leadership Forum, April 2002.

Japan and Africa after the Cold War

JUN MORIKAWA

ABSTRACT

The purposes of this article are twofold. The first is to discuss the factors that make inquiry into Japan's African diplomacy difficult, in connection with the elaborate publicity campaign run by the Ministry of Foreign Affairs (MOFA), focusing on the Tokyo International Conference on African Development (TICAD). The second is to examine the current status of, issues in and future of Japan's African diplomacy in the post-Cold War, post-apartheid era and the meaningful participation of Japanese citizens in formulating and implementing foreign policy in reference to the regional power of South Africa. The article concludes that there is a significant gap between words and action in Japan's African diplomacy that has led to a loss of credibility and that attempts by MOFA to recoup the loss using aid or rhetoric are likely to rather result in heightened distrust on the African side and that securing trust will require structural reform and building foreign policy that is based on the wishes and interests of the people and subject it to democratic control.

The Tokyo International Conference on African Development (TICAD): Image and Reality

The Tokyo International Conference on African Development (TICAD) was instituted at the Japanese government's initiative in the fall of 1993 when the transition to the post Cold War era had become apparent. The purposes of the Conference were stated as the heightening of the international community's interest in Africa, which had declined with the end of the Cold War, and for Japan to support and call on the international community to assist the self-help efforts of African nations in the form of democratization and the transition to market economies.[1]

That Japan had conceived, proposed, prepared and held an African development conference on a massive scale, bringing together actors including recipient and donor nations and the representatives of international organizations was met with astonishment, not only from the countries of Africa, but from the international community in general. This emanated from Japan previously having contented itself with playing a subordinate role as an external actor in international relations with Africa in comparison to European nations and the United States. Japan's efforts had been inconspicuous even in comparison with countries such as China and India.

TICAD has been the catalyst for international discussion and a great deal of debate about the Conference has ensued. The discussion has focused on its background, aims, significance, contributions to the African Union (AU) and the New Partnership for Africa's Development (NEPAD), which are features of the African self-help efforts, and the overall impact on Japan's diplomacy with Africa. However, this article does not join in this narrowly focused debate on Japan as a contributor to Africa. My rationale is that I judge TICAD to have been cleverly structured by the Japanese government as a grand diplomatic show for the purpose of creating an image. Put another way, the pursuit of a mirage-like international conference devoid of substance does not assist in the elucidation of Japan's diplomacy with Africa, but is rather highly likely to mislead those interested in the topic.

But TICAD, which has now been convened three times, in 1993, 1998 and 2003, has had a significant effect in improving Japan's image amongst the international community in general. The image constructed over the past decade emphasizes that TICAD is an African conference, for Africa, run by the international community, beginning with Africa and Japan and that image suggests that the diplomacy undertaken with Africa by Japan, the sponsor of such a major conference like TICAD, is nothing other than aid diplomacy based on altruism.

These positive views have been widely disseminated within and outside Japan by Ministry of Foreign Affairs publicity campaigns and sympathetic reports by the general Japanese mass media, which put the dramatic effect of TICAD to good use.[2]

---

[1] See Morikawa Jun. (1997). Japan and Africa – Big Business and Diplomacy. London: Hurst & Co., pp. 203-233 on Japan's African diplomacy and the relevance of 1st TICAD. For government documents on TICAD see The Tokyo International Conference on African Development accessed via the Ministry of Foreign Affairs website at http://www.mofa.go.jp/index.html (in English).

[2] The Ministry of Foreign Affairs 'Press Club', the Kasumi Kurabu, which has 20

As a result, despite a lack of evidence to substantiate these views, the image of Japan's diplomacy with Africa as being centered on aid diplomacy has begun to take on a life of its own. In such circumstances, the major debates focused on how to give aid for which Africa.[3]

Yet, the question remains. For what purpose and for whose interests is the Tokyo International Conference on African Development designed? It is necessary to give fresh consideration to this question even though the answer may initially seem self-evident. The following statements translated from Japan's *Diplomatic Bluebook* (1993) are instructive in terms of grasping this point.

> Aid for developing nations contributes to the improvement of economic development and welfare in the recipient country and is, in addition, an investment in Japan's national interests from a medium to long term perspective. In particular, due to Japan's 'peace constitution', ODA forms a stronger pillar of Japan's international contribution than is the case with other nations, and combined with diplomatic efforts in fields other than aid, ODA contributes to the economic development of developing nations, promotes friendly bilateral relations whilst heightening the trust of the international community in Japan's diplomatic position and leads to a boosting of Japan's weight in the international arena. This is why Japan has, in particular, exhibited initiatives in the area of aid, including in the 1st International Committee on the Reconstruction of Cambodia (ICORC), the Consultative Group Meeting for Mongolia and TICAD.[4]

---

members, is located on the 3rd Floor of the Ministry building. Each media organization reports by relying heavily on the information provided by the Ministry's Press Division. On the other hand, according to information obtained by the author in a private interview with the Kasumi Club, a meeting is held by senior Ministry officials to examine and assess the content of newspaper articles, incorporating discussion of restraints on the press, every morning at 10 am.

[3] The Africa-Japan Forum (AJF) was established in 1994 by a dozen Africa-related NGOs and scholars. The main purpose of the Forum was to ensure the backflow of ODA funds to NGOs. It was necessary to gain the trust of diplomats in order to receive funding grants. This actually led to the abandonment of surveys and research entailing the critical analysis of Japan's African diplomacy as well as watchdog activities and the proposing of alternative policies based on the same. However, a decade later, voices for change within the AJF prevailed and they reviewed their stance on collaboration with the government, which led to a reconfirmation of the importance of surveys and analysis on Japan's African diplomacy and advocacy based on the same. It will be interesting to observe how this review is reflected in the AJF's future activities.

The AJF has stated its long-term objectives in English as follows: "(purpose of forming a network) is to develop a mechanism and structure in which official funds can be directed to the activities of the local people, community-based organizations and NGOs. It means also that Africa-Japan Forum will submit concrete suggestions or recommendations making influence on the policy of Japanese government on aid to Africa. However, on those purpose, it is essential, first of all that Africa-Japan Forum has broad network and has credibility to be able to use official funds." [Africa-Japan Forum] February, 1994.

[4] Ministry of Foreign Affairs. (1993). Waga gaiko no kinkyo [Diplomatic Bluebook]: Tokyo, Okurasho Insatukyoku, p. 93.

The above statement is significant since it directly demonstrates that the purpose for holding the African Development Conference is not merely to hold such a conference. It is also a method for realizing Japan's larger long-term national interests. This naturally leads to a consideration of what aims have constituted Japan's larger long-term national interests since the beginning of the 1990's, when the transition to the post Cold War era became apparent. Japan's goals are to emphasize its appeal to the international community as a nation with "the will and capability to contribute to world peace and development as a global power" and to have Japan accepted as a major political power. This intent is reflected, for example, in the Japanese government's claims and conduct in seeking to have Japan granted a permanent seat on the United Nations Security Council (U.N.S.C.).[5]

Japan reminds its diplomats of the importance of doing as much as possible to increase the number of countries in the United Nations that support Japan in order to realize the above goals. From this perspective, obtaining the support of Africa, which represents a voting bloc of over 50 countries, has tremendous political significance. However, in order to achieve the goals, Japan needs to repair the deep-rooted criticism and distrust of African nations that have been brought about by Japan having promoted a pro-Pretoria policy (see below) during the Cold War era. Fortunately, both the confrontation between the United States and the U.S.S.R. and the apartheid regime departed the African continent around 1990. TICAD has been an effective tool for Japan since then as an influential diplomatic event that has helped repair Japan's damaged image and turn it into a positive image.

It is no coincidence whatsoever that Owada Hisashi, later Japan's Ambassador to the U.N., was the Vice Minister for Foreign Affairs from August 1991 to July 1993, immediately prior to the 1st Tokyo International Conference on African Development Conference. He played a crucial role as scriptwriter and stage manager from the initial planning stages of this dramatic diplomatic show. Owada is a strong proponent of the formation and operation of a 'New World Order' under *troika* (trilateral) collaboration between the U.S., Europe and Japan (Owada 1994: 227-228).[6] However, despite its professed passion, it is necessary to note that the attitude of the Ministry of Foreign Affairs to TICAD has rather been one of indifference. As is evidenced below, this is reflected in matters

[5] See for example Asahi Shimbun [Asahi Newspaper]: 18 March and 15 October 1994.
[6] Owada Hisashi (1994), Sanka kara sozo e – Nihon gaiko ga mezasu mono [From Participacion to Creation – Japan's Diplomacy Objectives]: Tokyo, Toshi Shuppan.

such as the characterization of the Conference, the substance of its resolutions, debates on how to put the resolutions into practice and the way in which the Conference is run.

Firstly, the position of the Japanese government, which is the sponsor of TICAD, has been clear from the outset. It has been repeatedly driven home that the Conference is not for the making of aid pledges. It is no more than a high-level forum for discussing principles and strategies for African development. However, numerous high-level forums have already been held on these matters by many organizations including the U.N. Considering the mountain of resolutions, declarations and concrete policy proposals on the shelves, the necessity and meaning of holding a new forum in the shape of TICAD was minimal from the outset.

The second matter the Japanese government has emphasized to participants from Africa is that both individual and collective self-help efforts are required before they can expect aid. In practical terms, self-help efforts mean economic reconstruction through democratization, 'good governance' and the introduction of 'structural adjustment programs'. It should be recalled here that, in the past, Japan's Cold War strategy was the same as that of the U.S., to consistently support Africa's most oppressive and corrupt regimes. These included the racist regime in South Africa, the Mobutu regime in Zaire, the Moi regime in Kenya and the Banda regime in Malawi, thus contributing to the perpetuation of 'bad governance'.

Thirdly, whilst Tokyo refers to 'self-help efforts', the fact is that the actual economic reconstruction and new development strategies concerned were not independently formulated by African nations. This is because the formula is for Africa to make self-help efforts within the prescriptive framework drawn up mainly by the World Bank and IMF, which are heavily influenced by Japan and its European and American partners. Since the West believes its victory in the East-West conflict makes the range of choices enunciated by Basil Davidson's *Which Way Africa?*[7] no longer valid, it follows that the only prescription is now for Africa to take the path of dependent capitalist development dictated by the donor nations, centering on Europe, the U.S. and Japan.

The substance of this scenario[8] is for the countries of Africa to faithfully implement structural adjustment policies, promote their transition

---

[7] Davidson, Basil (1971) [Which Way Africa? – The Search for a New Society –]: Penguin Books Ltd. Harmondsworth, UK. Third edition.

[8] Economic Cooperation Bureau, Ministry of Foreign Affairs [Japan's Official Development Assistance, White Paper 2002, "Strategy" and "Reform"]: Tokyo, Economic Cooperation Bureau, Ministry of Foreign Affairs, March 2004, p. 135.

to market economies and prepare an environment conducive to the activities of the private sector[9] (in other words, foreign capital) including multinational corporations, increase production and exports of internationally competitive goods and strive for increased integration with the world economy. By doing this, it is believed that the economic growth of African nations will be enhanced through acquiring cooperation such as ODA, direct private investment, trade and commerce and technical cooperation. However on careful consideration, most African countries have aimed at capitalist development using basic strategies and methods like those mentioned above after their independence. As for the result, whilst it is said that socialist development strategies failed in Africa, the question remains as to whether capitalist development strategies have succeeded.

If one is meticulous in reading between the lines of TICAD declarations, resolutions and action plans, the strong intent and preferences of the Japanese government become clear. It is obvious Japan, which had a deep involvement in the 'success story' of Asian capitalism through the above mentioned strategies including ODA, feels Africa should learn from this experience. The basic position of Japan's diplomats is typically expressed in the statements of Kono Masaharu (2004), Deputy Minister for African Affairs, who described TICAD as "a marketplace for participants to freely trade in ideas and policies on African development". An illustrative example of Kono's views from a 2004 edition of the Gaiko Forumu is translated below.

> In such a 'marketplace' Japan is more than a simple stall holder; Japan sets the agenda, drafts the written results and takes on a special role in managing the 'marketplace'. Stated another way, whilst the 'marketplace' itself is certainly free, it is Japan that controls its values and rules or 'currency' to the last. And furthermore, first of all, at the Opening Ceremony, Prime Minister Koizumi states Japan's Africa policy in front of unprecedented numbers and levels of participants. In other word, Japan's position at TICAD secures it the best position in the 'marketplace'. This is why it is no overstatement to say that TICAD is the most indispensable requirement in Japan's diplomacy with Africa.[10]

---

[9] For example the following wording from the Tokyo Declaration of the 1st TICAD is notable; "the Private sector is vital as an engine for sustainable development" and "application of successful development experiences in Asia to development activities in Africa and further expansion of South-South cooperation". In the 2nd TICAD the emphasis was on Africa's "integration into the global economy". Further, Japan's 1992 ODA Guidelines, which had been revised after the Cold War, expressly state that countries that endeavor to "introduce a market economy" will be given priority in grants of aid.

[10] Kono Masaharu. (2004) Gaiko foramu [Foreign Affairs Forum] 196 (Nov): Tokyo, Toshi Shuppan, pp. 82-83.

Fourthly, there is the emphasis placed by the Japanese government on the significance and importance of South-South cooperation. It must be added that Tokyo's South-South cooperation is founded on the paternalistic thinking and methodology whereby a developed nation of the North, in particular Japan, takes initiative under which mutual cooperation between the countries of Asia and Africa is promoted. Yet there is no doubt that the peoples of the South feel uneasy with the Japanese government's use of language. This is because South-South cooperation has been historically understood and put into practice as spontaneous and horizontal. It has the character and substance, in relation to the 'haves' in the North, of the 'have-nots' in the South seeking a change to a 'fair world order' on a case-by-case basis. The Bandung Conference, the 50th Anniversary of which falls this year, surely symbolized just that. The South-South cooperation of which Tokyo speaks, is rather large corporate Japan, mobilizing the small to medium-size enterprise (SME) rising nations of Asia, for example Malaysia,[11] which has adopted a 'Look East' policy, as sub-contractors to contribute to African development, evoking a pyramid-shaped design. In the case of Africa, Egypt,[12] Tunisia and South Africa are given the same sort of role as Malaysia.

The fifth issue is that TICAD gives the impression that Japan considers Africa as being more important than anywhere else. It is highly questionable whether this is actually the case. The following statement of a former Director-General of Economic Cooperation in the Ministry of Foreign Affairs (Kikuchi Kiyoaki 2003) is instructive in understanding this point:

> Japanese commentators often tell us that whilst it is good to view Asia as important, we should increasingly look at Africa as well. But other developed nations, such as Europe, view Africa as important and America considers Central and South America as important. Japan can hardly be told to give aid to the entire world, including Africa. It is obvious that we would focus on Asia.[13]

Sixthly, there is the fact of Japan's political intent and the view that it is acceptable to limit Japan's commitment to Africa, as seen in the

[11] Economic Cooperation Bureau, Ministry of Foreign Affairs (ed.). (2004). Seifu kaihatsu enjo (ODA) kunibetsu deta-bukku 2002 [ODA Country by Country Handbook – 2002]: Tokyo, Association for Promotion of International Cooperation, March 2004, p. 89.

[12] As for Egypt and Tunisia's role & their positions in the South – South Cooperation Strategy, See, *ibid.* (2002) p. 252 and pp. 272-273.

[13] Kikuchi Kiyoaki. (2003). Keizai gaiko no genba o kataru – gaiko jitsumuka no me [The Practice of Economic Diplomacy – Through the Eyes of a Diplomat]: Tokyo, Kajima Heiwa Kenkyujyo, pp. 227-228.

Director-General of Economic Cooperation's own words above,[14] lends support to the importance with which Asia is viewed.

The methods by which Africa's expectations of Japan would be met include significantly increasing Africa's share in the regional distribution of ODA and the cancellation of large foreign debts.[15] However, Tokyo does not have the political will required to implement these measures. This being the case, the only options actually left to Japan are the construction of a mountain of rhetoric, seeking individual and collective self-help efforts from the Africans, calling for support from the international community using the 'South-South cooperation' catchphrase and providing aid for basic human needs that is, in effect, mere lip service. Looking at the ability of Africa itself to absorb aid, the relationship between Japan and Africa and other factors, I feel that the appropriate share for Japan is probably 10%.[16]

This 10% share fluctuates slightly between fiscal years. It was 13.76% in 1988 when criticism of Japan's South Africa policy was heightened and rose well above 10% to 15.34% in 1989, the year of Emperor Hirohito's death, when Japan carried out 'condolence diplomacy' on a large scale, but it has basically been evenly maintained after 1990. On the other hand, Japan has been compelled to drastically reduce its ODA budget over the past decade due to the drawn-out recession and deepening financial crisis. Japan's ODA budget peaked in 1995 at USD 145 billion. By 2003, it had dropped by as much as 40% to USD 89 billion.[17] In other words, contrary to the strong impression of support for African development given by TICAD, the amount of Japan's aid to African nations has actually decreased.

In conclusion, it is necessary to recognize the difference between various images of TICAD and the reality. The public view is that the conference is a forum for international consultations on aid for Africa's development. But there is a tacit understanding in government and diplomatic circles that TICAD is not intended to directly cover the six nations of North Africa, Egypt, the Sudan, Tunisia, Libya, Algeria and Morocco,

---

[14] Matsuura Koichiro. (1990). Enjo gaiko no saizensen de kangaeta koto [Thoughts on the Frontline of Aid Diplomacy]: Tokyo, Association for Promotion of International Cooperation, p. 194.

[15] On the efforts of NGOs in relation to Japan's debt problem see "Jubilee 2000 Okinawa" AMPO Japan-Asia Quarterly, Tokyo, Pacific Asia Resource Center, 29(3).

[16] Matsuura Koichiro. (1990). Enjo gaiko no saizensen de kangaeta koto [Thoughts on the Frontline of Aid Diplomacy]: Tokyo, Association for Promotion of International Cooperation, p. 194.

[17] Asahi Shimbun [Asahi Newspaper]. 25 October 2004.

which are treated as belonging to the Middle East. This is because aid for these countries is handled on bilateral and multilateral levels within the framework of Japan's Middle East policy. Further, even in the sub-Saharan region, the Republic of South Africa is not covered by Japan's ODA policies, although small scale aid is carried out as a political gesture towards the black community of South Africa. This is because the Japanese bureaucrats concerned have historically treated South Africa as being a developed nation,[18] notwithstanding that it was a country that legalized racial discrimination. Another reason is that Japan has, in the case of South Africa, had the benefit of large-scale stable trade, direct private investment and technology transfers. In light of these understandings, the six North African nations, South Africa and the Western Sahara (since Japan does not recognize this country out of consideration for the position of its occupier, Morocco), are, in effect, removed and the countries entitled to the support of the Tokyo International Conference on African Development really number just 46 not 54.

This means that TICAD is a forum and opportunity for international consultations on the stability and development of only the countries sandwiched between North Africa[19] and South Africa and the neighboring island nations. However, Japan's treatment of even these 46 countries is not uniform. This is because, on the one hand, around a dozen nations, including Kenya, Tanzania, Ghana, Nigeria, Zambia, Zimbabwe, Ethiopia, Senegal and the Congo (formerly Zaire) have received preferential treatment[20] from Tokyo, including the establishment of Japanese embassies, aid distribution,[21] the dispatching of economic delegations and 'invitational diplomacy'. While on the other hand, the remaining 30 countries have been the subject of only secondary interest and treatment by Tokyo over the past four decades.

---

[18] Ministry of Foreign Affairs. (1983) Waga gaiko no kinkyo [Diplomatic Bluebook]: Tokyo, Okurasho Insatukyoku, p. 607.

[19] Egypt is the North African country Japan views as an important pillar. Preferential ODA is also given to Morocco and Tunisia, which act as supporting pillars on each side of Egypt and are pro-Europe and the U.S.

[20] The dominant explanation as to why Japan grants aid to specific countries is that given from the perspective of economic determinism. However, the importance with which, for example, Malawi and Tanzania, which lack attractiveness in both natural resources and markets have been viewed cannot be justified under that explanation. In the case of Tanzania it was necessary to neutralize President Nyerere, an international political figure deeply involved in the problems of southern Africa who was highly critical of Japan's 'dual diplomacy'.

[21] Economic Cooperation Bureau, Ministry of Foreign Affairs (ed.), (2002) Seifu Kaihatsu Enjo (ODA) kunibetu deta – bukku [ODA Handbook, Country by Country – 2002]: Tokyo, Association for Promotion of International Cooperation, pp. 325-327.

It is unfortunate that TICAD did not change this 'double-decker bus' approach to sub-Saharan Africa at the bilateral level. Moreover, the fact that the partnership of which Japanese bureaucrats speak is not with the countries of Africa or with the AU but actually with the countries of Europe and United States, the World Bank and the IMF, a fact which also increases frustrations on the African side. It was no doubt inevitable that the number of African nations participating in TICAD who are voicing discontent and dissatisfaction has increased as they become fed up with rhetoric and seek practical aid that treats African nations as equal partners. It is worth noting that the reality of TICAD was subject to severe criticism by Dr. Konare, Chairperson of the Commission of the African Union, during a symposium held in Kyoto on 16 October 2004: "The partnerships formed by Japan under TICAD have been with donor nations and the African Union has been made subordinate to those partnerships."[22]

In the context of the four-layer structure of Japan's Africa policy, however, this is not surprising. The fourth and bottom layer is made up of around 30 countries. The third layer down is made up of just over a dozen countries given preferential treatment. The second layer comprises Japan's regional partners like South Africa and Nigeria. The top layer of this structure systematically integrates the former colonial powers such as the U.S., the U.K. and France, as Japan's global partners.[23]

Japan's Diplomacy with Africa: South Africa as the Cornerstone

Africa is a diverse continent but in Japan's diplomacy with Africa, a homogenous image is constantly projected to the Japanese people. A one-sided image of Africa is placed at the fore portraying friendship with black Africa and development cooperation in the narrow sense described above. When contradictory images exist, such as Japan's relationship with the former white ruling powers of South Africa, whose economic influence is unchanged despite now being a minority, or Japan's involvement with North Africa, the Horn of Africa and East Africa and the closely connected problems of the Middle East, information on these topics is furnished in only a fragmentary manner. The result is that this has made it difficult for the Japanese public to comprehend the trials and errors of the stratified and inter-related African diplomacy practiced

[22] According to the report of Prof. Takabayashi Toshiyuki, who attended the Symposium.

[23] See for example, the 'New Japan-U.K. Action Plan – A Partnership Extending Globally' on p. 302 and 'Aid Cooperation in Africa' on p. 304 of the 1997 Gaiko seisho [Diplomatic Bluebook]: Tokyo, Okurasho Insatukyoku.

by Japan's diplomats or to have a constructive involvement and impact on Japan's African diplomacy.

This section begins with a consideration of the relationship between Japan and South Africa. The picture portrayed by the Ministry of Foreign Affairs is that it is no more than a trade and commerce-centered relationship that commenced in the 1960s. Moreover, as a result of Japan having introduced a series of sanctions in opposition to the apartheid policy, including not maintaining diplomatic relations with South Africa, the relationship was of a restricted nature.[24]

Portraying the situation in this way, it would follow that the intimacy of Japan's relationship with South Africa is a very recent phenomenon, dating from after 1994 when the Mandela administration was established. These assertions convey the contemporary message that the guiding principles of Japan's diplomacy with Africa, has always been anti-racism, anti-colonialism and support for the self-determination of the peoples of Africa in order to accelerate liberation. However, the question is whether this 'pro-black Africa' message propagated by Tokyo has been backed by practical action.

Firstly, it is necessary to recollect that the historical relationship between Tokyo and Pretoria had already been formed long before the Second World War. The background to the relationship is the development of bilateral trade in the interwar period, which led to Pretoria granting Japanese persons 'honorary white' status in 1930 and to the establishment of diplomatic relations in 1937. The aims of Japan's African diplomacy were the securing of export markets and resources and it should be noted that Japan was already more than willing to accept the methods of realpolitik where pre-existing oppressive and unjust systems were used in order to realize those aims.[25] Bilateral relations changed temporarily from friendship to enmity due to the Second World War. However, a relationship of friendship and cooperation was revived immediately after the war. The background to this was the intensification of the Cold War, having, even if indirectly, become allies through the bilateral security treaties each country concluded with America in 1951 and the mutual complementarity of the economic relationship. This is reflected in the recommencement of Japanese trade with South Africa in 1948, in Japan's major involvement as a rear base and the dispatching of the South

[24] Morikawa Jun. (1984). "The Anatomy of Japan's South African Policy." Journal of Modern African Studies 22 (1): Cambridge, Cambridge University Press.

[25] Morikawa Jun. (1985). "The Myth and Reality of Japan's Relations with Colonial Africa: 1885-1960." Journal of African Studies 12 (1): Los Angeles, the African Studies Center of the University of California.

African Air Force in the Korean War, in the announcement of a bilateral accord on the recommencement of diplomatic relations on 1 March 1961, in the opening of the South African Embassy in Tokyo on 13 January 1962.[26] It is also seen in the implementation of trade and direct private investment on a massive scale. By doing so, Japan ignored the calls for cooperation in economic sanctions from the international community (see below), and energized exchanges with the white ruling class as 'honorary white' Japanese whilst opposing the spread of liberation for the peoples of Africa and the anti-apartheid movement.

From the above, it is clear that Japan considered it very important not only to secure export markets and sites for investment but, to be involved in and contribute to the East-West confrontation as an influential member of the West through political diplomacy and economic measures. The activities of the 'Springbok Club', formed in 1977 by Japanese businessmen and diplomats in South Africa, is notable for its organization of exchanges with the white ruling class. The activities of the Japan-South Africa Parliamentarians Friendship League formed in 1984 by some 50 Liberal Democratic Party Diet Members with Ishihara Shintaro as Secretary General, for the purpose of achieving closer relations with the white minority government, was also significant.[27] The Ministry of Foreign Affairs gave its tacit consent in relation to the formation and activities of these pro-Pretoria organizations. However, the open activities of these pro-South African lobby groups were made difficult by the watchdog activities of the Japan Anti-Apartheid Committee. The fact that the founding members of the Japan-South Africa Parliamentarians Friendship League included several men who subsequently became Prime Minister (Takeshita Noboru, Hata Tsutomu, Obuchi Keizo), a Foreign Minister (Kakizawa Koji), Ministers of Economy, Trade and Industry (Hiranuma Takeo, Yosano Kaoru, Nakagawa Shoichi) and a Tokyo Governor (Ishihara Shintaro) is an indication that Japanese society is extremely tolerant of racists. The position taken by the Japanese government in opposition to the African liberation movement is also reflected in the friendly and cooperative relationships maintained and promoted with the white settlers of Rhodesia and the Portuguese colonialism that ruled Angola and Mozambique. These southern African regions were given a strategic status as a buffer zone protecting South Africa, the pillar of anti-Communism, from the advance of the Eastern bloc. Preferential

---

[26] Middle East and African Affairs Bureau. (2002) Ministry of Foreign Affairs – Afurika Binran – Sahara inan no kuniguni [Africa Handbook – Sub-Saharan Countries]: Africa Society of Japan, Tokyo, p. 99.

[27] See Morikawa (1997): 260 for a list of the members of the Japan-South Africa Parliamentarians Friendship League.

granting of ODA to the sole black African state to establish diplomatic relations with Pretoria, the Banda regime in Malawi, was also implemented in the context of support for a buffer state strategy. It is notable that the strategy of striving for the stabilization of the entire region by supporting the core country, South Africa, and neighboring countries friendly to South Africa continued even in the post-Cold War era. A relevant example is the Ministry of Foreign Affairs opposing the national liberation movement symbolized by the African National Congress (ANC) by regarding the ANC as an organization that carries out terrorism.

In relation to this point, the perception of Japan's domestic position on South Africa at the time can be seen in the 1983 *Diplomatic Bluebook*: "The destruction and terrorist activities that became frequent in 1981 were also widespread in 1982 and in December, the Kuberg Nuclear Station was bombed."[28]

If one accepts this logic, the above statement would suggest the Japanese government was willing to cast the South African liberation forces as 'terrorists' and to view the Pretoria administration and those who cooperated with it within and outside South Africa as 'freedom fighters'. The significance of this unusually frank statement is easy to grasp if one understands the diplomats' perceptions of what and to whom attention should be paid in order to make the alliance work.

> What is important, in order for Japan to strengthen our cooperation with developed democratic nations in future is, firstly, to achieve consensus with these countries in our basic understanding of international politics and economic conditions, to formulate agreement on basic strategies for dealing with the same and to be in constant dialogue and consultations with these countries in order to achieve this.[29]

If one asks with whom Japan was in constant dialogue and consultations on African problems in general, and in particular on South African problems, the answer is Washington, London, Brussels and Pretoria. It was certainly not Addis Ababa, where the headquarters of the Organization for African Unity was located, nor in Dar Es Salaam where President Nyerere was in residence. The Japanese government itself did not have the capacity to undertake the relevant information analysis and evaluations necessary and chose to rely on the governments of the U.K. and the U.S. and on the white minority government of South Africa.

---

[28] Ministry of Foreign Affairs. (1983) Waga gaiko no kinkyo [Diplomatic Bluebook]: Tokyo Okurasho insatukyoku, p. 216.

[29] Public Information and Cultural Affairs Bureau, Ministry of Foreign Affairs (ed.). (1982). Sekai no ugoki [Global trends]: (Nov) 398,Tokyo, Sekaino ugoki sha, p. 22.

The Japanese government's basic strategy followed and valued the initiatives and proposals of the U.S., the U.K. and Pretoria unquestioningly. The mistaken judgments and actions of Japan's political elite, who subordinated the idea of self-determination to Cold War strategy in Africa, have been repeated in Asia and Latin America as well. Nonetheless, the Japanese government's opposition to the ANC was to change under pressure from the victory of African liberation forces in various regions around southern Africa and the consolidation of the anti-apartheid movement within South Africa. This was apparent when the Ministry of Foreign Affairs dispatched the Director of the Second African Division in January 1986 to contact the ANC leadership.[30] In 1987, Oliver Tambo, Secretary-General of the ANC, was invited to visit Japan by a private body, The Africa Society of Japan, which was under the heavy influence of the Ministry. In 1988, permission was given to open an ANC liaison office in Tokyo. No doubt, the dramatic political upheavals of the second half of the 1980s also contributed to these changes. Among them were the advent of the Gorbachev administration in the Soviet Union, the dramatic easing of the Soviet confrontation with the U.S. in Africa, the increased isolation and weakening of the white minority government in South Africa, the development of the anti-apartheid movement within the international community, including America and the countries of NATO, and the intensification of international criticism of Japan's role as Pretoria's major trading partner. The appearance of these new circumstances made the Japanese government realize that the collapse of the apartheid administration and the birth of a majority black administration was only a matter of time. Eleven years after the publication of the 1983 *Diplomatic Bluebook* statements, the Japanese government invited South African President Nelson Mandela to Japan as a state guest, an individual who they had formerly considered to be the leader of a "terrorist" organization.

Japan's pro-South Africa policy developed in a more visible form in the economic field. Until the mid-1960's, Japan's trade with South Africa differed little in scale and rate of growth from that with Nigeria, Ghana or Kenya.[31] However, Japan's trade with black African nations was subsequently sluggish, due to the structural problems of Japan's massive trade surplus and the fall in purchasing power of the sub-Saharan African nations, which accompanied their economic difficulties. On the other

[30] Amaki Naoto. (2004) Mandera no Minami Afurika [Mandela's South Africa]: Tokyo, Tenbosha, pp. 130-131.

[31] Ministry of International Trade and Industry. (1968) Tusho Hakusho [MITI Whitepaper]: Kakuron, Tokyo, Okurasho insatukyoku, p. 511.

hand, Japan's trade with South Africa achieved spectacular growth, supported by the economic complementarity of exchanging manufactured goods for primary commodities. Naturally, it is inappropriate to search for the causes for the development of the trade relationship between Japan and South Africa in this complementarity alone. Through 'constructive engagement', strategic judgments and responses, namely the strengthening of the power bases of the weak anti-Communist minority white government through economic and technical measures and the securing of a stable supply of the rare metals indispensable to the support and development of Japan's high-tech industries,[32] brought about long-term expansion and balance in bilateral trade.

Historically, Japan's involvement in Cold War strategies became conspicuous from the mid 1970's, when the United States lost the Vietnam War and the 'domino phenomenon' appeared, advancing simultaneously in Indochina and southern Africa, to the early 1980s when the new Cold War commenced with the invasion of Afghanistan by Soviet forces. This diplomatic positioning by Japan was closely linked to its Africa and Middle East policies and was also reflected in its intervention in the strengthening of commerce and trade with South Africa. In terms of the former, the establishment in 1980 of the Second African Division in the Middle Eastern and African Affairs Bureau of the Ministry of Foreign Affairs is noteworthy. The Second African Division was responsible for a wide swathe of Southern Africa, from South Africa to the countries neighboring South Africa then passing across Kenya and Uganda to Ethiopia and Somalia. As usual, the Ministry did not give an explanation for the establishment of a Second African Division. However, it appears clear a major factor was responding effectively to the simultaneous advance of the former Soviet Union into southern Africa and the vicinity of the Arabian Peninsula, which were regarded as important to the security of the West.

In terms of the connection with the problems of the Middle East, a succession of pro-Soviet administrations had already been established in the 'weak links' in these two regions, in Afghanistan, South Yemen and the Sudan. Moreover, Ethiopia, off the southern coast of South Yemen, was increasingly strengthening its ties with the Soviet Union and South

[32] "It is necessary to consolidate the relations of interdependence with nations possessing resources and to promote resource exploration, development and technological advancement". See Outline of the 1982.

Outline of the Report by The Special Sub-Commitee on Economic Security of the Industrial Structure Council, Ministry of International Trade and Industry (ed.). Keizai anzen hosho no kakuritsu o mezashite [Towards Ensuring Economic Security]: Tokyo, Tusho Sangyo Chosakai, pp. 187-188.

Yemen and Libya formed a tripartite alliance with Ethiopia and South Yemen in 1981.[33] Moreover, the collapse of the pro-U.S. administration in Iran and the arrival of the regime of the Ayatollah Kohmeini and the ascendancy of Islamic fundamentalist forces greatly challenged the West-dominated regional order. Even in Southern Africa, factors such as the advance of the Soviet Union into Angola, the independence of Zimbabwe, the development of the struggle for liberation in Namibia and the growth of the anti-apartheid movement within South Africa meant that the system of white minority rule was collapsing from within. It was under these circumstances that the Japanese government strengthened its support for South Africa, Kenya and Egypt and the pro-Western nations surrounding those countries.

I would like to turn here to intervention in South Africa through economic measures. To illustrate, Japan's exports to South Africa amounted to USD 60 million in 1962, with imports worth USD 119 million. However, looking at the figures for 1980, there had been drastic increases, with exports at USD 1.8 billion and imports at USD 1.744 billion. This is dramatic growth, with exports rising by a factor of 30 and imports by a factor of 15 in 20 years. It is notable that the exports of this period include the exports of large scale industrial plants and related high-level technology to ISCOR, the South African national steel corporation, which were also highly significant in terms of military strategy. As a result, Japan was South Africa's largest trading partner in 1981 and again in 1982, or put another way, the largest violator of economic sanctions. It should also be noted there were significant disturbances in the system of white minority rule after the commencement of the 1980's and this led to a state of emergency being declared in July 1985 and June 1986. To demonstrate the magnitude of Japan's trade with South Africa from a different angle, trade with South Africa amounted to USD 3.325 billion in 1983, exceeding trade with France in the same year, which amounted to USD 3.312 billion. This made South Africa Japan's 18th largest global trading partner. Moreover, as of 1983, trade with South Africa occupied 32% of Japan's exports to Africa overall and 49% of Japan's imports from Africa overall. In the case of trade with the countries of sub-Saharan Africa, the status of South Africa rises even higher, to a level where it occupies a 49% share of all Japan's exports and a 62% share of Japan's imports.[34]

---

[33] Ministry of Foreign Affairs. (1982) Waga gaiko no kinkyo [Diplomatic Bluebook]: Tokyo, Okurasho Insatukyoku, p. 20.

[34] Morikawa Jun. (1988). Minami Afurika to Nihon – Kankei no rekishi, kozo, kadai

Japan's export trade to South Africa amounted to USD 2.047 billion in 1988. With imports worth USD 1.93 billion making the total trade figure USD 3.977 billion, Japan again became South Africa's largest trading partner. Japan's conduct in trading with South Africa was specifically pointed out and criticized in the General Assembly of the United Nations in December of that year. However, the problem was the fact that Japan had maintained an extremely high level of trade with Pretoria, worth USD 3.5 billion or more annually, throughout the 1980s. It should be pointed out that if imports of South African products via the third countries of Switzerland or Israel, such as gold or diamonds, were included, the real trade figures would quite likely be much higher. The 'separation of political and economic matters' argument used by the Japanese government in response to this criticism had no persuasive power whatsoever, as Japan had applied strict economic sanctions to the Soviet Union in the new Cold War conditions of the early 1980's following the invasion of Afghanistan. Further, the majority of goods imported from South Africa, for example iron ore, coal and agricultural products, were not necessities in terms of economic security and would be easy to source from countries other than South Africa should the Japanese government so desire. Ironically, even most of the rare metal platinum imported went not to Japan's high-tech industries but for use in women's accessories. The following testimony is no doubt relevant in terms of Japan's direct private investment into South Africa at the time:

> As Japanese business was progressively investing, even during the time of the economic sanctions, it is not expected that the lifting of the sanctions will, in itself, bring about a rapid increase in investment.[35]

The above discussion leads to the following conclusions. Firstly, the relationship between Japan and Pretoria has been, contrary to the claims of the Japanese government, long, close and comprehensive in historical terms. Secondly, South Africa has, in fact, been given a cornerstone status and role in Japan's African diplomacy. This cornerstone status and role increased as time passed and even had an impact on Middle East policy that cannot be ignored. It is important to recollect that South Africa had a close relationship with Israel.

[South Africa and Japan – History, Structure and Problems of the Relationship –]; Tokyo, Dobunkan, p. 171. Note that exports to Liberia are included in Ministry of Foreign Affairs export figures to Africa in general and to sub-Saharan Africa, however the majority of these exports were of vessels sailing under a flag-of-convenience and have been subtracted as not reflecting the real situation and the data re-calculated.

[35] Keidanren. (1994). Keidanren ho-NanA keizai misshon hokokusho: [Report of the Keidanren Economic Mission to South Africa]: (Nov), Tokyo, Keidanren, p. 87.

Of course, the position of the Japanese government at the beginning of the 1990s was not simple. This is because the ANC, after winning the struggle for liberation, expressed its readiness to apply sanctions to those who had cooperated with the white minority government. The Japanese government and Japanese businesses that had expanded into South Africa, including Toyota, commenced giving aid to the victims of apartheid, the black community, at the end of the 1980s.[36]

However, the response of the black South African community to this aid, designed to vindicate the Japanese and insure against future losses, was cold. Empty Japanese sanctions against South Africa also broadened distrust and criticism of Japan. The Japanese government did not conduct a comprehensive review of its past pro-South African policies and it had no intention of putting the practical lessons learned to good use in a fresh start. Tokyo decided to take a 'wait and see' approach in relation to the changes within and outside South Africa, partly in fear and partly in anticipation. The response of the Japanese government and the Federation of Economic Organizations (*Keidanren*) to the Mandela administration should have been relief, as it provided new opportunities for pardon and reconciliation for the former apartheid powers and those who cooperated with apartheid within and outside South Africa. The background to Mandela's rejection of bitterness was the pragmatic political judgment that the rebuilding of the South African economy and society could not be achieved by self-help efforts alone. The involvement of Europe, the U.S., Japan and capital from those sources would be indispensable. Instead of taking the opportunity it had been given by the ANC to humbly reflect on its past conduct and make a completely new start in bilateral relations, the Japanese government, simply invited President Mandela to Japan in July 1995 as a state guest. On 27 June, the Ministry of Foreign Affairs released a noteworthy document marking the visit, entitled "The Significance of President Mandela's Visit to Japan". The document is a direct expression of the Ministry's perceptions and position on African diplomacy in the post-Cold War, post-apartheid era. Its main points are introduced below:

> As South Africa has a pivotal position in the economic development of the African continent, taking up 40% of the GDP of sub-Saharan Africa and its stability and development are indispensable to southern Africa and to Africa as a whole, Japan's relationship with South Africa is the cornerstone of Japan's Africa diplomacy. With the passing of apartheid, President Mandela's

[36] Keidanren (ed.), Keizai dantai rengokai gojunenshi [A 50-Year History of the Keidanren]: Keidanren. (1999): Tokyo, Keidanren, p. 750.

> strong charismatic leadership will be indispensable to stable development and the preservation of the unity of multiracial South Africa. Japan hereby expresses its support for the President's leadership.[37]

Taken at face value, this means that Japan will implement its post-Cold War diplomacy with Africa by building on the centerpiece of South Africa. The question is whether this will lead to the South Africanization of Africa. This South Africa-centric policy was exemplified by the holding of the 1st Japan-South Africa Partnership Forum to "consult, not only on political and economic issues between Japan and South Africa but also on African development problems and global problems" in January 1999. The Ministry of Foreign Affairs made the following statement on the meaning of the Forum:

> In consideration of post-Cold War Africa and the world in the 21st century, Japan conducted an exchange of opinions with a practical focus on building Japan's first strategic partnership with an African nation.[38]

Bilateral human exchanges have also increased in volume over the preceding decade, becoming commonplace and bi-directional. Following the lead of the business community, there has been great activity in terms of reciprocal visits by political leaders as well. As a sequel to President Mandela's 1995 visit, President Mbeki was invited to visit Japan as a guest of state in 2001. From Japan, Prime Minister Yoshiro Mori visited South Africa in 2001, followed by Prime Minister Junichiro Koizumi in 2002.

The closer relationship between the Japanese business community and South Africa is illustrated by the *Keidanren* cooperating with the Ministry of Foreign Affairs to dispatch business missions to southern Africa in May 1992 and November 1996, holding a Japan-South Africa Business Forum every year since the 1st Forum in 2001 and the promotion, with the continued support of both governments, of exchanges with the white capital counterparts of 50 major Japanese business members of the *Keidanren* standing committee on sub-Saharan Africa, who have expanded into South Africa.

Closer bilateral relations were also realized in the economic field. Attention should be given to the maintenance of the value of Japanese exports to South Africa at an average of USD 1.7 billion since the early

[37] Ministry of Foreign Affaires, Mandera daitoryo no hounichi no igi [The significance of President Mandela's Visit to Japan]: June 27, 1995.

[38] Ministry of Foreign Affairs. 21 January 1999. Report of Visit to Africa by Senior Advisers to Prime Minister Hashimoto. Gaiyo to seika [Outline and Results]: Tokyo, Ministry of Foreign Affairs.

1990s and the further increase in imports from South Africa after 1996, which have been maintained at a high plateau of around USD 3.0 billion. 1996 was an epoch-making year from the perspective of the post-war history of Japan's trade and commerce with the sub-Saharan Africa. This is because this was the year in which the total value of Japan's trade with South Africa surpassed the value of Japan's trade with the 47 nations of sub-Saharan Africa. 2000 is also a year worthy of attention, as in this year, South Africa's share in Japan's total trade figures was 0.6%, whereas the average share of Japan's total trade taken up by all the other countries of sub-Saharan Africa was only 0.3%.[39] It is interesting to note that the combined total value of Japan's trade with sub-Saharan countries other than South Africa in that year, JPYen 313.1 billion, was less than the total value of Japan's trade with New Zealand, JPYen 372.4 billion.[40] Put another way, the value of black African nations for Japan in terms of export markets, has actually disappeared.

Conclusion: An Outline of Japan's Sub-Saharan Africa Policy and Overall Structural Reforms Required in Japan's Diplomacy with Africa

There are only 6 sub-Saharan African countries mentioned in the 2000 *White Paper on International Trade*; South Africa, Nigeria, Ethiopia, Kenya, Zambia and Liberia. Moreover, the 1999 *Diplomatic Bluebook* does no more than briefly list the 17 nations to which an ambassador has been dispatched. In 1961, when the African Division was established in the Middle Eastern Affairs Bureau of the Ministry of Foreign Affairs, sub-Saharan African countries attracted attention as export markets, sources of raw materials and for securing votes at the United Nations. However, interest in relation to markets and resources had faded by the late 1970's due to the economic woes of Africa and the failure of plans for the large-scale development and importation of natural resources from Zaire. Further, the acquisition of UN votes had also become difficult from as early as the mid 1960s due to the disillusionment and offence caused by Japan's dual diplomacy, speaking of friendship and cooperation with the sub-Saharan Africa while forming a close relationship with racist regimes.[41]

---

[39] According to JETRO materials; Wagakuni no tai nan a boeki 1993-2000 [Japan's Trade with South Africa 1993-2000].

[40] According to Ministry of Foreign Affairs Middle East and African Affairs Bureau, Second African Division materials; Wagakuni no chiikibetsu yushutsunyugaku [Japan's Import and Export Figures by Region].

[41] 1966. Ministry of Foreign Affairs. Waga gaiko no kinkyo, [Diplomatic Bluebook], Tokyo, Okurasho insatukyoku, p. 12.

This impediment has only been recently removed, allowing Japan to approach black Africa at the U.N. freely since the beginning of the 1990s, when by a stroke of good fortune the Cold War and apartheid suddenly disappeared. However the Foreign Ministry's dilemma is that although African support for Japan has been augmented through holding TICAD, the measures and resources Japan can use to meet the expectations of TICAD are limited. To illustrate, the ODA budget is shrinking and further, the countries to which preferential grants are given are fixed, because the financial circles on which the Ministry relies are also diffident about trade and direct private investment in sub-Saharan Africa. In such circumstances, the only choice left to the Ministry is a policy of effective appeals for the prioritization of Africa. These policies include emergency humanitarian aid by NGOs, the strengthening of basic human needs (BHN) aid, international conferences symbolized by TICAD and invitational diplomacy. Further, the roving post of Deputy Minister for African Affairs was newly created in May 2001 to energize lobbying of the African Union. In the same manner, Self-Defense Forces detachments were dispatched to Mozambique and Zaire in a move that was symbolic but highly effective in terms of publicity. However, the political and diplomatic impact of TICAD also continues to dim, since the European Union (E.U.), the U.S. and China have all held large-scale international conferences on aid for Africa. African expectations of the Japanese government and of Japanese society in general in these circumstances are no doubt for the kind of structural reforms outlined below.

Firstly, for the Japanese government and the Ministry of Foreign Affairs to consider Africa and, in particular, the peoples of Africa as important in African diplomacy, not external forces, and in particular not the wishes and interests of the 'Anglo-Saxon Club.' This requires moving from 'banana' like thought and behavior (yellow on the outside but white on the inside) and incorporating democratic values and aims, namely freedom, equality, social justice and human dignity into African diplomacy and augmenting the involvement of the Japanese people in the formation and implementation processes of African diplomacy.

Next would be for the Japanese people themselves to prioritize eliciting a more balanced interest and understanding of Africa instead of offering cheap sympathy. The Japanese people themselves should take a direct role, actively setting the agenda for the Ministry of Foreign Affairs and Japan's financial circles and promoting grassroots level exchanges and solidarity with Africa. These are no doubt the sort of expectations Africa would have. Put another way, it is important to not only have the unilateral expectation and demand that Africa will change, but for the Japanese government and Japanese society itself to make an effort to change. Under current conditions, the encouraging efforts being made by the Japanese people towards building relationships of mutual respect, in which mutual benefits are obtained, center on NGOs.[42]

It is unfortunate that no significant positive changes have been seen on the part of the Japanese government and the Ministry of Foreign Affairs, except for the efforts of Sadako Ogata, the former head of the UNHCR and current director of the Japan International Cooperation Agency (JICA), who has tried to give more priority to Africa and to give more decision-making ability to those JICA officials working on the ground in Africa.

Just as with Japan's history in Asia, there is a syndrome of not facing Japan's history in Africa squarely. The trend to cover up and justify inconsistencies in words and actions through the manipulation of information and perceptions is just as deep-rooted as ever. The result is a negative boomerang effect, inflicting great damage to Japan. Although 60 years have passed since the Second World War, it is debatable whether Japan as a nation has friends in Asia. It would appear that our diplomats are tremendously mistaken. The national interest is not something they can determine in their own minds and they are certainly arrogant if they judge it acceptable to manipulate African leaders and the Japanese people in order to realize their perception of Japanese national interest, which are to secure natural resources and U.N. votes in their quest for a seat on the U.N. Security Council and to support pro-American and pro-Western European African regimes. They need to recognize that it is by promoting wider, long-term and common global interests that Japan can best promote its own interests.

In fact, rather than being manipulated, it may well be that the Japanese government has already been seen as 'the Emperor with no clothes' by the highly politically aware African community. Japan failed to gain the votes of two thirds of the U.N. membership needed to win election as a non-permanent member of the U.N. Security Council in 1978. Japan

[42] There have been notable responses to Japan's policies on ODA for Africa from a small but effective number of Japanese NGOs. These include critical & analytical research, watch-dog and advocacy activities by the Japan Wildlife Conservation Society (JWCS) on the ivory issue, by the Friends of the Earth Japan (FoEJ) on the construction of a controversial dam project in Kenya, and by the NGO Mozambique-net, which has taken up the issue of exporting questionable pesticides and chemical fertilizers to Africa as aid to increase food production.

In the sphere of grass roots exchange activities to enhance mutual understanding and cooperation between Japan and Black Africa, the activities of the Kansai Southern Africa Network (KASAN) have been noteworthy.

* All translations from the Japanese are the responsibility of the author.

was elected in 1986 but with only a bare margin of four extra votes. In the end, the most important national interest to be considered in diplomacy is perhaps a country's credibility. The question is whether the Japanese government regards Japan as having a credible presence in Africa. Japan should not underestimate Africa's perspicacity.

References

Africa Society of Japan (n.d.) *Gekkan Afurika* [*Africa Monthly*]. Tokyo.

Africa Society of Japan (2002-2003) Gyomuhokoku [Annual Report]: Tokyo.

Association for Promotion of International Cooperation. (2000) Kaihatu tojokoku kunibetu keizaikyoryoku shirizu. Echiopia [Developing countries country by country economic cooperation series, Ethiopia]: Tokyo.

Association for Promotion of International Cooperation. (1998) Kaihatu tojokoku kunibetu keizaikyoryoku shirizu. Gahna [Developing countries country by country economic cooperation series, Ghana]: Tokyo.

Association for Promotion of International Cooperation. (1988) Kaihatu tojokoku kunibetu keizaikyoryoku shirizu. Kenia [Developing countries country by country economic cooperation series, Kenya]: Tokyo.

Association for Promotion of International Cooperation. (1996) Kaihatu tojokoku kunibetu keizaikyoryoku shirizu. Maraui [Developing countries country by country economic cooperation series, Malawi]: Tokyo.

Association for Promotion of International Cooperation. (1992) Kaihatu Tojokoku kunibetu keizaikyoryoku shirizu. Naijeria [Developing countries country by country economic cooperation series. Nigeria]: Tokyo.

Association for Promotion of International Cooperation. (1996) Kaihatu Tojokoku kunibetu keizaikyoryoku shirizu. Minamiafurika [Developing countries country by country economic cooperation series. South Africa]: Tokyo.

Association for Promotion of International Cooperation. (1997) Kaihatu tojokoku kunibetu keizaikyoryoku shirizu. Tanzania [Developing countries country by country economic cooperation series. Tanzania]: Tokyo.

Association for Promotion of International Cooperation. (2000) Kaihatu tojokoku kunibetu keizaikyoryoku shirizu. Ejiputo [Developing countries country by country economic cooperation series. Egypt]: Tokyo.

Association for Promotion of International Cooperation. (1992) Kaihatu tojokoku kunibetu keizaikyoryoku shirizu. Chunijia [Developing countries country by country economic cooperation series. Tunisia]: Tokyo.

Association for Promotion of International Cooperation. (1994) Kaihatu tojokoku kunibetu keizaikyouryoku shirizu. Morokko [Developing countries country by country economic cooperation series. Morocco]: Tokyo.

Chomsky, Noam. (2003) Media Control – The Spectacular Achievements of Propaganda. Tokyo. Syueisha Japanese translation edition. (Translated by Suzuki Chikara)

Davidson, Basil. (1971) Which Way Africa? The Search for a New Society. Harmondsworth. Penguin Books Ltd.

El-Khawas Mohamed, and Barry Cohen (eds). (1976) [The Kissinger Study of Southern Africa-National Security Study Memorandum 39-]: Westport, CT Lawrence Hill.

Gaikoforamu [*Foreign Affairs Forum*]. (Dec. 1993, Feb. 1996, Aug./Sep. 1998, Jun. 2001, 2004) Tokyo. Toshi Shuppan.

Irie Akira (1991) Shin nihon no gaiko [Japan's Diplomacy revised edition]: Tokyo. Chuokoronsha.

Itagaki Yuzo (ed.) (1991) Chuto anarishisu [Analysis of the Middle East]: Tokyo. Daisan shokan.

Japan Business History Council (ed.) (1978) *Keizai dantai rengokai sanjunenshi* [*A 30-Year History of the Keidanren*]. Tokyo. Keidanren.

Japan Business History Council (ed.). (1999) *Keizai dantai rengokai gojunenshi [A 50-Year History of the Keidanren]*. Tokyo. Keidanren.

Keidanren A Government dispatched Economic Misson to Africa (ed.) (1970) Hirakeyuku afurika [Developing Africa]: Tokyo.

Keidanren Keidanren Committee on Africa (ed.) (1988) Seifu haken afurika keizai misshon? [A Report of the Government dispatched economic mission to Africa]: Tokyo.

Keidanren Kokusai Keizaibu (ed.) (1991) Keidanren nan a keizai syakai shisatu misyon? houkokusho [A Report of the Keidanren Study Mission to South Africa]: Tokyo.

Keidanren Keizai Kyoryokubu (ed.) (1992) Seifu haken nanbu afurika keizai misshon? hokokusho [A report of the Government dispatched economic misson to Southern Africa]: Tokyo.

Kennan George. [American Diplomacy, Expanded Edition]: Chicago. The University of Chicago. Japanese edition (2000) by Iwanami Shoten Tokyo, Translated by Kondo Shin'ichi & Others.

Kitamura Hiroshi & Others. (1983) *Nichibei kankei o toitsumeru [Pressing for Answers in Japan-U.S. Relations]*. Tokyo. Sekai no Ugoki Sha.

Ministry of Economy, Trade and Industry (formerly Ministry of International Trade and Industry). (Since 19) *Tsusho hakusho [White Paper on Trade]*. Tokyo. Ministry of Finance Printing Bureau.

Ministry of Foreign Affairs. (n.d.) *Gaiko seisho [Diplomatic Bluebook]*. Tokyo. Ministry of Finance Printing Bureau.

Ministry of Foreign Affairs. (n.d.) Economic Cooperation Bureau. *Wagakuni no seifu kaihatsu enjo – ODA hakusho [White Paper on Japan's Official Development Assistance]*. Tokyo. Association for Promotion of International Cooperation.

Ministry of Foreign Affairs, Middle Eastern and African Affairs Bureau. (1980, 1983, 1986, 1990, 1993, 1998, 2002). *Afurika binran – Sahara inan no kuniguni [Africa Handbook – Sub-Saharan Countries]*. Tokyo.

Matuura Koichiro. (1990). Enjo gaiko no saizensen de kangaeta koto [Thoughts on the Frontline of Aid Diplomacy]: Tokyo. Association for Promotion of International Cooperation.

Muroi Yoshio. (1999). Nanboku nannan mondai [North-South & South-South Problems]: Tokyo. Yamakawa Syuppansha.

Nishikawa Jun. (ed.) (1998) Shakai kaihatu [The Social Development]: Tokyo. Yuhikaku.

Okamoto Mituo and Yokoyama Masaki. (ed.) (1999) Heiwagaku no genzai [Peace Studies in the Making]: Kyoto. Horitubunkasha.

Okazaki, Hisahiko. (1989). Senryakuteki shiko to wa nanika *[Defining Strategic Thought]* Tokyo. Chuokoronsha.

Owada, Hisashi. (1994). *Sankaku kara sozo e – Nihon gaiko ga mezasu mono [From Participation to Creation – Japan's Diplomacy Objectives]*. Tokyo. Toshi Shuppan.

Russell G. John. (1991). Nihonjin no kokujinkan [Japanese View of Black People]: Tokyo. Shinhyoron.

Tanaka Hiroshi. (1997). Zainichi gaikokujin [Foreign Residents of Japan. Revised edition]: Tokyo. Iwanami Shoten.

The Special Sub-Committee on Economic Security of the Industrial Structure Council, Ministry of International Trade and Industry (ed.) (1982).

Keizai anzen hosho no kakuritu o mezashite [Towards Ensuring Economic Security]: Tokyo. Tsusho Sangyo Chosakai.

Education and Modernization: An Examination of the Experiences of Japan and Ethiopia

GETACHEW FELLEKE

ABSTRACT

Japan has cultivated an immensely positive image among countries in the Sub-Saharan Region of Africa. Its industrial prowess, its post-war image as champion of peace, and its generous contributions of aid through its ODA lie behind this image. Beyond this, it also has long been regarded as a model of how a non-western and non-European country can successfully undertake a fast paced process of modernization. It is espccially appealing as a model for African states to emulate in that the country managed to achieve its modernization without having to bear an undue cost of erosion of sovereignty and cultural integrity. This paper is a comparative examination of the early and divergent approaches to modernization that were adopted by Japan and Ethiopia.

A commonly accepted strategy for economic development has been the availability of a sizable human resource with skills that are productive and growing. It is a strategy that was once widely accepted as a sure means for accelerating development. Hence the great commitment to investment in education that African states such as Ethiopia undertook during the first half of the Twentieth Century. Despite their considerable efforts to invest in education, however, it is now clear that the anticipated returns on their investment have failed to materialize. In terms of its capacity to bring social and economic progress for Africa, the role that modern education was intended to play appears to have somehow been blunted.

Yet, education has also proven an effective tool in other places and at other times. The experience of Japan is particularly instructive in this regard. A large and early investment in modern education laid the foundation for the effective mobilization of Japan's economic and social resources. How, then, did education deliver on its promises of progress and development in Japan but failed to do so in the context of African countries such as Ethiopia? This study examines the strategies for the adoption and dissemination of education in Japan and Ethiopia. In other words, the study will attempt to explore answers to the question: how did the strategy of education for accelerated development succeed in Japan but not in Ethiopia?

During the early decades of the 20th Century, Ethiopian intellectual leaders showed a desire to learn how the Japanese modernizers proved so effective in what they set out to do.[1] As a result, there has been a close scrutiny of key Japanese institutions that were thought to have spearheaded the country's modernization. Among these institutions, Japan's education system and the context in which it evolved and influenced the modernization process has been of a particularly high interest. Some of the progressive thinkers among Ethiopia's early 20th Century leaders were readily impressed by the successes achieved by the Japanese education system. Taking their cues from this Japanese success, they urged their compatriots to exert greater efforts to spread modern education in Ethiopia.[2]

This type of fascination with the Japanese way appeared to have captured the popular imagination of ordinary folks of the time as well. A reference to such popular sentiment is indicated by the following quotation.

> "The theme of modernization, for the sake of strength, likewise found expression in another poem, which declared, in the words of the Psalms, that counsel was beautiful for those who accepted it, and concluded:
>
> He who accepted it, fears no one.
> He will become like Japan, strong in everything."[3]

---

[1] Reflecting the strong impression that Japan had made on the thinking of Ethiopian intellectuals, an important work by an Ethiopian scholar, Bahru Zewde's *Pioneers of Change in Ethiopia: The Reformist Intellectuals of the Early Twentieth Century*, mentions Japan or Japanese on seventeen separate pages while Britain and the U.S.A. are together mentioned only on only ten separate pages.

[2] Notable among this group was Fitawrari Deresa Amante who brought to bear both his social standing as well as his personal resources to advance the cause of modern education in Ethiopia. See Bahru Zewde, p. 32. Also, among the early 20th Century contributions to Ethiopian literary work was Kebede Mikael's book: *Japan Indemin Seletenetch?* (This roughly translates as: "How did Japan Achieve Its Progress?")

[3] In Richard Pankhurst, History of Education, Printing and Literacy in Ethiopia, in *Addis Tribune Archives*, 02, 10, '98.

In Ethiopia, as, no doubt, in other developing regions as well, there clearly was a deep admiration for what Japan was able to achieve as a nation that set out to modernize its economy and society. There was also a conscious desire on the part of at least some Ethiopian leaders to emulate the Japanese, as can be gathered from their pronouncements and specific references regarding the Japanese experience. This offers the student of development an important question to investigate: Why has there existed a gap between the desire of these leaders to modernize their country, on the one hand, and the very limited achievements in education on the ground, on the other?

Modernization

A theme that underlies the discussion throughout this paper is the concept of modernization. The significance of modernization as an issue in this paper derives from two interrelated postulations: 1) Ethiopia's recurring social and economic problems reflect the detrimental effects of the country's weak institutions – institutions that have failed to modernize as they underwent little change over the course of several centuries; 2) Countries like Japan managed to overcome their social and economic problems mainly because they succeeded in a process of modernization that overhauled and upgraded their institutions, including their systems of education and technologies of production.

If we liken institutions to vehicles that transport society from one stage of its progress to another, modernization then becomes similar to the up-shifting of gears in order to effectively negotiate the changing terrains and inclines of social and economic challenges that every society comes to face. In some countries such as Ethiopia, population grows relentlessly even as some of the resource base needed for the production of customary provisions shrinks. In addition, changes in tastes and preferences lead to more intensive consumption by a new self-centered and insistent consumer class. The awareness of, and influences from, rapid changes around the world further add to the urgency of meeting these domestic challenges.

Those institutions that undergo modernization permit societies to make a rational, efficient and timely use of their resources to meet the evolving and expanding needs of their citizens. Institutions that fail to undergo such modernization will soon get overwhelmed by the demands of the new challenges. When further weighed down by the constraints of a degraded natural environment that a growing population triggers, the challenges may quickly spiral towards a national disaster. Ethiopia has experienced a number of these disasters in the past. A modernization process that is purposefully[4] pursued and effectively implemented equips societies with the methods with which to manage new challenges that inexorable change will continue to bring. At the very least, societies must review and revise the effectiveness of their existing inventories of institutions with the aim of systematically removing or modifying those that are a detriment to on-going adjustments to meet people's needs.

Education and Modernization

An important feature of modernization is that societies undergo varying levels of transformations in their social, cultural and economic lives. Education is perhaps the single most important medium through which the socially transforming influences of modernization are both received and disseminated. In that sense, the education system becomes the institutional face of the process of modernization. Some of these transformations are deliberately sought and embraced by those championing modernization. But some others are neither anticipated nor even universally welcomed. Inevitably, and early on, this may cast education either as something that bears hope for a society's future, or as a Trojan horse that would only bring its cultural ruin.

Whatever the public sentiment that it may engender, the education system of a country often plays far-reaching and lasting roles in redefining the direction and pace of social transformations. Thus, whenever it is allowed to take its own natural course of evolution, education inevitably implies change and transformation. Over the long term, the instance of such change as well as the pace and direction that it acquires tend to take a life of their own regardless of the intents and designs of any contemporary champions of education. However, this long term can be made even longer depending on the frequency and strength of resistance points that may get placed on the path of education reform in the interim. Accordingly, the impact that an education system can register in ushering in social and economic transformations varies from one society and one time period to another.

[4] The term modernization likely imparts a range of meanings, and it may be argued that not all those meanings may be socially redeeming. The modernization represented by the guillotine displacing the axe-wielding executioner is an example. But the term as it is applied here refers to a gradual process of overhauling the institutions and technology of a country with respect to their instrumentality for enhancing the quality of life of people in general. The abolishment of the death penalty, as opposed to its mere modification, would thus represent a more reliable measure of such progress in modernization. Or, more to the point, developing drought-resistant seeds or introducing affordable mechanical ploughs to replace the ox drawn ploughs that are still in use in Ethiopia are examples of purposeful modernization.

How is education connected to the social and economic transformation of societies? Other things being equal, a popular and practical function of education has been the production of specific skills that help solve the prevailing puzzles of life in a specific society at a specific time. The practicality and adequacy of an education system should rest on how well it tailors itself to meeting these specific societal puzzles as and when they arise. To that extent, a society needs to cultivate its own customized education system to solve its own puzzles. This is about making or selecting a tool that matches the requirements of the societal task at hand; it is about a society ensuring that its education system is relevant to its own particular needs. In short, it is about learning how to learn well in order to live well.

The benefits of education to society and the need for developing an education system that proves relevant to that society are seldom in question. But what strategy in education must a society follow to ensure such an outcome? Here, the answer to this last question is anything but simple or direct. A society is seldom endowed with a single end, even when that end concerns its choice of an education system. It has multiple and even conflicting ends with multiple stakeholders. An important question to ask then is "what consensus exists on the particular strategy of education that may be needed in a society at any one time?" And who says what education is needed? The following quotation further highlights this point:

> Education reflects a society's capacity to produce, reproduce, adapt, and consume itself because it is both an agent and a product of those pursuits. Diverse and often complex educational formations – each one distinguished by its own particular configuration of accepted knowledge, theory, practice, and institutions – that appear and disappear over the course of a society's history as it attempts to act upon itself and its environment, reproduce itself, and endow itself with meaning are neither created nor sanctioned by metasocial, evolutionary forces acting upon that society. Rather, they are produced by that society, within a "field of conflictive creation" that is marked by competing class interests and animated by "debates and conflicts, political initiatives and claims, ideologies and alienations."[5]

In other words, the contents and the relevance of an education system may be specific to a particular society and to a particular period in a country's history. But this specificity may not necessarily be a reflection of a "master plan" scheme to address some generally agreed-upon social and economic needs of society as a whole. Rather, at best, it may represent

[5] Beauchamp, Edward R., *Windows on Japanese Education*, New York: Greenwood Press, 1991, p. 2.

a compromise between the ever shifting, evolving, and mostly conflicting interests of various groups in society. And at worst, it may be imposed on society by the group that wields political authority. As the views, interests and preferences of the dominant group go, so go the form and content of education that are put in place. The system of education built around such compromise or dominance can last so long as either the coalition of interests or the monopoly of power from which it receives its support can be sustained.

For many developed as well as developing societies with education systems that are mostly of "home-grown" varieties, the role that education plays in society may be sheltered from controversies during long periods of social and economic stability. It may be assumed that, under a normal course of evolution, an education system's very existence evinces a gradual process of accommodations and adjustments to the social, cultural and idiosyncratic requirements by and within which it is formed. This is similar to the concept of what naturalists call "co-evolution." The system of education in place caters to the expressed requirements of the society, and the society comes to claim and protect the system as an asset that is uniquely its own. This process of accommodation and adjustment is what lends the education system its social relevance and shields it from challenges and attacks. Such social relevance of an education system is preserved for the duration that the social and economic environment in which it evolved is also preserved. But as soon as that social and economic environment faces challenges from internal or external sources, the existing system of education begins to appear lacking and outdated. This will soon invite overt challenges and calls for reform.

While challenges to existing education can develop fairly rapidly in the face of a social environment that is in crisis, attempts at reforming it are likely to prove both contentious and painfully time consuming. And where the threat to the social environment originates externally, the questioning and challenges that are directed at the existing system of education are often accompanied by a search for an external model of education that would prove more in tune with a society's current and future needs.

Some time during the second half of the 19th Century, two countries, Japan and Ethiopia, found their existing social and economic systems under challenge as a result of externally generated crisis that each country found itself ill prepared to face. One outcome of this social and economic crisis was the realization in each country that its existing system of education was too archaic and inadequate for the requirements of the time. There was an early recognition and commitment in Japan that major reforms in education needed to be implemented quickly. Ethiopia's efforts in bringing about such reforms was more measured and drawn-out than Japan's. But in both cases, each country sought to import and implement western education as a means of accelerating its economic and social modernization.

An imported system of education, unlike a home grown variety of education, cannot deflect controversies for long. Importing an entire education system carries much risk. It amounts to an experiment in which a society's transformation is entrusted to the guidance provided by an education that had evolved in societies with dissimilar economic, social and cultural needs and institutions. It is an experiment that can encounter numerous impediments. It is also an experiment that inevitably invites controversies.

This paper examines some of the conditions that surrounded the introduction of western education into Japan and Ethiopia during the early stages of their respective modernization. It will analyze the level of receptivity for adopting an imported system of education in the two countries. Official roles in the adoption of modern education in the two countries will be compared and contrasted. More importantly, the various factors that came into play in either impeding or enhancing attempts at education modernization in both countries will be studied. The paper will conclude by exploring and discussing some probable implications of the two countries' track records in modernizing their respective education systems.

Demand-pull Education

Applying a strictly economic model, a human resource perspective of education is perhaps the least complex of educational strategies to study. In its simplest form, it implies the generation and harnessing of knowledge for the purpose of enhancing society's productivity to shore up its cultural and material wellbeing. It is about the deployment of more economic resources through the formation of human capital. Education and education institutions serve as resource markets that produce and supply human capital. When they function efficiently, they respond to the changing requirements of market demand by making available the right quantity and quality of such a resource at the market clearing price. The institution of education that evolves will thus respond to the inducement (or pull) of demand for consumption of education.

As is the case with respect to other goods and services, the efficiency of the market is displayed in its capacity to provide answers to numerous demand and supply problems. How do we establish how much, and what type, of human capital is needed? How is this human capital to be produced and deployed? Do these and other complex questions present a challenge? That may be so. But these are precisely the types of questions for which the market is said to offer answers. For the subtle and not so subtle communication that goes on between suppliers and consumers of human capital will, sooner or later, find an efficient resolution to these questions. The supply in human capital surges and ebbs in response to the green and red light signals issued by market determined prices for specific skills. The market thus serves as an efficient clearing-house for sorting out the numerous decisions on the type and level of human capital to be produced.

Does the market offer all the necessary clues on means and methods of human capital formation? The answer to this has to be contingent on whether we can assume that information and all other market supporting institutions do exist for the market to function as it is intended to do. In other words, for decisions on human capital formation to rely on the market, the market has to exist first and an effective market demand has to be in play. But what if there is no market to speak of? What if there are no price-signals to guide decisions on human capital development? What if education as a modern-day resource remains a yet unfamiliar concept? What happens then?

Two Phases of Education

There are at least two problems that materialize when applying the market approach to the process of human capital development. The first problem has to do with the phases through which a society's education evolves. It is possible to identify two such phases, education for literacy and education for advancement. Education for literacy often precedes the formation of a viable market system, and its provision, therefore, is not market driven. Thus only one of these two phases, education for advancement, can be expected to respond to cues from the market. The second problem concerns the attempts to transfer modern education (in either of the two phases) to non-modern societies. This presents a problem because a great social, economic, and cultural disconnect exists between the point of "supply" where such education originates and the new point of "demand" where it is intended for consumption.

The first of these dual phases, education for literacy, involves the formal and organized means for reproducing and disseminating society's existing know-what and know-how. Such education serves as a means for the reproduction of existing knowledge. It is reproductive in its aims in that it is intended to increase the size of the population with access to an existing type and level of education. The type and level of education found in a few geographic or cultural corners of a country get disseminated to include a much larger and broader population group. To borrow a concept from development economics, education for literacy is a phase that can be described as education widening. Its accomplishments are measured by national statistics indicating number of schools or classrooms, number of students at the different levels of schools, national literacy rates, etc.

The second phase, education for advancement, is that of education serving as an incubator of new knowledge for purposefully tackling a society's pressing needs and problems. Such education is conducted at colleges, universities, research institutes and major laboratories. It serves as the driving force for invention, innovation, and diffusion of new knowledge. It is mostly concerned about building specialized skills and technologies for fixing some of society's knotty problems and challenges. This may be referred to as "education deepening" to underline its contributions to the broadening and enrichment of human knowledge. Progress in this type of education is measured by the number and prestige of academics and scientists as well as by the quantity and quality of higher education and R&D establishments within a country.

How does the above dichotomy of "education widening" and "education deepening" bear on our understanding of the issue of education and modernization? More specifically, what bearing does it have on our analysis of the market's role in the development of these two phases of education? Let us examine the potentials for such market role in each phase of education.

Education Deepening

Looking at "education deepening" first, its association with the development of specialized skills clearly hints at a role that the market can play. For example, if the costs of acquiring specialized skills are high, as they often tend to be, it follows that going for such skills represents an important investment decision on the part of both individuals and society. Given that, returns on investment must become important considerations in decisions to undertake education deepening. The strength of demand for such skills is what justifies investments to supply such skills. In this type of education, the market is at its best in doing its job of efficient allocation of a highly scarce resource. The tandem cues of market demand and supply are what will shape the development of this variant of education. Absent distortions and impediments originating in non-market sources, education deepening can respond well to the fairly accurate signals that flow from a well-developed and smooth functioning market.

Distortions and impediments can and do exist, however. It matters that the market signals which education deepening responds to do actually originate within the social environment of its eventual application and use. Where the market signals originate from across both geographic and cultural boundaries, distortions will occur that could impact on the relevance of education deepening. The triumph of a particular segment of computer engineering and engineers in a developed country such as England cannot be a basis for a national strategy on education deepening in Ethiopia. But, one may ask, decision makers in countries such as Ethiopia cannot knowingly commit such an obvious error, can they? The answer to this question is anything but simple.

Demand and supply decisions by market actors are often swayed by the amount of reliable and low-cost information available to them. Given the contemporary global market concentration in information production and dissemination, it is not unthinkable that Ethiopian educators and students are more informed about labor market prospects in England, U.S., and Canada than they are about that in their own country. Strategies for education deepening may end up responding to the only available "market signals," even when such signals may have little to say about the country's particular needs. Distorted signals lead to distorted policies and decisions. As the distortions grow, there widens the gulf between the skills and aspirations[6] of the "educated" and the capacity of their society to accommodate them. If and when that happens, education deepening can degenerate into a socially wasteful investment whose costs to society will end up exceeding any benefits that may accrue from it. The possibility of negative returns on investment can be real. An education-starved country may invest heavily to produce an over-educated class of individuals only to discover that it lacks the capacity to make full use of them.

It is important to note, though, that this mismatch between demand and supply in education deepening occurs not because market signals do not apply here, but because decision-makers tend to respond to the wrong market signals. The problem can be resolved when local and national market signals gain sufficient strength to become at least as compelling to the attentions and interest of decision-makers as the market signals from abroad. This occurs when various modern social and eco-

[6] In addition to weak accountability and oversight mechanisms, such frustrated aspirations may be one reason for the rampancy of corruption among technocrats in some poor countries. Unable to secure what they consider to be their due pecuniary rewards by legal means, the educated may fall prey to the temptation to slake their ambitions by rewarding themselves through non-legal means.

nomic institutions are already in place and provide the needed support for a market system to function properly. It is possible to conclude from this that making optimal decisions on education deepening faces a much better prospect during the later stages of a country's modernization than they do during the earlier stages.

Issues surrounding education deepening gain in significance at later stages of a country's modernization process. However, education widening presents a challenge right from the outset of that process. And as the focus of this paper is the challenge of education reform at the outset of a country's modernization efforts, we will now turn our focus on the aspect of reform that concerns education widening.

Education Widening

Education widening, as defined above, is about spreading out the benefits of education in its existing form. The driving force behind this is the recognition that this type of education is a "public good." That is, its acquisition by a part of society will have benefits for the whole of society. Given its "public good" nature, the market tends to understate the benefits and overstate the costs of such education. If so, the market is likely to "under-produce" this type of education. For this reason, the market is generally regarded not to be the most suitable mechanism for providing this variant of education. Accordingly, the production and dissemination of such education is largely dependent on public policy, and it is socially provided. That, after all, is why even the most advanced and market oriented nations have departments (or ministries) of education.

Given that such an education system is policy driven, it must be based on what policy makers have identified as the socially desirable ends that education can help a particular society attain. The identified ends will in turn help influence the selection of means and methods. With the help of a carefully crafted policy, the selection and implementation of means that are compatible with identified ends will help accelerate the development of an effective system of education widening.

This is all well and good so long as such education widening takes place within the confines of one societal boundary. It might even operate, perhaps with minor glitches here and there, in another society whose level of social, economic, and political development is comparable to that of the society where the education system originated. However, the history of the wholesale transfer of education systems has not been one of societies at one level of development adopting the education systems of other societies at the same level of development. Rather, the transfers of education systems have been between societies that are at unequal levels of development. And this leads us to the second of the two problems mentioned above.

Specifically, education systems have been borrowed by tradition-bound non-modern societies from the more modern industrialized societies. While this trend of education transfer is quite understandable, it is also recognizably problematic.

Key to the problem of education transfer from modern to non-modern societies has been the issue of receptivity, given the considerable differences in the values and needs of the two types of societies. What are the determinants of receptivity or resistance to the transfer of an education system from more modern to less modern societies? Looking at the experiences of the two countries, Japan and Ethiopia, how did each proceed with the task of selecting and adopting a modern education system? What were the levels of receptivity to the imported system of education? And what elements in each country's situation influenced the level of receptivity or resistance to imported education? The following discussion will address these questions.

Receptivity to Modern Education

Receptivity to an imported education system from abroad was significantly different in Ethiopia from that experienced in Japan. There are several factors that can account for the different outcomes. Some of these factors are quite obvious, but others are subtle. They include:

A. Geography (both physical features and location in relation to other countries)
B. The contemporary polity and the line-up of national policy priorities
C. The size and strength of groups resisting modernization
D. The type of lessons extracted from early (and traumatic) encounters with the west
E. The type and level of education already established within the country.

These factors and the manner in which they impacted on attempts at education reforms in the two countries are discussed below.

A. *Geography and Receptivity to Education Modernization*

Ethiopia

The role that geography plays on the movement and adoption of international cultures, including education, can be quite significant. In the case of Japan and Ethiopia, geography played quite contrasting roles. Ethiopia's geography is one of high plateaus surrounded by arid deserts or malaria prone lowlands. "Some of the highest, most rugged and inaccessible places on the African continent are found here . . ."[7] David Korten highlights these same geographic features of the land when he writes:

> Located between Asia and Africa, this plateau has stood as a nearly impregnable mountain fortress, set apart from the forbidding deserts surrounding it by steep slopes and escarpments of up to 4,000 feet high. The highland plateau is itself a virtual equatorial paradise, with cool climate, fertile soil, and abundant rainfall. It represents a dramatic contrast to the fierce heat and the barren soil of the eastern desert, which drops to some 400 feet below sea level. Ethiopia has stood from ancient history to modern times cut off from the remainder of the world, largely withstanding both the invasions of surrounding Moslem peoples and the European colonists who at one time occupied and ruled most of the remainder of the African continent.[8]

Before the onset of modern transportation, this geography made the country inaccessible except to the most inquisitive visitor from afar. This geography-induced state of physical isolation was to become a kind of default mode that would not require Ethiopians to build fortresses or lay obstacles to keep intruders at bay. While such isolation may have insulated and protected the land from unwanted intruders, it has had at least two significant and lasting effects on the country's situation.

First, there is little doubt that this state of relative isolation helped preserve the culture and tradition of the country by minimizing the introduction and incorporation of other cultures. It thus contributed to the fairly unique social and cultural identity of the country. It also served as a factor that helped preserve the country's independence over the centuries. But there is also a second – and perhaps not so benign – effect of this isolation. In effect, Ethiopia's geography offered its people the option of self-isolation with all its attendant detrimental consequences; and they willingly chose to exercise the option.

The isolation first imposed on a people by geography leads to the development of belief systems, institutions, and practices that gradually come to be regarded as "unique" national traits that sets the country apart from other countries. A growing sense of one's own uniqueness would, in turn, instill feelings of wariness or even suspicions and distrust against outside influences. A country's isolation can thus become self-enhancing over time. The result was that Ethiopia's geography both

[7] *Spectrum Guide to Ethiopia*, Nairobi: Camerapix Publishers International, 1995 Revised Edition, p. 19.

[8] David C. Korten, *Planned Change in a Traditional Society*, New York: Praeger Publishers, 1972, pp. 17-18.

induced and interacted with its people's sense of uniqueness to become an important factor in slowing down the introduction of new ideas and methods from abroad. Without links to the external world, the country's institutions, including its education, were deprived of the revitalizing benefits of new ideas and cultures. Such self-isolation left the country's social and economic progress lagging far behind that of other countries, including those that it may have once compared favorably with.

Japan

The geography of Japan, on the other hand, posed few obstacles to the flow of ideas and cultures from countries near and far. Being an island nation, practically all the coastal regions of the country have been relatively accessible by sea. This has historically made it easy for persons and things foreign to reach Japan, and it also made it easy for adventurous Japanese to travel in and out of the country. However, this is not to say that the country has been receptive to all intruders that arrived at its shores. It may be possible that Japan, just like Ethiopia, sought its security and national integrity in seclusion and insulation from the vagaries and potential dangers of foreign intrusions. In fact this may well be the natural tendency of all societies, if given the choice. Japan, too, resorted to various measures to accomplish that goal. The *Joi*, "Expel-the-Barbarian" policy attempted by the Shogunate is an example. Measures were also adopted to close Japanese ports to Western ships in the 1860s.

But unlike the situation with Ethiopia, geography made the option of a "default mode" self-isolation unavailable to the Japanese. Lacking a natural means with which to block out intruders, Japan sought to protect its isolation by expending energy on fighting off an endless parade of unwelcome intruders. But this amounted to little more than tilting at windmills. Sooner or later, it had to redirect its energy away from futile resistance and towards the managed accommodation of such intrusions. It is perhaps this reality that has shaped the character of Japan as an adaptable nation. Quoting Leonard Schoppa:

> Japan is known as an adaptable nation – famous for its success in achieving two great transformations in its modern history. First, following the Meiji Restoration in 1868, a cadre of reformists were able to transform feudal Japan into a fast growing modern nation state by directing all of the nation's energies toward the goal of catching up with 'the west'. Then, after the Second World War, Japan was able to adjust equally efficiently to a new world order dominated by the United States – incorporating new democratic institutions and continuing its campaign to achieve economic parity with the western powers. In each of these great transformations, education reform played a central role. In the Meiji period, the reformist leaders' decision to

> institute universal primary education and a meritocratic system gave Japan an educated and trainable workforce and a talented elite at a time when the nation needed to make maximum use of its human resources in its effort to catch up. Later, following the war, the reforms carried out under the Allied Occupation succeeded in creating a more egalitarian and democratic education system, making it even more efficiently meritocratic at a time when the nation needed skilled workers to power its post-war recovery.[9]

Additionally, the country's location has placed it in the proximity of some of the earliest and most advanced civilizations in the world. Ideas and practices that arrived from China, and also from as far away as India, had registered strong cultural impacts on Japan long before the arrival of Western influence. This is a direct upshot of the country's geography.

However, geography may also set in motion other secondary factors. The receptivity that was initially precipitated by geography will in turn lead to greater receptivity. That is because such receptivity to new ideas and cultures has a tendency to gradually become self-augmenting. For example, once Japan borrowed the writing system as well as the social-political philosophy of China, the sense of urgency to protect the "integrity" of Japanese society from things Chinese tends to diminish. The foreign and the foreigner now pose much lessened threats to cultural integrity. With a degree of comfort that is engendered by the familiar, Japanese authorities resorted to pragmatically and selectively adopting imported ideas so long as those ideas did not jeopardize their own privileged positions in society.

Following the Meiji Restoration, the country launched itself even more vigorously to function as an open system. This had its risks. The country did open itself up to both potential threats and opportunities that any open system faces. However, Japanese civic and political leaders seemed fully aware of this. They followed specific policies and undertook measures not to leave things to chance when deciding to adopt western ideas and methods.

B. *A Cohesive and Coherent Polity and Receptivity to Education Modernization*

The form and philosophy of government, the articulated policies of governance, and the institutions and mechanisms of government can strongly influence the receptivity of a society to imported education. Basic to this is the existence of a centralized form of government with authority to design and implement a national education policy that is consistent with national goals for social and economic development. It is interesting to

[9] Schoppa, Leonard J., *Education Reform in Japan*, pp. 1 & 2.

note that, both in Japan and Ethiopia, the *attempt* to introduce modern (i.e., western) education did not commence in full until each country set itself on a course of achieving a centralized form of government. The more successful the attempt at political centralization, the greater the sense of urgency with respect to education reform and the fewer the obstacles to the introduction of western education.

Ethiopia

Here again, the factor of polity did not favor Ethiopia's chances at modernizing its education. In significant ways, the "Zemene Mesafint" (or the "Era of Princes") did not in any real sense come to an end at the close of the 19th Century. Referring to Emperor Haile Selassie in the 1930s, John Markakis observes, "Although he had rid himself of the most recalcitrant members of the old nobility, the Emperor still had to reckon with several powerful provincial rulers."[10] As history indicates, loyalty to the Emperor and to the central authority in Addis Ababa remained tentative and conditional even on the eve of the Italian invasion.

What this means is that, even as late as two to three decades into the 20th Century, the Ethiopian polity had, underneath its veneer of modernity, basically remained feudal and traditional. Administration of the affairs of the people beyond the reach of the capital was left to the whims of hereditary lords and their subordinates. And in the zero-sum game proposition that characterizes relationships between the ruler and the ruled under a feudal system of government, "administration" seldom meant more than just protecting the power and expanding the wealth of the ruler at the expense of the ruled.

The tendency was for the more energetic and ambitious of the populace to gravitate towards a life of soldiering and indolence. This tendency was accelerated during Menelik's reign when the Empire underwent significant expansion through conquest. The growth in the material wealth of the conquerors was accompanied by the weak and the desperate falling into harsh life of tenant farming – a life of stunted productivity and crushing poverty. Unable to resist or escape, the peasantry was easily victimized by several layers of more or less idle classes that tightly held it in their clutches.

It may be argued that this group of powerful people provided a core of national military might. And this military might may have served to deter foreign invaders form having an easy pass to conquer the land.

[10] John Markakis, *Ethiopia: Anatomy of a Traditional Polity*, Oxford: Clarendon Press, 1974, p. 202.

Many see a legitimate argument in this. On balance, however, the military might of the group seemed to have been directed more often and with more devastating effect towards subjugating and repressing other Ethiopians. Military might was used on those that were least able to resist it; and it was an instrument for appropriating wealth from those who were least equipped to produce it. This has had a lasting and detrimental influence. By turning the gun into the most valued instrument for securing one's material wellbeing, the practice instilled a tradition of disdain for physical labor. This effectively diminished prospects for industry and enterprise among some of the most able members of society even as it sanctioned an unsustainable predilection for a life of leisure and comfort.

From the economic perspective, the classes that ruled over the peasantry could demand and receive practically all the labor that they required for free. Given that, the administration of their economic affairs did not necessitate the substitution of intensive labor use for extensive labor use. In their scheme of cost and benefit calculation, better labor, with the implication of investment in skills development, could not have been all that preferable to more labor. Building schools and educating Ethiopia's youth could hardly fit into this mode of economic management.

If a modern school system was both late and slow in making its appearance in the capital, it was even later and slower in working its way to the provinces. Reflecting the narrow span of central authority control over developments in the land, Ethiopia's early education modernization efforts were confined only to the capital city, the part of the country that was under the direct control of the Emperor. Even then, however, powerful regional lords assumed the role of sponsors of the few students that attended the modern schools.[11] The official justification for this unusual practice was that these promising students lacked any other source of support to pursue their education. Practically, however, the practice could have been intended to ensure the loyalty and commitment the students so sponsored to serve the interests of their powerful benefactors. The arrangement could also prevent any type of teaching that could undermine the interests of the old order. The potential of modern education and the educated to transform the Ethiopian society thus had little chance of being realized.

In the context of the Ethiopian society of the time, the practice just described may not be all that surprising. In other countries, the introduction of a modern education system was generally preceded by some

---

[11] A few examples of this practice is discussed in Bahru Zewde, pp. 26 ff.

form of a nationalist revolution. Such a revolution succeeds in significantly curtailing or even eliminating the powers and privileges of the aristocracy. The new education system would thus face little resistance as it is deployed to advance the national interest, however that may be defined. But this was not the case in Ethiopia.

At the beginning of the Twentieth Century, the power of the Ethiopian Emperor was absolute, and remained so practically until the 1970's. This absolute power was mostly employed to keep the ambitions of rival lords in check. Political stability and defending the national boundary were other areas of concerned that absorbed their energies. When they were not engaged in defending the borders, a lot of their attentions were devoted to putting down internal dissension.[12] Throughout the reigns of both Emperors Menelik and Haile Selassie, maintaining authority over the different regions of the country became an all-consuming task that elevated matters relating to military campaigns to the highest level of their leadership priority. This sapped much resource and energy to the detriment of modernization on other fronts, including the education front.

Where the Emperors may have shown sufficient commitment to promoting modern education, many of the lords surrounding them were outright hostile to it. National development or national education goals could not be designed and promoted under those conditions. National resources could not be mobilized to underwrite modern education on a national scale.

Finally, the autocratic form of government that had ruled Ethiopia was itself a major point of resistance to education reform for much of the first half of the century. The monarchy was at the apex of a delicately balanced structure of social and economic relationships whose core organizing methods were religious mythology, coercion, and fear. These arrangements had to be protected if the monarchy was to survive. But there were also practical problems with attempting to reform just education while leaving intact these other aspects of society. The need for modernization was thus pitted against the instinctive desire for self-preservation. As a result, successive autocratic governments could not afford to do more than just pay lip service to education reform. In general, when it came to addressing their basic social and economic needs, Ethiopians came to expect and ask little from their autocratic leaders, and they received little from them. Absent the mechanisms of meaningful elections and other measures of accountability, the concept of

[12] While involving much destruction in life and property, many of these campaigns against "dissensions" were mere power struggles with little implication to nation building or securing national integrity. The campaigns also fed into the myth of the warrior/soldier as occupying an important place in national life.

government leaders as servants of the public interest remained an alien notion. This was the situation that prevailed in Ethiopia until the eve of the Second World War.

Japan

Although beset for several centuries by political fragmentation and feuds between regional warlord similar to those experienced by Ethiopia, Japan's 19th Century attempts at political centralization proved relatively more successful. The era that is known as the Meiji restoration came to represent an enduring and genuine establishment of centralized authority at the expense of the power of the regional lords known as Daimios.

> The Meiji Restoration in Japan, dating from 1868, . . . was ostensibly to restore the emperor of Japan to a position of primacy that was obscured during the Tokugawa and earlier shogunates. In practice, however, the emperor ended up with little more power than before, and real power passed to a different group of samurai who instituted a constitutional monarchy. This form of government was chosen in conscious imitation of what the Japanese modernising elite saw as the most effective forms of government in Europe and the Americas, and as they were willing to borrow wholesale a form of government, they were willing and eager to borrow other institutions including an educational system.[13]

This made it possible to create the political, legal, and administrative basis for developing modern institutions, including a modern education system. The centralized authority was able to provide direction for the development of society, and education was given full support as a means to achieving those goals. As an example, a frequently enunciated goal of the Meiji era was "catching up with the west" militarily, economically, and technologically. This goal in turn paved the way for the rapid introduction and diffusion of western type education throughout Japan.

> If the prime model for government was the UK, the prime models for education were the USA and France. The USA impressed the Japanese with the way it managed to get a great number of children into schools, and France impressed the Japanese with its high level of advanced training for a political and technological elite. So the ruling groups in Japan made the decision to establish a system of universal, compulsory elementary schooling and very high quality selective post-compulsory training. While this was based on a foreign model, it is hardly surprising that the foreign model chosen was very compatible with the traditional elite and hierarchical nature of Japanese culture.[14]

[13] James, Estelle and Benjamin, Gail, *Public Policy and Private Education in Japan*, New York: St. Martin's Press, 1988, p. 11.

[14] *Ibid.*, p. 12.

Beyond the establishment of a centralized authority, the interpretation and formulation of national priorities are important factors in determining a society's receptivity to the modernization of its education. Such interpretation in turn rests on the perception of sources of threats and security. If the perceived threat of security is the warlord in the adjoining province, any security benefits that a modern system of education may offer is not readily seen. If, on the other hand, the threat is perceived to come from a more technologically advanced country with a modern economy and military, a centralized authority would sooner or later recognize that its relative backwardness is its number-one enemy. Having recognized that, it would be keen on acquiring the benefits of modern education.

A key distinction that exists between the experiences of the two countries should be noted here. Japan succeeded in establishing both a centralized government authority and at the same time committed itself to the goal of modernizing its education. These two developments complemented each other, thus making possible the rapid modernization of Japanese education. But Ethiopia was unable to achieve effective centralization during the critical decades of the late 19th and early 20th Centuries, and that undermined its commitments to, and efforts at, education modernization.

C. *Domestic Resistance and Receptivity to Education Modernization*

By its nature one normal function of education is to instill change in ideas, attitudes, and the ways in which individuals and groups within society relate to one another. There was strong resistance to the introduction of foreign education both in Japan, until the start of the Meiji era, and in Ethiopia as late as the eve of the Second World War. However, the sources of resistance were different in each country.

Ethiopia

In the case of Ethiopia, one can detect both parallels and distinctions with the type of resistance to modern education that was experienced in Japan. There is a parallel in that one basis of such resistance is the commitment to orthodoxy in education. As in Tokugawa Japan, the view prevailed in Ethiopia that all that is knowable was already known. That being so, there was no need to introduce or even tolerate reforms in the existing (i.e., church based) form of education. But there was also a distinction.

As was indicated above, Ethiopia's geography made national insulation an option that was both possible and practicable up to a point. Such self-insulation was defended in the name of the protection and preservation of national identity. Topping the list of elements of national identity that became the fountain of resistance to education reform was the Ethiopian Orthodox Church. The Orthodox Church enjoyed a monopoly on the education taught at many of the important centers of national power. Practically all of the education to which the Christian population had access was entirely being provided by the church.

How important was this domination of Ethiopia's education by the church? According to Dr. Teshome, "Church education . . . aimed to prepare priests, monks, *debtera*, and teachers to serve in the church's programs. Church education also produced civil servants, however, such as judges, governors, scribes, treasurers, and general administrators. There was no other source of trained personnel, and most civil servants shouldered the dual responsibility of serving both church and state."[15]

Was this education adequate to the task of preparing monks and administrators? The church, which for several centuries enjoyed an uncontested control over education in the highland region of the country, held on to a rather static view of education and learning. It had become a virtual museum of the knowledge and learning that was in vogue in the 4th Century AD, the time of the introduction of Christianity to the country. Its clergy flatly maintained that all knowledge was under the exclusive realm of God. Human attempts at seeking and expanding knowledge could, therefore, only be a mark of hubris that amounted to tampering with that which was forbidden to humans. Having embraced this anti-intellectual and anti-knowledge position, the clergy appears to have practiced what it preached. A sampling of observations from a parade of early travelers in Ethiopia draws an unflattering picture of the group:

> Most travelers use extremely depreciatory words of the clergy, such as 'ignorant', 'besotted', 'lazy', and 'degraded'. Through the centuries, beginning even with the tolerant Alvarez, the criticism of the clergy has been almost unbroken. Ludolphus recorded that 'both the Patriarch and his Clergy are a poor sort of contemptible and rustic People and void of all common endowments'. 'Twelve thousand clerical drones . . . fatten in idleness on the labour of the working classes', declared Harris. Plowden speaks of 'the almost daily spectacle of their drunkenness, excesses, and immorality'. Coulbeaux has equally hard things to say at greater length. Rey writes that they are ignorant and illiterate parasites. Baum speaks of the country as 'woefully priest-ridden'. Even Mrs. Sanford, latest and most sympathetic of commentators, stigmatizes the priesthood as 'ignorant, primitive and superstitious'.[16]

---

[15] Wagaw, Teshome G., *Education in Ethiopia*, Ann Arbor: University of Michigan Press, 1979, pp. 10-11.

[16] Margery Perham, *The Government of Ethiopia*, Evanston: Northwestern University Press, 1969, p. 111.

This is not exactly the sort of group that can offer enlightenment to a nation. However, it is too easy to conclude that the church, strangely enough, presided over an education system that championed ignorance. But this will be missing the point. Though it found itself in a position of monopoly with respect to the provision of Christian Ethiopia's education, the clergy's primary duty was never the dissemination of education. Its primary duty was the spreading (or, more accurately, the celebrating) of the Orthodox Christian faith. That does not mean that it did not interfere in the social and political life of the people; it did do that in very significant ways. The church clergy did not limit its influences and activities to matters of the faith. In fact, it freely interfered in all aspects of the social and economic life of Ethiopians. It is precisely the type and level of meddling in the everyday lives of the people that opens it up to criticism.

The open hostility of the Ethiopian clergy to modernization of any form is legendary and well documented.[17] Early movements to bring modernization to Ethiopia were seen as representing threats to the privileged status of the Church. The clergy were not entirely wrong in their perception of modernization as a source of threats. A new and modern education promised change. The longer Ethiopia and Ethiopian institutions had remained in isolation from the rest of the world, the more drastic the change that modernization and education reform threatened to bring. The strength of their resistance seemed to match the size of the threats that loomed over the future of the church and its clergy. For many in and out of the clergy, however, threats to the church were treated as being synonymous with threats to the country as a whole.

As a powerful institution with far-reaching influences in the land, the Church did not stand alone in its resistance to education reform. It enjoyed the support of conservative feudal lords and, until the ascendance of Menelik II to the throne, the acquiescence and protection of the kings and emperors as well. Quoting Dr. Teshome again, "Never once, however, until the beginning of the present (i.e., the 20th) century, had any ruler sought to establish a secular program of education. Had one tried, he would perhaps have aroused the indignation of the church, as Emperors Menelik and Haile Selassie did later."[18]

[17] Bahru Zewde describes the fate of an Ethiopian scholar who, two years after his return from extensive travels and studies abroad, was thrown in jail and placed in chains. His crimes were that "he disputed the intercession of saints, . . . that he claimed that one can attain divine grace through good deeds . . . and that he held fasting to be of no value if not attended by abstinence from sinful acts . . ." *Pioneers of Change*, pp. 68-69.

[18] Wagaw, p. 22.

Resistance to modernization from the conservative religious community was very persistent and at times led to ineffective measures and compromises that could only result in cumbersome and self-defeating policies. This was the case when the Ethiopian government first set about hiring foreign teachers or sending its students for study abroad. The conservative community's fear and distrust of foreign influence was such that the acceptable site for recruitment of teachers was another site of Orthodox Christianity, Alexandria, Egypt. Ethiopian students selected for study abroad also ended up being sent to colleges in Alexandria.[19] That Egypt itself was a developing country with little of the advanced culture that the students were intended to assimilate was of little significance. What was more important was that they received little exposure to things western that might pose threats to the traditional establishment. In the tug of war being played out between the forces of tradition and the impulse for modernization, the arrangement favored a victory by the former.

Unlike in Japan where Confucian philosophy and tradition had long nurtured respect for and the promotion of education at least at the level of the upper stratum of society, education in general and secular education in particular did not seem to enjoy the high regard of the Ethiopian populace. A curious early popular saying cited in Dr. Pankhurst's 1998 article in Addis Tribune concludes that: "The worst of animals is a scorpion; and the worst of men is a scholar."[20] Without weighing the quality of insight and the degree of veracity that may or may not be contained in the saying itself, what a popular sentiment like this reveals is the huge gulf that had separated Ethiopian scholars and scholarship from the everyday lives and concerns of ordinary folks.[21] Church educated scholars devoted their time to reading from the scriptures and conducting religious rituals. When not engaged in such rituals, some even dabbled in magic and sorcery. The few scholars that had acquired foreign education carried the added burden of being too closely associated with foreigners and foreign interests. As a result, and quoting Dr. Teshome, "The influence of the foreign educated in the times of Emperors Tewodros, Yohannes, and Menelik was not so significant because of their affiliation with foreign missions, foreign ideas, or foreign religions. Such suspicions were real and difficult to overcome."[22]

---

[19] Bahru Zewde, *Pioneers of Change*, p. 81.

[20] Pankhurst, Richard, History of Education, Printing and Literacy in Ethiopia, from *Addis Tribune Archives*, 09, 18, '98.

[21] One comes across such distrust and criticism of Ethiopia's scholars even today. And the criticism comes not from the uneducated public, but from other Ethiopian scholars. The words "elite" and "elitism" are used to describe the unhealthy gulf that lies between Ethiopian scholars and the general Ethiopian public.

[22] Wagaw, p. 27.

But even under the more recent leaders, the hands of these few educated Ethiopians were not set free to apply their skills and knowledge in the service of their country and people. For all his reputation as a modernizing leader, Emperor Haile Selassie did not go far enough in making use of the precious little human capital that he had at his disposal. As Perham points out:

> The Emperor found it necessary in many cases to appoint older men of standing as ministers, and they, for the most part, were very naturally unable to appreciate the purposes or conduct the business of a ministry. To compensate for this deficiency, and also to give scope and practical expression to the desire for reforms of the younger men who had received some education, the Emperor appointed some of these as directors of departments under the ministers. This sometimes tended to produce friction or even deadlock, as the Emperor did not yet feel able to give strong support to the young reformers against their conservative superiors.[23]

This was a strategy more for assuaging the ambitions of powerful traditionalists and less for ushering modernization into a country that was already severely lagging in development. The ominous long-term implications of this arrangement could not have been hidden from these "directors of departments." Aside from the frustrations and disappointments that these early Ethiopian scholars with modern education may have felt, their experience bespeaks of the numerous and persistent obstacles that lay in the way of introducing the benefits of modern education into the country.

In denying these educated Ethiopians a meaningful role in shaping and directing the affairs of the country in a new direction, the leaders of Ethiopia squandered a golden opportunity to set the nation's future on a course of steady progress. That was a critical juncture in the history of the nation. But the tradition-bound aristocratic leaders of the land were both unwilling and unable to seize the moment and to provide the kind of bold leadership that the occasion called for.

The potential benefits and relevance of education appeared to be concealed not only from the ordinary folks, but from members of the Ethiopian aristocracy as well. Again quoting Dr. Pankhurst, "Most Ethiopian noblemen of this period are said to have been largely, if not fully, illiterate, and employed Church educated youths, to carry out their correspondence."[24] This translated into an unfavorable environment for the dissemination of education and the onset of modernization through-

[23] Perham, p. 90.
[24] Pankhurst.

out the country. As Perham points out, "... little machinery existed for executing outside the capital the measures drawn up within it. The tendency, therefore, was for the activities connected with social services, public works, police, finance and the rest to be concentrated mainly in and around Addis Ababa."[25]

The Ethiopia of late 19th and early 20th century thus appeared to be a hostile environment for the kind of education reform that Japan pursued with an unmitigated vigor. In the self-serving calculation of Ethiopia's leaders of the time, modern education promised more threats and costs than benefits. Ethiopia's clergy and aristocracy saw only risks to their privileges. The emperors, even in those rare instances when they themselves were committed to education reform, were reluctant to anger the Church and the aristocracy whose support and loyalty were crucial for their own survival. The rest of society had no civic voice and was not yet experiencing sufficient autonomy in social and economic matters to make its own demand for reforms in education. It was a situation in which there was plenty of resistance and little impetus to the introduction of modern education on a national scale.

Japan

Resistance to newly imported education in Japan, which ended with the Tokugawa era, was mostly from political authorities that were unnerved by the implications of rapid education-inspired changes in social and political relationships. This concern of authorities with the unwelcome implications of imported education is illustrated in various sources. The following decree was part of the series of measures that constituted the Kansei Reform (Kansei no kaikaku), that were intended to insulate the Tokugawa rulers from rapidly evolving changes in various aspects of life.

> In 1790, Matsudaira Sadanobu, chief councillor of the Tokugawa bakkufu and regent to the shogun, issued a decree to Hayashi Kimpo, rector of the Shoeiko, where the study and explication of neo-Confucianism had enjoyed official support since 1630. It warned that:
>
> Since the Keicho era (1596-1614), all generations have put their trust in Neo-Confucianism, and your house has been ordered to support that doctrine. Therefore, you should watchfully encourage that orthodoxy and promote its students. Recently, however, the world has witnessed the rise of several new doctrines; heterodoxy has become a fashion; customs have suffered from it; and orthodoxy [seigaku, written with characters, meaning

[25] Perham, p. 90.

> 'correct learning' or 'sacred learning'] has declined. This is a deeply regrettable situation. Even among your pupils, it is said, impure doctrines have spread. I hereby order you to discipline the school strictly. . . . Regardless of whose students they are, they should study orthodoxy, and in this way you should apply yourself to promoting the formation of talented men.[26]

A closer look reveals this to be a remarkable passage in that it captures the contradictions and conflicts inherent in policies on education under autocratic regimes. It is the contradiction that results from the fact that education is a vehicle for change, and yet change is what an established authoritarian system is bound to fear the most.

The "orthodoxy" that the Japanese authorities of the time favored, with its emphasis on textual learning and rituals, blocked the onset of the vitality and dynamism that is inherent in heterodoxy. The former conceived of a world of knowledge that is long established and static. The latter treats knowledge as both fluid and ever expanding. It is fundamentally about multiple interpretations and reinterpretations of the human experience in the light of new and changing facts and perspectives. The former seeks to legitimize and preserve the status quo, but the latter often sets the stage for the challenging and dismantling of the same.

Orthodoxy was the form of education that advocated a single world view which successive Tokugawa regimes found compatible with the protection of their own feudal political power. It was not unlike the church-controlled system in Ethiopia in that it placed education and knowledge in a straightjacket since it too maintained that knowledge is fixed and that the existing type and level of knowledge contained all that can be known by humans. The "heterodoxy" that the Tokugawa authorities found so objectionable was education in its more modern form, one that allowed for different perceptions and interpretations of human experiences. Heterodoxy recognized that human knowledge is ever changing and expanding. This is education in its ideal progressive form. But, ideal or not, it was not hard for the authorities to recognize that heterodoxy could easily plant the seeds of critical thinking that would lead to the pursuit of forms of political and social relationships that are quite different from the ones that they had come to embrace.

To summarize the preceding point, the resistance by the authorities during the closing days of the Tokugawa era is directed not so much to education or even the dissemination of education itself, but to the

[26] Beauchamp, Edward R., Windows on Japanese Education, New York: Greenwood Press, 1991, p. 1.

emergence of new forms of education that promised new views and attitudes. The source of resistance came from the highest Japanese authorities of the time. Yet these authorities had, in the past, displayed sufficient support for some form of education to expand in various parts of the land, an education system that had gradually expanded in content and geographic reach as it sought to accommodate changing commercial and administrative needs in the land. This earlier education had helped produce merchants, teachers, and other groups with their own specific social and economic interests. These interests eventually formed the basis for the growing call for reform in Japanese education. Equally important to the promotion of education in Japan, the Japanese authorities were themselves highly literate and, therefore, were invested in and appreciative of the benefits of education as such. If they had growing concerns with respect to education, it was in that they were beginning to sense major changes in the air that threatened to upset established traditions.

In one sense, the Tokugawa rulers had good cause to be nervous about the "heterodoxy" in education since its arrival coincided with rapidly unfolding changes throughout society itself. Both the regime and its resistance to the new form of education came to an end with the arrival of the Meiji era in 1867. Once the regional shogunates were dismantled, the ranks of the noblemen lost their lands and political authorities. Having lost their traditional base of power, they quickly became part of the modernizing force in the land as many of the off-springs of this class of Japanese joined service in the new government. Many others of the group started modern-sector businesses, or traveled abroad to acquire modern education.

D. *Lessons of 19th Century Encounter with the West and Receptivity to Education Modernization*

Both Japan and Ethiopia had experienced unwelcome encounter with powerful western nations during the second half of the 19th Century. Any ambivalence towards acquiring western education that the two countries may have had was put to rest when the U.S. subjected Tokyo harbor to naval bombardment in the 1860s and Italy invaded Ethiopia in the 1890s. The two western nations employed their technological advancement and industrial might to project their military power against countries on distant continents. These events represented defining moments for both Japan and Ethiopia in that each country could weigh and assess its condition and standing in relation to the rest of the world. But the two events had different outcomes in both the immediate conclusions of the encounters as well as the lessons that each country was able to draw.

Ethiopia

For Ethiopia, the encounter with Italy in 1896 may have also prompted some form of soul-searching, but any impetus for full-throttle modernization that it could have generated was blunted by the fact that the invader was defeated. It was defeated in spite of its superior technology and sophisticated military organization. This could hardly be the basis for Ethiopians admiring and emulating western education in the ensuing years. The Ethiopian spear proved mightier than the Italian tank. Or so it seemed then. Who would need to acquire the education that helped build the tank? In winning the battle of Adua, the Ethiopians lost the element of anxiety that could have served as an impetus for further national progress. Count Gleichen of the 1897 British diplomatic mission wrote:

> Up to this time all Europeans had been looked up to in Abyssinia with respect, if not fear. Adua, to use a vulgarism, upset the apple cart and entirely altered the views of the natives. The body of the Abyssinian people even now imagines that their victory has laid not only Italy, but the whole of Europe, at their feet and their heads are proportionately elevated.[27]

To the extent that the Emperor recognized the need to bring modernization to Ethiopia, he sought to do so with the cooperation and assistance of European countries. Referring to this sentiment of the Emperor, Gleichen wrote, "He has recognised that the only way of bringing his country into line with the other Powers of the world is to keep in touch with them, and as far as possible to imitate their mode of progress and civilisation. His 'line', therefore, is to make friends with European nations, and with their help, to develop his country."[28] At a time when almost all the important European nations were set on a path of colonizing Africa, the Emperor's wish to draft European assistance to modernize his nation was not realistic.

This "the Europeans can do it for us" sentiment is in stark contrast to the "can do" attitude of Japanese leaders. Instead of placing Ethiopia's future at the mercy of the goodwill of European powers, the occasion called for the country's leaders to crisscross the length and breadth of the land drumming up support for education, building new schools, recruiting teachers, and browbeating parents to send their children to school. They could have sent young Ethiopian to Europe by the hundreds, as did Japan, to bolster the ranks of the educated. They could have

[27] Pankhurst, Richard, "Late Nineteenth Century Images of Ethiopia, in Addis Tribune," March 9, 01.

[28] *Ibid.*

issued edicts, promulgated laws, garnered all necessary resources and placed the weight of their offices and personal prestige to remove the stubborn obstacles to modernization that existed throughout the empire. The Emperor's leadership would have been crucial, but it was not forthcoming. It took twelve years after Adua before the barest minimum foundation for a modern school was laid with the opening of Menelik II School in 1908. Access to this one school was not for everyone either – "A group of young nobles were selected to attend, among them being two future emperors: Lij Yasu, who succeeded Menelik, and Dejazmatch Tafari Makonnen, who was to become Emperor Haile Selassie."[29] The Emperor died in 1913 without building another school. It then took another eighteen years after the opening of Menelik II School before another school "for the nobility" was opened in Addis Ababa by the then Regent, Tafari Makonnen.

That does not mean that Emperor Menelik himself was not sincere about wishing to bring modernization to Ethiopia. All evidences suggest that he was. Visitors who met him marveled at his curiosity and interest in novel ideas and gadgets. His wish to see Europeans help him bring modernization to his country indicated the depth of his interest. But the leadership requirements of the period went far beyond mere wishful thinking and a tendency to lean on imaginary friendships. The notion that any one of the nations that were parties to the Berlin Conference would positively respond to his wishes was both a measure of his misreading of the geopolitical signs of his age as well as of the desperate lack of domestic support for his ambitions. In either case, the Emperor showed no desire to expend his considerable political capital to overcome the numerous obstacles that stymied efforts to transform Ethiopia's archaic education. That was a serious lapse of leadership. It was a lapse in leadership that condemned the nation to decades of social and economic weakness. It was also a lapse in leadership that left the door open for Maichew and the devastating attacks against the very causes that the Adua's patriots fought and died for.

The down side to the Adua encounter with the west is, therefore, that it left Ethiopians more contented than before with who they were and where their society stood in the closing years of the 19th Century. If there were ominous signals in the encounter to alert them of the momentous changes that would soon occur in their global environment, and there clearly were, they chose to ignore them. Unable to discern any national disadvantage in the country's position *vis-a-vis* the rest of the

---

[29] Markakis, p. 145.

world, Ethiopians returned from their victory with no sense of urgency to address the country's severe deficit of modern infrastructures. The "Hidden Kingdom" chose to hide from the hard existential realities that confronted it.

Meanwhile events and developments in the world did not stand still. The ground on which the country's traditional relationship with the outside world had rested was now shifting from underneath its feet. The industrial revolution was in full swing in Europe and America, and its impacts were transforming societies. A new era was dawning in which any future victory of any kind must first be preceded by peacetime victory in the development of factory towns, industrial centers, and expanding institutions of education. Industrial and economic power was supplanting military power as the only relevant foundation for national security.

Japan

For Japan, the bombardment of its capital city by a distant nation was a wake-up call that became a stark reminder of its technological backwardness and its vulnerability to foreign invasions. The event also accelerated the demise of the Tokugawa regime, which regime was shown above to be opposed to education reforms and modernization. It also strengthened the voices of reformers who advocated the modernization of Japanese society according to European and American models. "Catching up with the west" became the rallying cry of reformers. And the first catching up to be accomplished was in the area of the modernization of Japanese education. The drive for modernization had the backing of the highest Meiji government authorities, and members of the former samurai class were sent abroad to acquire western education. By 1893, a total of 23,960 schools had been built, and the total number of students, in both public and private schools, stood at 3.34 million.[30] The commitment to modernization was strong, and Japanese authorities never looked back.

The encounter with the west left different impressions and impacts in the two countries. In 1905, some forty years after the bombardment of Tokyo harbor, Japan had mastered western naval technology sufficiently to build its own battle ships and defeat Tsarist Russia's navy in a major naval battle. The world was put on notice that Japan had made good on its vow to catch up. In 1935, also some forty years after the battle of Adua, Mussolini's Italy invaded and occupied Ethiopia. The Italians

[30] James and Benjamin, p. 13.

had war aircraft and chemical weapons in their arsenal when they made their call this time around. The Ethiopians headed to battle with practically the same spears and swords that they deployed against the enemy forty years earlier. The Ethiopian Emperor fled his country to seek the "protection" that the principle of collective security implied from the very same forces whose quiet schemes led to his nation's downfall.[31] Yet, these forces had already determined that the Emperor's Ethiopia was too backward to merit their intervention, a measure which they were required to undertake as signatories to the Charter of the League of Nations. For Ethiopia, backwardness and defeat became the price of lessons that the country's leaders failed to learn.

These outcomes illustrate the stark contrast in the lessons that each country was able to draw from its first encounter with the forces of the modernized west. Japan committed itself to "catch-up" with the west. Critics may argue that, in so doing, the country traded its own national identity because it consciously decided to imitate the west. Another interpretation would be that Japan was able to preserve its independence and identity precisely because it successfully imitated the west in those areas of economy and technology that could contribute to its national integrity and resilience.

It is difficult not to conclude that, as far as Ethiopia was concerned, victory on the battlefront spelt defeat on the modernization front. Can it then be concluded that it would have been better for the Ethiopians if they had lost the battle of Adua?

In comparing the two countries' responses to encounters with the west, it is important to note the distinctions in the natures and implications of the encounters themselves. When on July 8, 1953, Commodore Matthew Perry of the United States Navy sailed into Tokyo harbor and forced Japan to enter into trade with the United States, he was neither prepared nor did he intend to occupy any of the Japanese islands. All he demanded was a treaty that allowed trade and the opening of Japanese ports to U.S. merchant ships. The impression that the incident made on the Japanese was more as one of an awakening call than as an instrument of destruction and loss. It was an inexpensive but valuable lesson for the Japanese to eventually benefit by. That, however, cannot be said about Ethiopia's encounter with the Italians at Adua.

The Italians came to Adua for the purpose of invading and occupying the entire country. A defeat in the hands of the Italians would have

[31] See Spencer, John H., *Ethiopia at Bay: A Personal Account of the Haile Sellassie Years*. Algonac, Michigan: Reference Publications, 1984, pp. 71-88.

destroyed everything the Ethiopians treasured. Without a country that they could call their own, the idea of "learning lessons from defeat" would have been of no consequence to them. For those who suggest that colonization could have brought with it modernization, it should be pointed out that a defeated Ethiopia would have fared no better than does the former Italian colony of Somalia today. The Ethiopians' victory at Adua may not have helped launch their nation on a path of modernization. But it did enable them to serve a crushing blow to a dangerous enemy, enhance their country's standing within the community of nations, and secure for themselves the right to remain masters of their own destiny. These are not gains to scoff at. If flaws can be pointed out, it is in that the victorious nation failed to build on its gains. It was unable to chart strategies and to mobilize resources on the domestic development front with the same zeal and determination that it had on the battle front.

E. *Already Existing Level of Education and Receptivity to Education Modernization*

As pointed out at the beginning of this paper, education, when allowed its own natural course of development, can be a self-augmenting process. This simply means that more education begets more education. Likewise, the receptivity to the introduction of a new system of education is likely to be better enhanced if there exists an already developed system of education. This is so because the country would already have in place the manpower as well as the institutional resources that are needed to receive and effectively utilize the new system of education. Other things being equal, the better developed the education system, the smoother the receptivity to the new education. While it is possible for resistance to arise from groups with vested interest in preserving the established system of education, there will be other groups, and in greater numbers, to overcome such resistance and press for the promises and benefits of education reform.

How did the type and level of established education systems found in the two countries compare with one another?

Ethiopia

With respect to Ethiopia, it may be argued that the existing type and level of education, while limited in its reach and narrow in scope, was still adequate to the task for which it was applied at the time. After all, it did sustain a national literary culture for several centuries, albeit a literary culture that was narrowly confined to the church. In fact some even assert that "Traditional Christian Ethiopia is a literate society possessing its own highly developed written language and body of literature comprising religious and historical works."[32] And one might argue that the existence of such culture proves that Ethiopia was and is self-reliant in education. But this is an argument that can be made only if education is stripped of its numerous and significant social and economic roles.

In general, education that was rooted in early religious institutions was not of the type that prompted a more diverse and expanded education, except in the furtherance of narrowly defined dogma. That is because those early churches tended to see life and the conditions that surround it as basically pre-ordained and its purposes and goals well-settled once and for all. Their teachings were backward-looking and future-shy. The result was that all new ideas came to be regarded with deep suspicions by the church clergy. It is reported that Negus Sahlesellasie quickly abandoned any idea of introducing windmills in Debre Berhan when the clergy of the time declared the contraptions "works of the devil." They could just as readily declare many elements of modern secular education "works of the devil." The church "educators"' prescription for addressing all sorts of societal crisis was to rush the faithful to mass prayers. If evidence is needed to show the shortcomings of that strategy, one finds it etched in the myriad of social and economic problems that has beset the country over several decades. Accordingly, while there was established education on the ground in Ethiopia, it was one that made little contribution to the improvement of the lives of the people. It also blocked other avenues for such improvement as it openly and staunchly opposed the introduction of modern secular education.

The system was probably quite capable of producing scholars that were expected to dedicate their lives to the service of the church. But by refusing to recognize the legitimacy of other alternative uses of education, it may have also prevented the domestic cultivation of other forms of education that could address the more mundane and pressing needs of society. As Perham observes, ". . . it was uncertain at the beginning of this [20th] century whether a movement of educational reform could be made to flow into this extensive but conservative system or whether entirely new channels must be made for it. The education system given by the church, whether or not it was still effective for the training of boys to fill its own several orders, appeared to be out of touch with the needs and the awakening desires of the new century."[33]

While Japan at the turn of century could boast over 3.3 millions students, Ethiopia's public school system was still nonexistent. According to

[32] Markakis, p. 144.
[33] Perham, The Government of Ethiopia, p. 247.

one source, there were fewer than ten thousand students in the entire country on the eve of the second Italian invasion in 1935. "In 1925 the government adopted a plan to expand secular education, but ten years later there were only 8,000 students enrolled in twenty public schools. A few students also studied abroad on government scholarships. Schools closed during the Italian occupation of 1936-41."[34] In spite of the very low level of education development throughout the first half of the 20th century, government commitment to build up the education infrastructure of the country remained weak. This is nowhere more evident than in the budget allocation priorities of the government.

> A measure of the inadequacy of financial investment in education is provided by a comparison of actual performance with the goals set in a development plan adopted by the Ethiopian Government in 1961. This plan was the result of the recommendations adopted by the Addis Ababa Conference on Education, co-sponsored by the Economic Commission for Africa and UNESCO with the participation of the ministers of education of African states, in 1961. . . . It was recommended that state investment in education should reach 4 per cent of the national income by 1965 and 6 per cent by 1980. The publication of the Report proved an acute embarrassment to the host country because statistics showed Ethiopia ranking among the lowest in the field of educational development.[35]

The actual budget allocations for the specified period fell far short of the target and came to less than 2 per cent of the national income. This is all the more surprising given the embarrassing evidence the conference provided of the country's lag in education behind most of the newly independent African countries – the very African countries that the Emperor's government sought to provide leadership for.

Japan

It was pointed out above that the Tokugawa rulers grew increasingly nervous about the direction that education under their realm was taking. It should be noted, however, that resistance to heterodoxy in education by the Tokugawa rulers was not the same thing as resistance to education itself. Starting from 1603 and continuing until 1867, these rulers managed to end Japan's regional warfare and established a level of peace that aided economic progress and led to the rise of a merchant class.

---

[34] University of Louisville Ekstrom Library, Government Publications, URL: http://www.louisville.edu/library/ekstrom/govpubs/international/ethiopia/ethed.html.

[35] Markakis, *ibid.*, p. 153. (In spite of its already low starting level relative to other African countries, the author points out that Ethiopia's investment in education was actually less than 2 per cent of its national income in 1965.)

This condition favored the development of schools first based in temples but gradually spreading to towns and villages. The structure and content of education were, however, of the "orthodoxy" type that authorities approved. The shogunate itself built schools where members of the samurai class could study Confucianism, a philosophy that was quite in tune with the ideology of feudalism. Within the confines of orthodoxy in education, schools offered lessons in a relatively wide range of studies. Scholars who have studied the Tokugawa Shogunate point to the considerable progress that was made in the development of schools.

These schools consisted mainly of two types: the *hanko* for the samurai class and the *terakoya* for commoners. Between the two systems of education, the curriculum covered was fairly extensive. The *hanko* included the study of books written in Chinese, Classics of Confucianism, historical works, anthologies of Chinese poems, brush writing, study of Japanese thinkers, and medicine. The *terakoya* served like modern day primary schools and taught reading, writing and mathematics. As James and Benjamin argue,

> Largely because of the educational legacy of two such systems already in place during Tokugawa times, Japan was able to move quickly and effectively to enlarge its educational reach. Education was compulsory and roughly uniform for all at the primary level, i.e. for the first six years. Beyond that, however, education was differentiated, vocational and highly selective. In its widespread compulsory primary stage the Japanese system was similar to the American; in its limited differentiated post-primary stage it was similar to systems prevailing in England, France and other European countries, which featured highly selective education . . . By 1902, 90 per cent of the children were attending school (at the compulsory level).[36]

In so far as the level of its educational development was concerned, it is clear that Japan was on a par with the most advanced industrial countries of the late 19th and early 20th centuries. If there was any controversy regarding modern education in Japan at the time, it was one that related to the level of government involvement in education or the degree to which principles of civil liberties and individual rights should be incorporated in the new education system.

Conclusion

Education in a society has dual roles that exist in tension with one another. On the one hand, it is a tool that society wields to reproduce itself. As such, its significant effect is to preserve the beliefs and practices

---

[36] James *et al.*, p. 12.

that a particular society has come to identify itself with. But education also plays a different and highly sought-after role. That role is the introduction of new and better ideas and practices that will result in great benefits to both individuals and society. Which role of education prevails in society at any one time depends on the existence of several key factors and the alignment of various stakeholders.

The early experiences of Japan and Ethiopia with the acquisition of modern education have some similarities but many more differences. Japanese society had been at the receiving end of successive waves of ideas and practices from abroad. What was a foreign idea at the point of its arrival was soon converted into a Japanese idea with which both political authorities and scholars identified. Two critical factors worked in favor of education transfer and education development in Japan. The first was geography, both in the sense of the ease of accessibility of the land by sea and the country's proximity to major centers of world civilization, including China. The second was the favorable disposition of the lords and the samurai class towards at least some types of secular education. As a result, Japan did not show strong inhibitions towards importing and utilizing modern education. Instead, it systematically identified and selected the most promising education systems from around the world. It then proceeded to extract the practical social and economic benefits of the imported education while taking measures to preserve its base of cultural identity.

In the case of Ethiopia, the same two critical factors were present. But, instead of being favorable, these factors tended to work against education transfer and education development. Geography helped insulate the land and its people from influences from abroad. The only way that new ideas embodied in new education could leapfrog the formidable barrier of geography was if Ethiopian rulers threw their authority and resources behind the effort. But neither the monarchy nor the aristocracy felt the need to do so. Add to this the ever-watchful opposition of the Ethiopian Orthodox Church to any thing new and foreign, and the early introduction of modern education into the country never had a chance. Without the influx of new ideas, the country's social and economic life was condemned to stagnation.

A theme that is briefly introduced above is that the widespread benefits of a modern education system cannot be fully realized if it is not preceded by social and political transformations on a national level. Such transformations help usher in the context in which policies that place the national interest above all others can be developed and promoted. This is where a key distinction arose between the experiences of the two countries with respect to their adoption of a modern education system.

Where Japan undertook the modernization of its education in tandem with the transformation of its social and political systems, Ethiopia tried to do so while leaving intact all aspects of its traditional ways. Ethiopia's approach left a hostile environment in place as far as the modernizing potential of education was concerned. The forces of tradition were not predisposed to readily recognize the benefits of such education. Given the tepid interest with which it was received, the benefits that modern education could offer remained sub-optimal at best. Unable to harness the developmental potentials of education, the country has remained economically weak and socially vulnerable. And among the first victims of such vulnerability would be the very forces of tradition that sought to keep modernization at bay.

Tradition or modernization can never be the question. It is a false and untenable dichotomy. Each generation has both the opportunity and duty to build for itself and its progeny a life that is superior to the one preceding it. Modernization and progress is an obligatory task for survival. Beyond that, a generation's ability to preserve its legacies from the past is contingent on its success in building a better life for itself in the present. The glory of the past will quickly fade if it does not get affirmed and reflected in the accomplishments of the present. The critical need for widespread and forward-looking education is one that Ethiopia's leaders failed to heed at great cost to the nation. A generation is yet to respond to the call of honoring the past with its deeds and, in the words of the poet, make Ethiopia ". . . like Japan, strong in everything."

References

Adams, Don, et al.

1969 *Education in Developing Areas* New York: David McKay Company, Inc.

Bahru Zewde's

2002 *Pioneers of Change in Ethiopia: The Reformist Intellectuals of the Early Twentieth Century* Addis Ababa: Addis Ababa University Press.

2001 *A History of Modern Ethiopia* Addis Ababa: Addis Ababa University Press, Second Edition.

Beauchamp, Edward R. ed.

1991 *Windows on Japanese Education* New York: Greenwood Press.

Carnoy, Martin, et al.

1990 *Education and Social Transition in the Third World* Princeton, New Jersey: Princeton University Press.

Desta, Asayehgn

1979 *Socio-economic and Educational Reforms in Ethiopia 1942-1947: Correspondence and Contradictions* Paris: UNESCO, International Institute for Educational Planning.

Duke, Benjamin

1986 *The Japanese School* New York: Praeger.

Fasil R. Kiros

1990 *Implementing Educational Policies in Ethiopia* Washington, D.C.: World Bank.

Haiducek, Nicholas J.
1991 *Japanese Education Made in the U.S.A.* New York: Praeger.
Horio, Teruhisa
1988 *Educational Thought and Ideology in Modern Japan* Tokyo: University of Tokyo Press.
James, Estelle, et al.
1995 Lincicome, Mark E. *Principles, Praxis, and the Politics of Educational Reform in Meiji Japan* Honolulu: University of Hawaii Press.
1988 *Public Policy and Private Education in Japan* New York: St. Martin's Press.
1972 Korten, David C. *Planned Change in a Traditional Society* New York: Praeger Publishers.
Markakis, John
1974 *Ethiopia: Anatomy of a Traditional Polity*, Oxford: Clarendon Press.
Ministry of Education, Japan
1989 *Outline of Education in Japan* Tokyo: Ministry of Education, Science and Culture, Government of Japan.
Nagai, Michio
1971 *Higher Education in Japan* Tokyo: University of Tokyo Press.
Perham, Margery
1969 *The Government of Ethiopia* Evanston: Northwestern University Press.
Schoppa, Leonard James
1991 *Education Reform in Japan* London: Routledge.
Spencer, John H.
1984 *Ethiopia at Bay: A Personal Account of the Haile Sellassie Years* Algonac, Michigan: Reference Publications.
Wagaw, Teshome G.
1979 *Education in Ethiopia: Prospect and Retrospect* Ann Arbor: University of Michigan Press.
Wirt, Frederick M., et al.
1986 *Education, Recession and the World Village: A Comparative Political Economy of Education* London: The Falmer Press.
Zewde, Bahru
2002 *Pioneers of Change in Ethiopia: The Reformist Intellectuals of the Early Twentieth Century* Athens: Ohio University Press.

Nigeria's Fledgling Friendship with Japan: The Beginning of a 'Special Partnership'?

KWEKU AMPIAH

ABSTRACT

Since the inauguration of President Olusegun Obasanjo as President of Nigeria Japan's attitude towards the West African state seems to have been positively transformed. The relationship between the two countries kicked-off with panache after the President's first visit to Tokyo in April 1999 as President elect to renew acquaintances. The two countries are now bound together in a "Special Relationship", which provides them with a coherent framework for regular and constructive consultations. The recent developments replace a period of immobilist diplomacy between Tokyo and Abuja especially during when Nigerian domestic politics was infested with military dictatorships.

Tokyo's recent initiatives toward Abuja have to be seen within the context of Japan's invigorated diplomatic initiatives toward sub-Saharan Africa as manifested through the Tokyo International Conference on African Development. The relationship is also premised on Nigeria's hegemonic position within the sub-region of West Africa. As a result, Japan has relatively increased its economic assistance to Nigeria in recent years and is seemingly showing signs of interest in the economic development of Nigeria. On his part, President Obasanjo has pledged his country's determination "to change from the way and manner business was done in Nigeria in the recent past in order to institute a new regime of accountability and transparency in conformity with internationally accepted codes of business ethics".

Introduction

For some time between the 1960s and the end of the 1980s, Japan and Nigeria had a notable economic relationship although it seemed to have been an exercise that provided Nigeria with few rewards but significant problems. As Obafemi Awolowo confirmed, the nature of the relationship "reached a disaster pitch" in the early 1980s. He felt, rather strongly, that Nigeria ". . . cannot afford to go on year in year out to lose money to a very rich – almost over-rich country like Japan".[1] Awolowo was speaking in relation to the country's trade balance with Japan, which had remained in the latter's favour since at least 1962, except for 1973 and 1974 when the energy crisis – orchestrated by the Arab oil exporting countries – forced Japan to purchase more crude oil from Nigeria. Indeed, in the early 1960s the Nigerian government imposed differential tariffs and quotas on imports from Japan and also invoked GATT Article 35 (dealing with trade reciprocity) against Tokyo. The situation, however, was not alleviated by these measures. By 1976 the balance in Japan's favour was close to half a billion US dollars and progressively rose to US$1.4 billion in 1980 (as shown in Table 3); the 'disaster pitch' as Awolowo called it. This demanded some firm action on the part of both countries as Nigerian policy-makers threatened further sanctions against Japanese exports. In the end, however, the large decrease in Nigeria's deficit to Japan was mainly a result of the economic recession in Nigeria itself and "the resultant fall in the country's purchasing power rather than an increase in Japanese patronage of Nigeria's exports".[2]

Speaking in December 2002, the Japanese Ambassador to Nigeria, Mr. Akira Matsui, noted that Japan had up to 40 companies (with about 18,000 Nigerian employees) in Nigeria in the 1980s. Indeed, between 1951 and 1990 there were 93 cases of actual Japanese investments in Nigeria, with the cumulative value of $159 million, although it represented a mere 0.1 percent of Japanese overseas investments during that period. Most of Japan's investments in Nigeria were in the manufacturing sector, producing tradables as in manufactured goods like textiles.[3] Incidentally, there are now only 14 Japanese companies, in Nigeria, as shown in Table 5, with about 145 local employees.

---

[1] Quoted in Jide Owoeye, "Nigeria and Japan: A Study of Trade Relations", G.O. Olusanya and R.A. Akindele, *Nigeria's External Relations: The First Twenty-Five Years*, Ibadan: University Press Limited, 1986, p. 319.

[2] *Ibid.*, p. 328.

[3] Kweku Ampiah, *The Dynamics of Japan's Relations with Africa: South Africa, Tanzania and Nigeria*, London: Routledge, 1997. Chapter 4.

It is imperative to note firstly that these investments were (and still are) hardly raw materials-oriented. Implicit in this is the fact that Japan's dependence on external sources for almost all her raw material requirements hardly contributed to Japanese investment interests in Nigeria. Given the abundance of good quality (low sulphur) oil in Nigeria, and in view of Japan's imports of all her oil needs, it is striking that Japanese oil refining firms have had no substantial investment interests in Nigeria. The second point to make is that the said Japanese investments in Nigeria primarily revolved around the country's potentially massive internal market. Because of Nigeria's huge population – by far the largest in sub-Saharan Africa – and given its exponential increase in wealth as a result of the oil boom in the 1970s, it was expected that the Japanese manufacturing companies would thrive in the country. These ventures either went bankrupt or were transferred to the co-operating local companies, thus confirming our third point which is that Japanese investments in sub-Saharan Africa have tended to be transitory.

As is evident enough, Japan is not renowned for its investment prowess in sub-Saharan Africa. For example, the value of Japanese investments in the region in 1998 was US$434 million, a mere fraction of the US$ 38.3 billion worth of the global investments it made for that year. By far the greatest share of its investments in sub-Saharan Africa that year was accounted for by investments in Liberian flags of convenience, which increased by 150% from the previous year. This leaves only five investments (worth US$57 million) outside those enjoying Liberia's flag of convenience. Nor is Japan renowned for its diplomatic and political astuteness in the area, although this may be partly due to its insistence on keeping a low profile in its operations in Africa.[4] There are, however, now indications that Japan is keen to increase its interests in Nigeria, and indeed in the African political-economy as a whole. Thus, this paper attempts to bring into focus Japan's recent initiatives towards Nigeria and addresses the relationship between the two countries since the latter half of the 1990s. Specifically, we shall examine the diplomatic, trade and investment relations between the two countries. The nuances of Japan's economic assistance to Nigeria will also be explored. Suffice to say, these recent developments between the two countries have to be seen within the context of Japan's new overtures towards Africa as a whole, as engineered since 1993 through the Tokyo International Conference on African Development (TICAD), a brain-child of the Japanese government.

[4] See Kweku Ampiah, "Japanese Aid to Tanzania: The Political Marketing of Japan in Africa", *African Affairs*, vol. 95, no. 378. January 1996.

TICAD is perceived as a process – development in progress, as it were, and evokes what Chris Alden rightly refers to as "an all-encompassing approach to growth and development"[5] which has integrated into its wider dimensions aspects of the neo-liberal stipulations for "good governance" and economic growth. Officially, it is defined as a "regional initiative for Africa" spearheaded by the joint support of the Government of Japan, the United Nations (UN) and the Global Coalition for Africa (GCA). It is also seen as ". . . involv[ing] a variety of stakeholders including all [the] African countries, international agencies and the civil society".[6] To date there have been three main sessions of the TICAD process, all of which were held in Tokyo and paid for by the Japanese government. The first session was held in 1993, the second in 1998 and the last one in 2003, and there is every indication that a fourth session will be held in 2008. Meanwhile, various preparatory and ministerial meetings will take place (as was the case with the previous sessions) before the actual event, roughly five years from now.

In his keynote speech at TICAD III, the Japanese Prime Minister, Junichiro Koizumi,[7] enumerated what he referred to as the three pillars that comprise Japan's initiative for assistance to Africa within the TICAD framework. These are "human-centred development", "poverty reduction through economic growth", and the "consolidation of peace". Koizumi also mentioned that since the initiation of TICAD 10 years ago, Japan has implemented economic assistance amounting to $12 billion to Africa. Essentially, the TICAD suggests that there has been a grand shift in Japan's attitude towards Africa and the region's developmental problems since the end of the Cold War, as well as marked positive effects on the politics of the region, including the end of the Apartheid regime in South Africa.[8] To emphasise the uniqueness of the process as a formula for the development of Africa, Koizumi presented TICAD as a comprehensive exercise "to bring together knowledge and the experiences of the international community in African development in support of the New Partnership for Africa's Development (NEPAD)".

NEPAD, which President Olusegun Obasanjo has actively helped to promote, is also seen as a comprehensive program for the socio-politi-

[5] Chris Alden, "The Chrysanthemum and the Protea: Re-inventing Japanese-South African Relations after Apartheid", *African Affairs*, vol. 101, no. 404, July 2002, p. 383.

[6] See the TICAD website, www.gca-cma.org/eticad.htm.

[7] Keynote Speech by Prime Minister Junichiro Koizumi at the Third Tokyo International Conference on African Development (TICAD III) (Provisional Translation), 29 September 2003.

[8] Ogura Kazuo, "Afurika o miru me no tenkan: gyakuten no hassô ni yoru afurika gaikô o motemete", *Gaikô Forumu*, No. 18, October 2003, pp. 12-14.

cal and economic development of all the African countries, with the primary objective of achieving sustainable growth and better life chances for Africans and, most importantly created by Africans themselves. Consequently, as Obasanjo recently confirmed, NEPAD's relationship with the Regional Economic Communities (RECs) of the area is an integral aspect of, and central to, its operations.[9] In his speech, the Japanese Prime Minister's reference to NEPAD was meant to convey the message that "Japan . . . respects the will of Africans themselves to make the 21st century the African century".[10] In essence, Japanese policy-makers are aware that they have to tread carefully in their dealings with Africa, in part because they want to avoid the mistakes the European countries made in the region. At the same time, they do not want the European countries and America to feel that Japan is encroaching on their interests in the region as it flexes its taut muscles in their face. Thus, the TICAD process is seemingly designed to involve all the relevant donors as well, including the other G7 member countries. The novelty of the process is also inherent in its determination to apply the formula for the East Asian economic achievements to the African situation. Consequently TICAD is additionally about South-South co-operation.

The Determinants of the Relationship

There are certain indicators that emerge from the bilateral relationship between Japan and Nigeria that need examining here. The first is that although the two countries are regional powers in their own right, their relationship is not based on an equal partnership. By the very nature of its economic power and its pre-eminent role in international politics, whereby Tokyo is a member of the G7 countries precisely because it is the second largest economy in the world, Japan is the dominant partner in the relationship. The relationship is sustained, first and foremost, by this understanding and moreover confirmed by Nigeria's expectations of what it could possibly gain by way of economic assistance from Japan. Japan's eminent predominance of the relationship is equally observable even at the multilateral level. For example, for the first time in the history of the G7 summit meetings, it was the Japanese Prime Minister, Yoshiro Mori, who made it possible for leaders of the emerging economies (including the President of Nigeria) to attend the summit in Tokyo in the summer of 2000. In doing so he provided President Obasanjo, as

[9] Statement by His Excellency President Olusegun Obasanjo On the Occasion of TICAD III, September 26, 2003, p. 3.

[10] Keynote Speech by Prime Minister Junichiro Koizumi. 29 September, 2003.

well as leaders from Algeria, South Africa and Thailand, with the opportunity to express their concerns about the negative effects of the global economy on their respective countries. The prestige Japan has gained from the event is enormous, not least because it elevated Tokyo into a champion of the emerging economies in their crusade for debt relief and equitable international trade.[11]

However, all states are also marred by a fundamental weakness which manifests itself differently, depending on the country and the issue(s) at hand, and Japan is no exception. Indeed, Japan's recent gestures towards the African states are carefully managed and monitored by the Japan Federation of Economic Organization, the *Keidanren*. In other words, these initiatives are led first and foremost by the potential economic gains that may be accrued by Japan *as well*. Fundamentally, Japan's recent enthusiastic approaches to Nigeria (and sub-Saharan Africa as a whole) are partly a product of Japan's depressed economy since the latter part of the 1990s, for which Japanese policy-makers have been frantically looking for remedies. Basically, Tokyo is attempting to find a solution to its ailing economy by applying its economic prowess and diplomatic skills more effectively in Africa than it did before the end of the Cold War. If our analysis is even remotely correct, then it is tempting to suggest that sub-Saharan Africa may well become Japan's Southeast Asia in the twenty-first century. As is well documented, Southeast Asia served as Japan's source for raw-materials and markets as well as the workshop for its manufacturing companies in the early post-World War II era when it kick-started the revitalisation of its economy. In that sense, Nigeria's potential importance to Tokyo cannot be over-stated if only because of its huge population, which is a potential market for Japanese products at the very least. In addition, Nigeria has low-sulphur crude oil, gas and other strategic natural resources. It demands then that Japan take Nigeria seriously, at least within the context of its relations with Africa, irrespective of the fact that Nigeria is the minor partner in the bilateral relationship.

Japan's relations with Nigeria is also premised on, and somewhat dictated to, by the fact that Nigeria is seen as a regional power by Japan's Ministry of Foreign Affairs (MOFA). This makes Abuja one of the three regional powers in sub-Saharan Africa with which Japan's policy-makers would discuss and negotiate broader issues concerning Africa and consequently other international matters of major importance. Specifically,

---

[11] Marc Castellano, "Mori Meets With Developing-Country Leaders", *Japan Economic Institute Report*, No. 29, July 28, 2000.

Nigeria is formally designated as the bellwether for the sub-region of West Africa in Japan's newly-formulated diplomacy towards the continent. Within that construct, South Africa and Kenya are the main reference points in Japan's diplomacy towards Southern Africa and East Africa, respectively. The economic implications of this diplomatic formula is that all three countries, obviously because of their relative economic strengths in their respective sub-regions, would attract more investment than the other countries in the same areas. They would then invariably serve as the countries from where the 'in-house' Japanese manufactured products would be exported to other markets in the region, and perhaps even to countries outside Africa.[12] Mitsubishi Corporation, for example, is currently involved in such a venture as evidenced by The MOZAL Aluminium Smelting project in Southern Africa, which is apparently the largest of its kind in the world,[13] and exports a share of its finished product to customers in East Asia, including Japan and China. The MOZAL project is also indicative of the public-private co-operation between Japan and sub-Saharan Africa that TICAD may well make a reality. We shall revisit this issue in due course.

Finally, despite the imbalanced nature of the relationship, there is a point at which the power configuration between the two countries may become obfuscated. Their mutual interests in reforming the United Nations Security Council, for example, may be a case in point where Japan and Nigeria could seemingly emerge on the same side in the arena of power politics as small powers intent on correcting an anomaly in the international political system. This may well turn out to be one of the outcomes of the agreement that the two countries reached in 2001 whereby they would establish a "Special Partnership" that will concern itself with global issues as well. Which of the two countries is dominant in this particular arrangement is hard to discern, although it has been suggested by some observers that Japan may be merely attempting to use Nigeria as well as the other African countries to achieve its long-standing objective of acquiring a permanent seat at the Security Council (SC). This is yet another issue to which we would have to return.

---

[12] Kweku Ampiah, "Japanese Investments in South Africa, 1992-1996: The State, Private Enterprise and Strategic Minerals", in Chris Alden and Katsumi Hirano eds., *Distant Mirror: Japan and South Africa in a Globalising World*, London: Ashgate, 2003.

[13] "Minami afurika kyowakoku no tôshi kankyô: moza-ru projecto no gaiyô ni tsuite (The Investment Environment in South Africa: An outline of the Mozal Project)" *JOI*, May 2002; Keynote Speech by Prime Minister Koizumi, p. 3.

A Fledgling Diplomacy

The relationship between Japan and Nigeria seems to have developed momentum with the inauguration of Obasanjo as President of Nigeria. The relationship kicked off with panache after the President's first visit Tokyo in April 1999 as President elect to renew acquaintances. His visit to Japan in July 2000 with Alhaji Sule Lamido (Minister of Foreign Affairs) to attend a G8 Summit consultation meeting consolidated the relationship. But the recent developments between Japan and Nigeria were bolstered by the visit of the Japanese Prime Minister, Yoshiro Mori, to Nigeria in January 2001, and by the fact that Mori and Obasanjo apparently got on very well. Mori's visit to Nigeria was significant for the following reasons: it was the first time a Japanese Prime Minister in office had visited Africa; Nigeria was one of only three countries in sub-Saharan Africa that Mori visited, an obvious indication that Japan recognises Nigeria's leadership role in African politics. Since the other countries that Mori went to were South Africa and Kenya, the Prime Minister's trip was designed to underline the power points, or the major focal points, in Japan's relations with sub-Saharan Africa in the 21st century. Invariably, this is a confirmation of Japan's attempts to co-ordinate its relations with Africa in the post-Cold War era through its triangular relations with South Africa, Kenya and Nigeria as its 'strategic points of reference and operation' in Southern Africa, East Africa, and West Africa, respectively. Importantly, the three countries are Japan's prominent trade partners in the region and not surprisingly central to the Southern African Development Co-ordination Conference (SADCC), the East Africa Community (EAC), and the Economic Community of West African States (ECOWAS), respectively. It is also no coincidence that all three countries enjoy vast coastlines, crucial for international trade.

The Prime Minister's visit to Nigeria in 2001 was preceded much earlier in May 1999 by that of Mr. Ryutaro Hashimoto (Senior Foreign Policy Advisor to Mori, and former Prime Minister), who attended President Obasanjo's inauguration ceremony.[14] At the summit meeting between Obasanjo and Mori in January 2001, the Japanese Prime Minister expressed his country's commitment to its proposals for the resolution of Africa's problems. In what has now become a landmark gesture towards the development of Africa, Mori proclaimed that "there would be no stability and prosperity in the world in the 21st century unless the problems of Africa were resolved." In the same breath he announced

[14] P.C. Asiodu, Presidential Adviser on Economic Matters also went to Tokyo in March 2000, and in September Mr. Yasukuni Enoki, Director-General of Middle East and African Affairs, went to Abuja in preparation for Prime Minister Mori's visit.

that support for economic development, conflict prevention and aid to refugees were as central to Japan's new policy towards Africa as "two wheels of a cart", adding that "Japan was resolved to co-operate in the priority area of Basic Human Needs" (BHN). He anticipates that Japan's efforts in the area of BHN will directly benefit the people of Nigeria. As he also noted, however, he expects Nigeria to contribute towards the processes of democratisation of the region, not to mention economic reform and regional stability, an indication that Japan fully appreciates Nigeria's hegemonic responsibilities within the region.

In May 2001, President Obasanjo reciprocated Mori's visit and the two countries signed what is now recognised as "very important bilateral agreements including the agreement to dispatch an Investment Mission to Nigeria, and establish the Japan-Nigeria 'Special Partnership'". As Julius Bala (Director, Policy Advocacy and External Relations, Nigeria Investment Promotion Commission) has correctly perceived, the establishment of the 'Special Partnership' provides the two countries with a coherent framework for regular and constructive consultations compared with the ad hoc manner according to which they conducted their relationship in the past.[15] The inaugural consultative meeting to formalise the 'Special Relationship' was held in Abuja on December 2001 and was led on the Japanese side by Mr. Nobutake Odano, Director of Sub-Saharan African Affairs, while Ambassador T. Daniel-Hart led the Nigerian delegation. This was followed by the first bilateral consultative meeting, which was held in Tokyo on 26 July 2002, and then by the second bilateral consultative meeting from 3-5 November 2003, also held in Tokyo. The indications are therefore that Japan and Nigeria are engaged in attempts to positively redefine their bilateral relationship towards strengthening their political and economic engagements with each other. Thus, at a dinner hosted by the new Japanese Prime Minister, Junichiro Koizumi, during Obasanjo's visit in May 2001, the President accepted the opportunity to raise the issue of debt relief for the poor nations, noting that it was the greatest obstacle to progress in Africa. He was therefore very clear in his affirmation that ". . . ultimately the surest remedy to unshackle the economies of [the] African countries is through remission of debts, with determined and realistic developmental programmes." He admitted, however, that "there are many ways this can be achieved. And we are going to remain engaged in seeking mutually acceptable solutions."[16]

[15] Julius Bala, p. 13, 1.

[16] Nigeria-Japan Bilateral Relations – At Dinner Hosted by Junichiro Koizumi, Honourable Prime Minister of Japan, Tokyo, Japan, 21 May, 2001, p. 3.

In saying that, Obasanjo was perhaps responding to Prime Minister Mori's comment in January 2001, that although the debt problem was a serious issue for Nigeria, debt relief was not the ultimate panacea for poverty reduction and economic development. The Japanese Prime Minister had emphasised the importance of strengthening efforts towards matters relating to development itself.[17] This is not at all surprising since aid administrators in MOFA and in particular the Japan Ministry of Economy, Trade and Industry (METI) have been traditionally averse to the concept of debt relief and have tended to see it as worth considering only as a last resort. Nevertheless, as stated above, this has not stopped Japan's leaders from rallying support for the debt relief program, at least in relation to TICAD. In fact as Mr. Kiyoshi Kodera (Temporary Governor, Ministry of Finance)[18] pointed out in June 2003, Japan's contribution towards debt relief under the Highly Indebted Poor Countries (HIPC) Initiative was the highest among the donor countries. Japan, as he promised, was "prepared to provide the heavily indebted poor countries of Africa with debt relief amounting to approximately US$3 billion."

Following discussions about debt relief with Koizumi in May, Obasanjo turned his attention to issues specific to his country and drew the Prime Minister's attention to Nigeria's desire to strengthen its economic relations with Japan, pointing out the vast areas of opportunities in Nigeria for Japanese companies. He was hopeful that his visit would provide the opportunity for the two countries to deliberate over and agree on other areas of co-operation; and that the policy-makers of the two countries "will work on the finer details of outstanding bilateral agreements in order to speed up conclusion and implementation". Effectively, the President was appealing for Japanese investments and thus enumerating the areas that he hoped would be able to attract foreign investment. These were the machine-tool fabrication sector, steel aluminium, mining and solid mineral extraction, sugar and cement production, finance and banking, hotels, and tourism. He then invited Japanese investors "to avail themselves of the immense and ample opportunities available for profitable investment in Nigeria . . ." while boldly predicting that the

[17] Summit Meeting Between Japan and the Federal Republic of Nigeria and Discussion with the Chairman of the Economic Community of West African States (ECOWAS) (Summary), 12 January 2001.

[18] Statement by Mr. Kiyoshi Kodera, Temporary Governor, Ministry of Finance (Japan), At the Annual Meetings of the African Development Bank and the African Development Fund, Addis Ababa, Ethiopia, 3 June 2003. Japan's method of debt relief is by writing-off relevant ODA debts owed to the Japan Bank for International Co-operation, as opposed to the old method of providing grant aid for debt relief.

"next market, and the market of the millennium, in the making is Nigeria and covering the West Africa region."[19]

As is obvious from the above, Obansanjo's comments underscored Nigeria's sub-regional responsibilities as a prominent member of ECOWAS, as well as Nigeria's specific national interests. On a much wider regional level, he hoped that Japan and Nigeria would be able to harmonise their positions on a number of matters affecting Africa and other issues of international concern, especially international peace, conflict management and security. Hence, with respect to peace and security in West Africa, Obasanjo mentioned Nigeria's responsibilities within the Economic Community of West African States Monitoring Group (ECOMOG), pointing out Abuja's huge financial commitments to the region's security.[20] He also noted that ECOMOG had deployed 1,600 troops to the tension ridden Mano River zone between Liberia, Sierra Leone and Guinea. Presumably, this was meant to give some assurance to potential Japanese investors to Nigeria and the other countries in the region that adequate security would be provided for all foreign investments in the country.

Japan and Nigeria on Reforming the United Nations Security Council

More recently, Japan's diplomatic advances toward the African countries have no doubt been intensified and at no other place than the United Nations, a fact that has been commented on by a number of observers. This is in relation to what has been popularly referred to as 'Japan's attempts to gain a permanent seat at the UN Security Council'. The debate takes its cue from the momentum towards the reform of the Security Council (SC)[21] since the beginning of the 1990s, and part of the argument is that Japan is attempting to 'use' the African countries to attain a permanent seat at the SC. One of the supposed 'satellite states' that is prepared to help Japan wrestle a permanent seat at the SC is said to be Nigeria. In accordance with this, during his visit to Japan in May 2001, Obasanjo did confirm that "Just like Japan, and in line with the principles of democratization sweeping across the globe, we have called for the reforms of the United Nations, particularly the

[19] Nigeria-Japan Bilateral Relations, 21 May, 2001, p. 3.

[20] For a comprehensive analysis of Nigeria's role in the ECOMOG see Adekeye Adebajo, *Liberia's Civil War: Nigeria, ECOMOG and Regional Security in West Africa*, London: Lynne Reinner, 2002, p. 73 ff.

[21] Shinyo Takahiro, "The United Nations at the Crossroads: Security Council Reform and Japan", *Gaiko Forum*, Winter 2004.

Security Council, to make it more representative." He further proclaimed that "Japan by all objective criteria deserves a permanent place in the enlarged Security Council."[22]

Earlier that year in Lagos, Mori had reiterated that the reform of the SC was urgent for the easy resolution of conflict, and expressed the opinion that "it would be appropriate for an enlarged Security Council to have 24 Seats". Implicit in Mori's statement is the assumption that an enlarged SC might include Nigeria and – or – South Africa, suggesting (in view of Obasanjo's statement above) that Japan and the two African countries are perhaps working as a team in relation to the debate about SC reforms. MOFA seems to confirm this in its statement that "it is absolutely necessary to expand the permanent membership with the addition of both developed and developing countries which possess the ability and willingness to assume global responsibility for international peace and security."[23] It seems, therefore, that both South Africa and Nigeria are supporting Japan's candidature for a permanent seat in exchange for support for their own bid. Thus, the differences in their international positions of power – Japan's pre-eminent spot among the G7, the fact that it is the second largest economy in the world and by extension the second leading aid donor – does not seem to compromise their mutual objectives on this matter. In that sense, a global economic power (Japan) and a regional power (Nigeria) have joined hands to challenge and possibly change the existing structure of the United Nations Security Council which they both view as unfairly dominated by the original permanent members.

Nevertheless, one critical observer has argued that Japan is using its foreign aid policy to cajole the African states into supporting its bid, further suggesting that TICAD is designed to 'buy' African support for Japan's candidature. As he pointedly put it, "The Ministry of Foreign Affairs . . . considers the African countries' support for the bid as decisive. Given their high dependence on aid and their often autocratic political system, it is obvious that they are particularly receptive to what Japan as the top world ODA donor can offer".[24] This criticism notwithstanding, there is no doubt that constructive reforms to the SC are long overdue and that Japan should be made a permanent member of the SC if only because it provides "approximately 20.6 percent of the United

[22] Nigeria-Japan Bilateral Relations, 21 May, 2001, pp. 3-4.

[23] The Ministry of Foreign Affairs of Japan, "Security Council Reform". http://www.mofa.go.jp/policy/un/reform/role21.html

[24] Reinhard Drifte, *Japan's Quest for a Permanent Security Council: A Matter of Pride or Justice?* London: Macmillan Press Ltd., 2000, p. 146 and pp. 145-154.

Nations budget, and is second only to the United States in its financial support of the Organization." Moreover, "Leaving out the United States, Japan's financial contributions exceed the combined contributions of the four remaining permanent members of the Security Council".[25] But in terms of military power Japan has also been one of the least aggressive countries in the world since the end of WW II, despite its wealth and technological advancement. This is partly because since its defeat in the war it has concentrated on the application of economic rather than military prowess in its dealings in international politics and by so doing has enforced a new dimension to the concept of state power and its wider implications.

The issue of a permanent seat for Japan aside, the reforms of the SC would also demand, as the logic of international relations in the 21st century should dictate, the provision of permanent African representation in it. That said, international politics is infested with hypocritical behaviour in a fashion that makes its operations unpredictable even at the best of times. It would therefore not be remarkable if the demands for the reform of the SC were totally rejected or if the reforms were effected without a permanent sub-Saharan African representation. If the latter should happen but Japan's bid for a permanent seat was accepted, it might be conceived that Japan has indeed 'used' the sub-Saharan African countries to win a permanent seat at the SC. This brings us directly to the issue of Japanese economic assistance to Nigeria.

Nigeria's Expectations: Economic Assistance

Before 1981, Nigeria was not qualified as a grant aid recipient from Japan because it was technically classified as a wealthy nation in view of its booming economy in the 1970s. Nigeria was, however, the recipient of some ¥en loans in the 1960s through to 1988; an indication that Japan felt confident about the Nigerian economy and therefore Nigeria's ability to honour its debts. It was in the latter part of the 1960s when Nigeria received the first of Japan's ¥en credit to the country, totalling ¥10,800 mn.[26] The loan was designated for the development of the following sectors and projects: the Arewa Textile Mill in Kaduna (¥1.2 mn),

[25] The Ministry of Foreign Affairs of Japan, An Argument for Japan's Becoming a Permanent Member, http://www.mofa.go.jp/policy/un/japan.html. High-ranking African diplomats in Tokyo support the inclusion of Japan as a permanent member of the Security Council.

[26] The value of the ¥en stood at ¥360 to the US$1 from 1949-1971; in 1973 it was ¥271 – US$1 and between 1974-1976 it ranged from ¥290 to ¥300 – US$1. It was ¥128 – US$1 in 1988.

the United Textile Mill in Kaduna (¥1.5 mn), the Dieselisation of the Nigerian Railway Corporation (¥1.2 mn), and the Wire and Cable in Ibadan (¥5.3 mn). In September 1972, Japan provided Nigeria with a second package of ¥en loans amounting to ¥ 6,200 mn[27] intended for the Kainji Dam Hydro-Electric power station, Phase I (¥1.5 mn) and Phase II (¥2.4 mn). ¥1.6 mn of the amount also went to the Mobile Transformer project. The third Japanese ¥en credit of ¥6.2 mn came in June 1974 and was designated for the purchase of 700 coaches for the Nigerian Railways Corporation. The ¥en loan to Nigeria after that amounted to $200 mn in 1988, and was to be used in relation to the country's Structural Adjustment Programme. It is also worth noting that Japan gave no loan to Nigeria between 1974 and 1987 although from 1981 to the early 1990s it extended Grant Aid to the country. It is equally significant that the loans (except for the last one) were given to Nigeria when the country's economy was performing relatively well. Moreover, some of the loans, as is clearly evident, were given for the purposes of developing certain areas of the country's infrastructure, obviously because they were necessary for Japan's growing investments in the country. The loan to the Arewa Textile Mills (which was established in 1965) was conceivably given because the Mill had equity from the Japanese private sector. The point to stress here is that the Japanese participants in the above operation (with the assistance of the Japanese government) were trying, by producing locally, to circumvent the debilitating problem of unpacking Japanese products on Nigeria.[28] In other words, the loans were also an attempt on the part of Tokyo to get Lagos to relax the restrictions it had imposed on Japanese exports to the country as a way of controlling the spiralling balance of payments in Japan's favour.

The 1980s brought with it the extension of Japanese Grant Aid to Nigeria, but from 1994 (as shown in Table 1) this was reduced drastically (and restricted to humanitarian aid only) as part of the sanctions regime that was imposed on Nigeria during the rule of General Abacha. During part of the sanction period, between 1992-1996, Japan disbursed about US$494 mn in humanitarian grant aid, including grant aid for increased food production and water supply for middle and large-scale villages in the North-Western states. Part of the funds was also used for technical co-operation. Suffice to say, Japan lifted the sanctions against

[27] There was apparently an unused balance of ¥3.1 mn.

[28] Kweku Ampiah, *The Dynamics of Japan's Relations with Africa*, Chapter 4.

Table 1. Japan's ODA Disbursements to Nigeria

US$ Million

Year	Grants			Loan Aid		
	Grant Aid	Technical Co-operation	Total	Gross	Net	Total
1994	6.72	3.15	9.87	–	−19.25	−9.39
1995	4.25	2.71	6.96	6.34	6.34	13.03
1996		1.63	1.63	–	−3.68	−2.05
1997		0.64	0.64	–	–	0.64
1998		0.62	0.62	–	−11.47	−10.85
Total	144.44	77.17	221.61	381.67	262.23	483.83

Source: Ministry of Foreign Affairs, Japan

Nigeria in 1999. In essence, the re-emergence of civilian rule that year made it possible for the Japanese government to review its policy of 1994 and to pledge assistance in Nigeria's efforts for political reform and economic development. Since then, Japan's economic assistance to Nigeria has picked up pace although it is still very paltry compared to Nigeria's expectations.

For instance, in 2000 a Grant Aid of US$120 mn was given to Nigeria for rural electrification projects in Awe and Keana in Nasarrawa State and parts of Borno and Gombe State. A further Grant Aid of US$49,196 was also given for the construction of wells in four regions in Ibadan, and US$48,000 was designated for the construction of more wells in Ijabe town, Osun State, both as part of the Child Health initiative. Within that same framework, over US$5 million was assigned to the eradication of polio. As Table 2 also shows, both 2001 and 2002 brought in some more Japanese ODA but no Loan Aid was given in either of those years. In 2002 Nigeria received US$16.85 mn and US$2.14 mn for Grant Aid and Technical Aid, respectively.

In the area of Technical Co-operation there has been a cumulative total of 933 technical trainees from Nigeria to Japan, while Japan has dispatched 218 experts to assist in the development efforts of Nigeria.[29] What should also be mentioned here is the long-standing co-operation between the Japan Co-operation Centre, Petroleum (JCCP) and the Nigerian National Petroleum Corporation (NNPC) which entails regular dispatches of Nigerian technicians in the oil sector for training in Japan

[29] JICA Annual Report, 2002, p. 197.

under the auspices of the JCCP every year. While the activities of JCCP are not considered in the analyses of Japanese Overseas Development Assistance (ODA), since its inception roughly 20 years ago JCCP has trained 534 of NNPC's staff in Japan. It has also sent Japanese experts in the oil and energy sector to Nigeria to assist and give training in the relevant areas. The annual programs of JCCP include courses on Development and Implementation of Refinery Maintenance, Project Management for Mechanical Engineers, Lubricating Oil Production, Petroleum Marketing, Quality Control and Assurance and Gas Processing for LNG. For the 2004-2005 academic year, for example, JCCP will run 25 courses including the ones mentioned above.

Further background information about the organisation would be useful at this stage as its functions are not well known. As part of the policy to ensure a stable and reliable supply of energy to the country, in 1981, soon after the 1973 and 1979 energy crises, JCCP was founded under the auspices of the then Ministry of International Trade and Industry (currently Ministry of Economic, Trade and Industry). In fact it was the major Japanese oil companies and engineering firms who founded the organisation. The grand idea behind it was to promote technical co-operation and personnel exchanges with the oil producing countries outside Europe and the United States and to ensure, through this relationship, that Japan obtains a steady supply of oil. It is also worth noting that although Japan's oil companies and engineering firms established JCCP, over 95 percent of its budget comes from the Japanese government, confirming that JCCP as an organisation is an essential tool in the armoury of the country's foreign policy and diplomacy. What is particularly striking for our purposes is that although during the period of sanctions against Nigeria economic assistance to the country (including technical co-operation) was drastically reduced, co-operation between JCCP and NNPC continued without a hitch. This was because it served Japan's interests. After all, to reiterate the point, JCCP was essentially designed to lubricate the relationship between Japan and the downstream sector of the energy industry. In other words, Japan saw it as strategically sensible to keep the relationship between JCCP and NNPC going because of the importance of oil to its own national security, but then the relationship also seemed to be serving Nigeria rather well.

On the specific matter of Japan's ODA to Nigeria, according to the Japanese Ambassador to Abuja, Akira Matsui, Japan has spent a total of US$73.2 in aid to Nigeria since the inauguration of Obasanjo as President of the country. He further revealed that about 98 percent of the total amount has been used to develop and enhance the health and agricultural sectors, and for rural electrification. He also mentioned the

Table 2. Japan's ODA to Nigeria, 2000-2002

¥100 mn

Year	Grant Aid	Technical Co-operation	Loan Aid
2000	21.53	1.71	0
2001	27.36	2.11	0
2002	31.73	1.32	0

JICA, "Naijeria ni okeru JICA jigyo no gaiyo", Afurika. Chûkintô. Ôshû bu (Afurika ka), January 2004.
Slightly modified by author.

fight against polio as one of the priority areas towards which the funds were directed; and confirmed that US$500,000 was used to assist in the Bar Beach erosion control project. All this, as has been noted above, is certainly nothing more than a drop in the ocean of requirements for a country the size and scale of Nigeria. Let us now turn our attention to the question of trade and investment.

Trade and Investment

Tokyo's main export items to Abuja have consistently remained machinery equipment, motor vehicles, electrical machines, telecommunication equipment, and metal products such as iron and steel, and galvanised metals. In other words, mainly expensive manufactured items. Its imports, on the other hand, are predominantly primary commodities. The volume of trade between Japan and Nigeria in 2000 was a little over $500 mn, as shown in Table 3, of which roughly $289 mn, comprised exports and $217 mn imports, leaving Nigeria with a trade deficit of about US$72,313 mn. Not surprisingly, in 2001 as well the trade deficit remained in favour of Japan except that the deficit was much higher at US$170 mn and reminiscent of the trade conflict of earlier years.

The situation changed dramatically in 2002. As Table 3 again shows, Japan's imports came to about US$748,068 compared to its exports, which amounted to roughly US$259,538, leaving Nigeria with a favourable balance of US$488,527,549. This was a major development in the trade relations between the two countries since 1974. The explanation for this is the recent increases in Japan's imports of fuel products from Nigeria. While Japan's imports of mineral fuel have increased consistently since 2000, there was a vast increase in imports from this sector in 2002, accounting for over US$733 mn of Nigeria's exports to Japan that year. Crude oil alone accounted for US$161,303 mn and US$599,812 mn of Nigeria's exports to Japan in 2000 and 2002 respectively. There has also

Table 3. Trade Between Japan and Nigeria, 1968-2002

Unit: US$ mn.s

Year	Japan's exports to Nigeria	Japan's imports from Nigeria	Nigeria's Trade balance with Japan
1968	14.5	13	−1.4
1969	28.6	12.9	−15.7
1970	62.8	12.8	−50
1971	95.9	27.1	−68.8
1972	125.9	79.9	−46
1973	141.1	189	47.8
1974	284.6	448.8	164.1
1975	585.3	178.5	−306.7
1976	537.7	108.7	−465
1977	1,009.50	20.2	−946.2
1978	954.4	47.5	−946.9
1979	806.8	42.4	−764.4
1980	1,526.60	117.9	−1,408.70
1983	567.5	6.7	−560.7
1984	445.5	7	−438.5
1985	342	5.8	−336.1
1986	194.7	5.1	−189.5
1987	345.9	5.2	−340.7
1988	293.1	5.3	−261.4
1989	266.1	4.7	−261.4
1996	309.7	165.6	−144
1997	213.6	198.8	−15
1998	229.2	84.2	−145
1999	246	206.8	−40
2000	289,344,070	217,031,052	−72,313,018
2001	444,002,235	276,831,029	−167,171,206
2002	259,538,598	748,066,147	488,527,549

Source for the figures for 1968-1999: Japan Tariff Association.
The figures for 2000-2002 are taken from JETRO.

been a rise in Japanese imports of liquefied gas from Nigeria as the production of this lucrative energy resource escalates.[30]

The sudden growth in Nigeria's exports of mineral fuels to Japan is attributable to two main factors: the recent developments in Iraq[31] which have caused a reduction in the amount of oil supplies to the global market from the Persian-Gulf, and the refusal of Saudi Arabia to renew the prospecting license to the Arabian Oil Corporation in February 2000. Unfortunately, the upsurge in Japanese imports of mineral fuels from

[30] *Ibid.*

[31] JETRO, *JETRO Boeki Toshi Hakusho*, 2003, p. 390.

Nigeria may not last, as occurred in the early 1970s, because ultimately the events leading to the increase in imports are external to both Tokyo and Abuja. Consequently, and quite rightly, Nigerian policy-makers have tried to sustain and improve upon their country's trade relations with Japan. As the Chief Adviser to the President, Dr. Magnus L. Kpakol, noted in 2002 "Japan is the second largest economy in the world and we cannot ignore that kind of market, so we have to work hard to develop and strengthen trade ties with the country". It is worth pointing out that Nigeria's other exports to Japan, including raw materials such as cocoa, oil seeds, hides and skins and other leather products, have not been seen as competitive enough by Japan for these to make any impact on the Japanese market. In 2000, 2001 and 2002, for example, raw materials accounted for a mere US$17,528,167 mn, US$28,919,720 mn, and US$13,456,190 mn, respectively, of the grand total of Japan's imports from Nigeria. Moreover, food items only marginally contributed to the total of exports to Japan, with the figures standing at US$505,297, US$1,840,739, and US$1,332,462, respectively, during the same period. Thus, the Japanese Ambassador to Nigeria, Akira Matsui, has pointed out that while in the past Japan depended on Nigeria for its supply of

Table 4. Main Items of Trade Between Japan and Nigeria

US$1000

	2001 Amount	2002 Amount	2002 The component Ratio	Percentage Difference
Total Exports(+others)	444,002	259,539	100.0	Δ 41.5
Steel		58,591	22.6	Δ 22.6
	75,738			
Automobiles	41,473	31,618	12.2	Δ 23.8
Passenger cars	34,253	23,815	9.2	Δ 30.5
Two wheel drives	23,363	20,886	8.0	Δ 10.6
Freight cars	32,239	18,120	7.0	Δ 43.8
Total Imports(+others)				
Crude Oil		748,066	100.0	170.2
	276,831			
Liquefied Propane		599,812	80.2	271.9
	161,303			
Liquefied Butane		45,308	6.1	29
	35,132			
Gasoline. Manufactured products	0	13,179	1.8	
Sesame seed oil	21,429	13,176	1.8	Δ 38.5

Source: JETRO Boeki Toshi Hakusho (Author's translation)

shrimps and other sea food items, "it is sad to note that these sectors [have] been neglected".[32]

Thus, Nigeria's positive balance of payments vis-à-vis Japan in 2002 is also partly to do with the fact that there was a drastic reduction in imports from Japan, as shown in Table 3. The importation of general machinery, for example, was reduced by 11.2 percent while that of electrical machines dropped by 7.9 percent.[33] Meanwhile, the importation of electrical plants and equipment for oil refinery projects also slumped. Moreover, although the imports of car tyres remained satisfactory in the first half of the year, that of automobiles suffered.

The Issue of Japanese Investments (or lack of it) in Nigeria

A little distressing for Nigeria is the fact that since 1995[34] there has not been any form of direct investment in the non-oil sector from Japan to the country. Nevertheless, with an ambition to expand the export of its non-oil products, the Nigerian government still has strong expectations for Japanese investments in the country's economy. It is tempting, although perhaps slightly optimistic to say that, given Japan's new initiatives towards sub-Saharan Africa, under the rubric of TICAD, it is highly conceivable that the Japanese business community may also be looking into the investment opportunities that Nigeria can offer them. Recently, in relation to Japan's "frantic search for an alternative source of stable oil supply"[35] it was confirmed that "Nigeria may be one of the favoured partners". A request was also made to the effect that "Some kind of concession should be considered for the Japanese to enable them to participate in the bidding process and consequently exploration of Nigerian crude [oil]". It was also stipulated that Japan "should be encouraged to enter into [a] joint venture partnership with Nigeria in the downstream sector of the oil industry with [a] view to refining and bottling gas for local and export needs".[36] Apparently, the Japan National Oil Corporation (JNOC) has been involved in negotiations with its Nigerian counterpart, although the Japanese government would prefer the realisation of such projects to be conducted through the private trading houses.

---

[32] Quoted in Eugene Agba, "Japan Donates US$73.2 m to Nigeria" *THISDAY online*, http://thisdayonline.com/news/20030730news41.html

[33] JETRO, *JETRO Boeki Toshi Hakusho*, 2003, p. 390.

[34] JETRO, *JETRO Boeki Toshi Hakusho*, 2003, p. 390. According to Table 3 the last Japanese direct investment was made in May 1995.

[35] From document obtained from Nigerian Embassy, Tokyo, January, 2004.

[36] From document obtained from Nigerian Embassy, Tokyo, January, 2004.

Table 5. Japanese Private Firms (Investments) in Nigeria

Name of Firm	Year Established	Percentage of Investment	Line of Business
Chiyoda Nigeria Ltd.	1963.6	Chiyoda kakôkensetsu 100%.	Plant construction and repairs.
Honda Manufacturing	1981.1	Honda 30%.	Sale of automobiles and spare parts.
ITOCHU Nigeria Ltd.	1978.10	Itôchu 100%.	Market Research.
JGC Nigeria Ltd.	1991.3	Niki 100%.	Various types of Plant design, supply, construction
MBK Nigeria Ltd.	1969.5	Mitsui Bussan 86.8%, Local Partners 13.2%.	Trade.
Marubeni Nigeria Ltd.	1970.3	Marubeni 100%.	Trade.
Meisei Nigeria Ltd.		Meisei kôgyo, 100%.	Construction of Wells.
Mitsubishi Shoji Kaisha	1969.7	Mitsubishi shôji, 100%.	Import and Export.
Nishizawa (Nigeria) Ltd.	1969.4	Nishizawa, 50%. Local Partners, 50%	
Nissho Iwai (Nigeria) Ltd.	1979.10	Nisshô Iwai, 96.7%.	Import and Export.
SEI Nigeria Ltd.	1978.5	Sumitomo Denki Kôgyo, 40%; 2 others, 60%.	Construction of Communication systems.
Taisei (West Africa) Ltd.	1979.4	Taisei Kensetsu, 40%. Howas Services, 35%. Bells Holding, 25%.	
West African Seasoning Co.	1991.5		Importing seasonings, etc
Yamaha Manufacturing (Nigeria) Ltd.	1981.2	Sales of motor bike and Yamaha, 17.5%, Mitsui Bussan	Parts. 17.5%, Others, 65%.

Tôyô keizai, *Kaigai shinshitsu kigyo sôran*, 2003 (Author's translation). The investments by Marubeni Nigeria Ltd., Mitsubishi Shoji Kaisha (Nigeria) Ltd., Nishizawa (Nigeria) Ltd., and Nissho Iwai (Nigeria) Ltd., were made in March 1970, July 1969, April 1969 and October 1979 respectively.

Certainly, in early 1999 Japanese government officials went to Nigeria to discuss and identify specific areas of development assistance required by Nigeria. The first ever Japanese Economic Mission to Nigeria then took place not long after that under the leadership of the Chairman and Chief Executive of the Japan External Trade Organisation (JETRO),

Mr. Noboru Hatakeyama.[37] As can be expected, the delegation included top-level *keidanren* officials including representatives of companies with business interests in Nigeria such as trading companies, engineering firms, general and electrical machinery companies, and construction companies. The Japan International Co-operation Agency (JICA) and the Japan Bank for International Co-operation (JBIC) also sent representatives with the aim of meeting and discussing with Nigeria's leading policy-makers and business officials to decide on ways and means of improving the economic relations between their two countries. The 30 representatives also met with the President.

Following this representation from Japan, Mr. Bala (the Director of the Nigerian Investment Promotion Commission) was invited to Japan by JETRO to promote the economic potentials of Nigeria and attract investments into the food-processing industry. Mr. Bala noted that during the three weeks he was in Tokyo and Nagoya in November 2000, he visited 11 companies in the vegetable oil, cocoa and chocolate, and spices businesses, and did not miss going to the JBIC and the Japan International Development Association (JAIDO). As a follow-up to this, in May 2002 a Japanese Investment Mission visited Nigeria and found "the food-processing industry as having the most potential for investment . . ."[38] Consequently, JETRO commissioned research into the possibility for investment into the processing of yam and cassava, two of the major staple foods in West Africa, including Nigeria. The trading company, Marubeni Corporation, has also produced research that shows there is potential for profitable investment in the production of vegetable oil and the processing of fruits in Nigeria.

Marubeni also found tantalite, a mineral used in alloys for strength and higher melting as well as in the production of glass and surgical steel, as having a high potential for profitable investment in Nigeria based on its 2001 research in Nasarawa State. Bala further confirmed that "Another Japanese company has sent an expert to undertake a comprehensive survey of the solid minerals sector in Nigeria."[39] Meanwhile, Nigeria is making efforts to attract Japanese investments into the oil and gas sectors, not to mention such areas as telecommunications, manufacturing and the service industry. All the same, Japanese investments

---

[37] Julius J. Bala (Director, Policy Advocacy and External Relations, Nigeria Investment Promotion Commission), "The Challenges and Opportunities of the Investment Environment in Nigeria". Paper Presented at the International Meeting for the Promotion of Investment to Africa, Organised by the Ministry of Foreign Affairs of Japan, 26 February 2003.

[38] Julius Bala, p. 11.

[39] Julius Bala, p. 12.

in Nigeria are hardly noticeable, as they stand as shown in Table 5, not least because the highest employer listed among the 14 Japanese firms, Yamaha Manufacturing (Nigeria) Ltd., employs no more than 30 local workers. Moreover, the financial commitment of some of the firms is minimal as in the case of Marubeni Nigeria Ltd., Mitsubishi Shoji Kaisha (Nigeria) Ltd., Nishizawa (Nigeria) Ltd., and Nissho Iwai (Nigeria) Ltd., all of which invested N6,000, N7,000, N5,000 and N6,000, respectively. The firm with the highest investment is Honda Manufacturing (Nigeria) Ltd., which committed N1,575,000 to its project in 1981.[40]

But the impediments to Japanese investments in Nigeria are also many and in certain cases quite enormous. Mr. Yuichi Ishimaru (Senior Vice-President/Director of Marubeni Corporation and Member of the Honorary Presidential Advisory Council on Investment in Nigeria)[41] spelt out some of these, including

1. Over-dependence on the oil sector for foreign currency income and the national budget.
2. National budget deficit and the external debt.
3. Inadequate infrastructure and concerns about security conditions.
4. Administrative corruption.
5. Unreliable institutional structures.

We will touch on just a couple of these. The issue of over-dependence on a single source of income is fundamental to the poverty of the African economies, as is well known. In the case of Nigeria, the oil sector alone accounts for 95 percent of its foreign currency and 80 percent of the national budget. This on its own is bound to undermine the country's efforts to attract foreign investors, if only because it gives the impression that oil is Nigeria's only viable commercial commodity. In other words, by diversifying the economy, not only would the country potentially strengthen its export economy but also it would attract more investors into the different fields of Nigeria's economic activities. Additionally, diversification of its export economy would invariably augment the infrastructure that remains minimal when there is an over-dependence on a single source for the national budget. Indeed, Nigeria's 'indulgence' in a mono-economy since the 1970s also succeeded in destroying the railways as a major means for transporting goods. Relevant to this is the fact that because the South African economy is more diversified

---

[40] Toyo keizi. The employment figure for Honda Manufacturing (Nigeria) Ltd. was not available. The investments by Marubeni Nigeria Ltd., Mitsubishi Shoji Kaisha (Nigeria) Ltd., Nishizawa (Nigeria) Ltd., and Nissho Iwai (Nigeria) Ltd., were made in March 1970, July 1969, April 1969, and October 1979 respectively.

[41] Julius Bala, p. 3.

and the country's infrastructure is also relatively more expansive and reliable, Japanese investors are more inclined to pursue investment projects there than anywhere else in sub-Saharan Africa.

There is no doubt that the Japanese government, through its ODA programs, would contribute to the development of a better infrastructure in the host country if the host economy is perceived by the Japanese business community as potentially viable. It was demonstrated above that in the latter part of the 1960s and the early 1970s, the Japanese government did attempt to contribute to the development of the Nigerian infrastructure, obviously because it would have served the interest of Japanese investors in the country as well. Nigeria therefore has to make its economy attractive by departing from its over-dependence on oil and making its other minerals such as limestone, coal, manganese, iron ore, and bitumen, to name a few, accessible for foreign investment. It would also have to demonstrate that it is actively trying to improve its infrastructure. The fact that the Nigeria National Electric Power Authority (NEPA) and Marubeni Corporation signed a pact of US$62 mn in February 2001[42] to rehabilitate and enhance Nigeria's electric power might well serve as an incentive to some of the potential investors from Japan to pursue their investment interests in the country.

During his visit to Tokyo in May 2001, Obasanjo confirmed that "since the inception of the new civilian administration, Nigeria has effected "the appropriate legal framework for the protection of foreign investment and the repatriation of legitimate profit." He further assured his Japanese audience that Nigeria's programme of privatisation was devised to "substantially disengage government from direct involvement in business". Thus, he pledged his country's determination "to change from the way and manner business was done in Nigeria in the recent past in order to institute a new regime of accountability and transparency in conformity with internationally accepted codes of business ethics". On the last point, he was referring to the problem of administrative corruption that plagues the Nigerian economy and society. Specifically, he was alluding to the Anti-Corruption and Other Offences Act of 2000, which his government has instituted into law. Certainly, an effective application of the Act would help attract potential Japanese investors since there is concern among the Japanese business establishment that there are many administrative problems that need attention in Nigeria.[43]

---

[42] Angela Sayer-Farely, "Nigeria: Emerging from the Darkness", ESI Africa, 2, 2001. www.esi-africa.com/last/ESI22001/ESI22001_012_1.htm.

[43] JETRO, *Boeki Toshi Hakusho*, 2003, p. 390.

Conclusion

There appears to have been a significant change in the Japanese attitude towards Nigeria compared to the reticent nature with which it dealt with the West African state in the early 1990s, for example. As has been pointed out above, the two countries are now seemingly bound together in a 'Special Partnership', which provides them with a coherent framework for regular and constructive consultation. The indications are that the two countries would use this new partnership in ways that would be beneficial to their mutual interests. Japan would attempt to gain access to Nigeria's potential market as well as to its natural resources if the conditions were conducive to this. Nigeria, on its part, would endeavour to attract as much economic assistance from Japan and since JICA is looking into expanding its office in Nigeria,[44] it seems that the country would be at the receiving end of more Japanese economic assistance. Most importantly, however, Abuja would continue to aim to attract as much Japanese investment as possible.

As has been argued above, Japan's initiatives toward Nigeria are, to some extent, a reflection of Japan's recent enthusiastic attitude towards Africa and its developmental problems. We have argued that Japan is operating within the TICAD framework to assist the African countries in creating better life chances for their citizens. We have, however, also argued that Japan's efforts through TICAD are partly motivated by its search for a solution to its own economic malaise: the on-going economic depression that began in the early 1990s. Thus, the change in the Japanese attitude towards Africa may be emanating from Japan's desperate attempts to correct its decade long economic downturn. The assumption is that if it is able to assist in re-ordering Africa into a viable economic entity, as well as a buoyant market for Japanese products and a source for lucrative raw materials, then it might be able to give its companies a new lease of life which would ultimately save the country from its economic problems. Japan's recent initiatives toward Africa could therefore be seen as perhaps similar to its relations with the Southeast Asian countries from the 1960s through to the latter part of the 1980s. During that period, these countries served as a source for the strategic mineral resources that the Japanese companies depended on, and provided Japan with the market for its manufactured products. On the other hand, through its programmes at economic assistance to these countries, including loans and human development initiatives, and with the vast

[44] Conversation with a JICA official (in Tokyo), 23 January, 2004. The JICA office is currently being run by only one person.

inflow of Japanese private investments, the Southeast Asian countries were able to develop their economies and provide their citizens with a better standard of living. But these new overtures toward Africa are also designed to bring prestige to Japan and that is one reason why the Japanese policy-makers, having committed themselves to the TICAD process, will endeavour to make it a success.

We have also noted that in 1999 the Japanese government reviewed its 1994 policy of sanctions against the Abacha administration and has since provided Nigeria with different types of economic assistance as shown above. Nigeria, not surprisingly, will need and ask for more, not least because of its size and scale. Japan, on the other hand, would submit to these requests only if it would also gain from what it is acquiescing to. Meanwhile, Japanese policy-makers are concerned about the various administrative problems in Nigeria. There is also reservation about the unstable regulatory and institutional environment, and the problem of the national budget deficit and both public and private debt financing. Meanwhile, on the Nigerian side there is obvious concern that the Japanese private companies have consistently shied away from investing in Nigeria, at least since the 1980s, and continue to do so despite Nigeria's strenuous efforts to engage them. This begs a few questions. Surely if TICAD is about developing the economies of the African countries, then why is it that 10 years after its inauguration there are still hardly any Japanese investments in sub-Saharan Africa and certainly in Nigeria of all places? And why is that in 2001, 56.6 percent of Japanese aid went to Asia and only 14.6 percent was directed towards Africa while the same region received only 9.4 percent of the total amount Japan allocated towards technical co-operation in the same year? Conversely, Asia, a relatively rich region, received 37 percent of the amount for technical co-operation. Moreover, with regard to grant aid for the same year, Africa received 35.4 percent of the US$1.9 billion Japan allocated to it while Asia received 38.2 percent. Nevertheless, there is also concern that whenever Japan gives project-related economic assistance to Nigeria Japanese trading companies and contractors end up managing the initiatives, thereby making it impossible for local companies to gain from such projects and contracts. In other words Japanese aid is 'tied' to Japan's own economic interests.

All this notwithstanding, on the diplomatic front the two countries seem determined to make the 'Special Relationship' a constructive engagement. They will both attempt to use it to gain a permanent seat at the SC for example, and may well be successful in their endeavours. On that very issue, however, if the contest for a permanent sub-Saharan African representation is between South Africa and Nigeria, no one is sure which of these countries Japan will support since, after all, in taking its cue from Nigeria, South Africa has also forged a 'Special Relationship' with Japan. Nor is there any certainty as to whether Japan will support Nigeria or South Africa if the contest for a permanent African seat at the SC involved Egypt. Ultimately, however, it is how the economic relationship between Japan and Nigeria develops that will confirm whether there is indeed a 'Special Relationship' between the two countries.

Japanese Contribution to Malaysian Economic Development: Lessons for Africa

Toyomu Masaki

Abstract

This paper does not deal directly with the relations between Japan and Africa; instead it looks at Malaysia and Côte d'Ivoire with the objective of portraying Japanese contribution to Malaysian economic development and identifying some lessons that can be learnt by Africa from it. Both countries had a comparable macroeconomic outlook until 1980, with economies based on similar primary goods such as cocoa, coffee, palm oil, timber etc., which are typical of tropical climates. However, following the sharp decline in international prices since 1980, Malaysia registered a high economic growth and became successfully industrialized, Côte d'Ivoire suffered an economic crisis and a balance of payment deficit. Moreover, the latter is not a special case among African countries. The paper also seeks to advance some hypotheses in order to explain the phenomena.

1. Introduction

As Figure 1 shows Malaysia and Côte d'Ivoire had a comparable macroeconomic outlook until 1980, with economies based on similar primary goods such as cocoa, coffee, palm oil, timber etc., which are typical of tropical climates. These products accounted for approximately 90% of the export income of the two countries. However, following the sharp decline in international prices since 1980, Malaysia registered a high economic growth and became successfully industrialized, Côte d'Ivoire suffered an economic crisis and a balance of payment deficit. Moreover, the latter is not a special case among African countries.

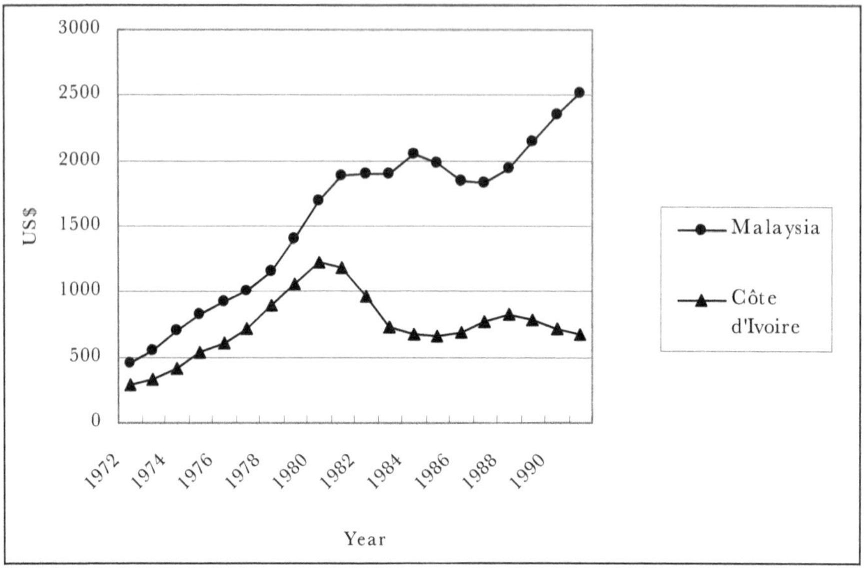

Figure 1. GNP per capita of Malaysia and Côte d'Ivoire

The actual Malaysian GDI per capita exceeds US$3500. Under the government of the ex-prime minister, Mahathir, who promulgated the South-South Cooperation, Malaysia emerged as a strong opinion leader among developing as well as Islamic countries. On the other hand, the GNI par capita of Côte d'Ivoire has declined to US$600 due to the economic crisis of the 1980s as well as several political crises since 1999. It is ironic that the former's success and the latter's failure both took place under the common phenomenon of globalization wherein a market-oriented economic policy is implemented. In the late 1980s, Malaysia changed its economic policy from protectionism to open economy, which resulted in substantial success in attracting foreign investments from multinational firms, especially in the electrical and electronic sector. These sectors can be considered to have played important role from the viewpoint of transfer of technology from developed countries, particularly from Japan to Malaysia. On the other hand, Côte d'Ivoire appeared to have suffered due to structural adjustment policies based on the neoclassical economic theory implemented by the Bretton Woods Institutions. In fact, the suspension of lending from these institutions because of the government's failure to implement some of the conditionalities contributed directly to the financial crisis and indirectly to the political instability of Côte d'Ivoire.

This paper seeks to examine the various reasons for the drastic difference in performance between Malaysia and Côte d'Ivoire despite the fact that the two countries were faced with the same phenomenon of globalization with similar initial economic conditions, and also attempts to make some observations that could have implications for the future of Africa.

2. Globalization and Developing Countries

Labor wage in rich countries tends to be higher than in poor countries, whereas the rental cost of capital in the former is apt to be lower than that in the latter because while capital is abundant in developed countries, the labor supply is relatively scarce compared to the demand. Therefore, neoclassical schools insist, based on the factor price equalization theorem, that in order to equalize labor prices across the world, free displacement of labor or capital is required because, theoretically, the economic gap between countries can be bridged when all the factors of production flow from a low-price area towards a high-returns areas under a condition of no governmental intervention. However, in reality, this economic conversion mechanism is rarely observed. Neoclassical theory suggests the inadequate liberalization of the economy as a probable reason and emphasizes that there exists a need to eliminate economic barriers in order to narrow the economic disparity between them.

In contrast to this viewpoint of economic liberalism, Myrdal, G. (1957) proposes the backwash and spread effects. The backwash effects refer to the situation wherein the free movement of the factors of production and products tends to favor the rapidly-growing communities and disfavor those that are stagnant. For example, since migration is always selective, the regions that attract migrants, particularly those that are young, ambitious and productive, enjoy a significant advantage with respect to production as compared to other regions. In contrast to the backwash effects, spread effects imply the expansionary momentum from economic centers to stagnant regions. Increased demand of primary products from developing regions and technical diffusion from the economic centers to the stagnant regions are examples of the spread effects. These two effects are stimulated by migration, capital movements and trade in both economic and non-economic factors. According to Myrdal, the free flow of factors of production and products between underdeveloped and developed regions may further expand these economic gaps because the backwash effects are often stronger than the spread effects in the absence of the welfare state. Myrdal states that:

> there is a tendency inherent in the free play of market forces to create regional inequalities, and that this tendency becomes the more dominant

the poorer a country is, two of the most important laws of economic underdevelopment and development under *laissez-faire*.[1]

This theory of circular and cumulative causation, explains the drift towards regional economic inequalities in a country under conditions of non-intervention and can also be applied to the problem of inequality between nations in the globalization era.

However, the two theories, as noted above, appear to be incompatible. The question that arises is whether the free global displacement of the factors of production and products results in a more equalized or disequalized world. This question can be answered by observing the regional disparities in countries, wherein in general, no economic barriers exist between sub-regions. Myrdal indicates that the regional inequalities between sub-regions have been diminishing in rich countries, whereas the reverse phenomenon is observed in less developed countries.[2] In this respect, Williamson, J.G. (1965), on the basis of an empirical analysis of the United States, also discovered the existence of an inverted U-shaped relationship between a country's economic level and its internal economic disparity. He argued that the economic disparity between regions within a country grows during the early stages; however, this disparity shrinks following the turning point at which the country is sufficiently developed. In the globalization era, the world has undoubtedly become smaller, similar in some ways to a country or a village. If Williamson's assumption is correct, in this circumstance, while the development of the world economy as a whole may increase the disparity between nations in the early stages, it could lead to a more equalized world after sufficient development has been attained. The emergence of the 'new trade theory' in the 1980s, which is based on increasing returns or monopolistic competitions also serves to demonstrate the feasibility of Williamson's hypothesis even on the global level.

Paul Krugman and Anthony J. Venebles, the pioneers of the new trade theory, have also contributed to the academic discourse about the relationship between globalization and the inequality among nations. By employing sophisticated analytic tools and the notion of transportation costs, they obtained results that led to a conclusion similar to that of Williamson, J.G. (1965), that global economic growth would inevitably result in the declining of transportation costs. For example, Krugman, P. and Venebles, A.J. (1995) assume that the world can be divided into two regions, namely, the North and the South and two sectors, namely,

[1] Myrdal, G. (1957), p. 34.
[2] *Ibid.*, p. 33.

agricultural and manufacturing. Agricultural goods are produced with constant returns to scale and the manufacturing sector is subject to increasing returns production curves and produces both finished goods that are sold to consumers and intermediate goods used as inputs in the production of manufactures. In the early stage, all countries are equally proficient in both sectors, implying that neither region has any inherent comparative advantage in manufacturing. At this stage, when the transportation costs between the two regions are very high, each region will be essentially self-sufficient and will produce both manufactured and agricultural goods. However, reduction in the transportation costs promotes the trade between the two regions. Further, the region, which for some reason has a larger manufacturing sector becomes more attractive as locations of manufacturing facilities (backward linkages). In summary, the region that produces a greater variety of intermediate goods can produce finished goods at a lower cost (forward linkages). This cumulative process leads to a world economy that consists of an industrialized core and a deindustrialized periphery. Moreover, real wages will fall in the region that suffers an outflow in the manufacturing sector and rise in the region that becomes the industrialized core. Krugman and Venebles thus argue that global economic integration leads to uneven development.

However, Krugman, P. and Venebles A.J. (1995) continue to assume further reduction in transportation costs. This implies that access to both the regions becomes easier and geographical proximity becomes less important. Their conclusion may be summarized as follows. The peripheral region will offer potential producers the advantage of a lower wage rate. At some point, the decline in transportation costs will be adequate such that the lower wage rate in the periphery would more than compensate for the disadvantage of its distant location from the markets and suppliers. At this point, the manufacturing sector will once again have an incentive to move from the core to the periphery, thereby forcing a convergence of wage rates.[3]

This theory, proposed by the pioneers of the new trade theory, seems to have been vindicated in the East Asian economic growth, since the late 1980s. For example, China, a country, that was nothing more than a periphery 20 years ago, has undoubtedly transformed itself into a global manufacturing and production centre by taking advantage of low labour wages and globalisation. Such success stories have emerged owing to the Foreign Direct Investment (FDI) by multinational firms from developed countries that are faced with high production costs and are seeking new

[3] Krugman, P. and Venebles, A.J. (1995), p. 861.

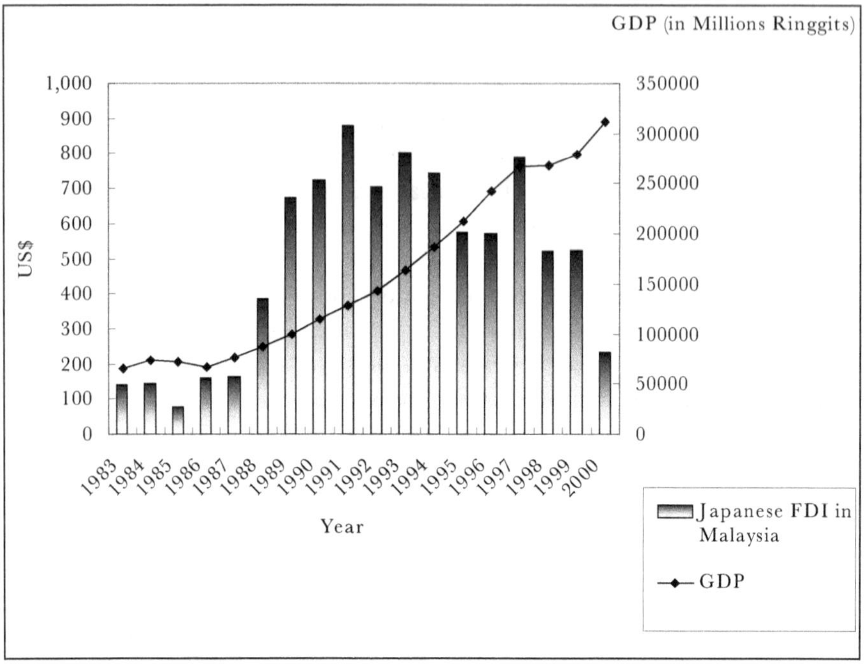

Source: GNP, *Key Indicators 2001*, Asian Development Bank.
Japanese FDI in Malaysia, Jetro, http://www.jetro.go.jp/jpn/stats/fdi/

Figure 2. Malaysia: Japanese FDI and Economic Growth

manufacturing locations in order to strengthen their competitive advantage. In this respect, a suitable example would be that of Malaysia, which achieved rapid growth after 1988. As figure 2 shows, this economic growth was not unrelated to the rapid inflow of FDI, particularly from Japan. Mahathir, who reigned as the prime minister between 1981 and 2004, continued to implement several measures since 1985 in order to gain the attention of multinational firms. As Krugman, P. and Venebles, A.J. (1995) and Myrdal, G. (1957) indicate, the displacement of capital from the developed world to developing countries can become a key factor in the convergence of development. The next section briefly describes the Malaysian economic development process since the 1980s and also examines the relation between the type of investment and development.

3. Malaysian Development and Japanese Capitals

3-1 *Malaysian Development after 1980*

Figure 3 indicates the composition of total Japanese FDI in the manufacturing sector between 1980 and 2003 in the world. It shows that

Japanese investment is characterized by the strong dominance of assembling industries such as machinery manufacturing, electrical & electronic products and transport equipment. Products in such industries consist of a number of intermediate materials and Japanese strength in these industries due to its specific ability to coordinate several intermediate goods is well known. Aoki Masahiko (2000) focuses on institutional analysis and explains that the strong competitiveness of Japanese firms in the assembling industry arises from its horizontal hierarchical organizational structure.[4] According to Aoki, strong 'complementarity' exists between tasks when many parts have to be assembled into various products on a single assembly line due to the diversification of products. Japanese institutional organizations, unlike those in the United States, permit workshops to innovatively handle the increase in complementarity between operational tasks that has resulted from the diversification and increased product complexity.[5]

Since its independence, Malaysia has always demonstrated an insatiable ambition for industrialization. In 1968, the government implemented the Promotion of Investment Act and provided several tax benefits to export-oriented companies, which were primarily American or Japanese electrical and electronics industrial firms that had penetrated into the Free Trade Zone (FTZ). However, low economic linkages between local and foreign firms are considered problematic. In this context, under the New Economic Policy introduced in 1971 and the Industrial Coordination Act introduced in 1975, which was revised from the Promotion of Investment Act, the government restricts foreign investment and prohibits foreign-affiliated companies from holding more than 50% of their share in joint ventures with local firms. This regulation is considered to have positively impacted the local economy from the viewpoint that foreign manufacturing firms, including a variety of small and medium supporting companies, were required for the establishment of joint ventures with local partners.

In 1980, the Heavy Industry Commission of Malaysia (HICOM) was established under government control for the purpose of stimulating the growth of the steel and iron manufacturing industry. Through collaboration with Japanese companies, HICOM intensified its efforts to boost

---

[4] Aoki, M. (2000), Chapter 2.

[5] *Ibid.*, p. 39. On the contrary, Japan, unlike the United States, which has implemented a functional hierarchical organizational structure all the way down to the workshop level, is less competitive in technologically mature industries such as the petrochemical industry. According to Aoki, in these industries, since uncertainties between processes can be handled largely through technological means, efficiency demands the existence of a structure in which the idiosyncratic information regarding the downstream market for processed goods is quickly and accurately assessed and reflected in the upstream supply system of intermediate materials.

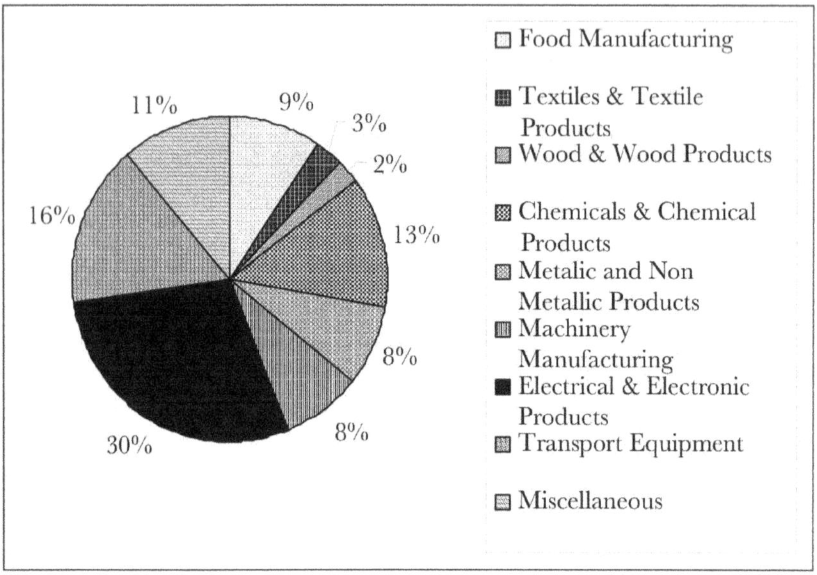

Source: JETRO, http://www.jetro.go.jp/jpn/stats/fdi/

Figure 3. Total Japanese FDI between 1980 and 2003 in the Manufacturing Sector (US$ millions)

the steel, motorcycle and automobile industries. In this regard, Proton, a national vehicle-manufacturing company established as a joint venture with the Japanese automaker, Mitsubishi Motor Corporation, is especially well known. Mahathir, who became prime minister in 1981, pursued the policy of import-substitution for heavy industries. However, a small country like Malaysia, with a population of just over 14 million at that time, this strategy may not have been appropriate since substituted products become expensive in the absence of scale merit.

In the mid-1980s, this strategy was abruptly replaced by export-oriented industrialization, and Mahathir decided to channel FDI into the electrical and electronic equipment industries. Although at that point in time, Japanese firms were the most competitive in these industries, Japan was faced with a decline in industrial competitiveness due to the appreciation of the yen following the Plaza Accord in 1985. The Malaysian inclination towards industrialization corresponded favourably with the strategy of Japanese firms, which were intent on cost reduction. As a result, Japanese FDI into Malaysia increased dramatically since 1988. The value of the annual Japanese FDI flows into East Asia[6] never sur-

[6] Asia NIES, ASEAN 4 and China.

passed US$1.5 billion until 1985; however, it rose to over US$8 billion in 1989.[7]

According to Tanaka, S. and Kenney, M. (1996), between 1985 and 1993 Japanese consumer electronics firms established 39 new manufacturing facilities in Malaysia, including companies such as Sony, Aiwa, JVC (Victor) and Pioneer.[8] In general, the Japanese electronics companies operating in Malaysia in the 1980s tended to invest in the manufacturing of consumer electronics such as refrigerators, radios, televisions etc. for the domestic as well as the foreign market.[9] American companies, on the other hand, preferred to invest in semiconductor and hard disk drive (HDD) and HDD parts' industries for re-export. In summary, Japanese electronics investment in Malaysia was significantly more diverse than that of the United States.[10]

During the early stages, the assembling sector was located in Malaysia and it imported the intermediate goods it required from Japan. However, as the scale of the Malaysian assembling sector increased beyond a critical level, a group of intermediate product suppliers were encouraged to localize in the proximity of the assembling plants because suppliers such as plastic injection molding or metal stamped parts firms are often highly concerned with the decisions made by the major assemblers. In this manner, if the development of the assembling sector in Malaysia led to the development of an agglomeration of a variety of input sectors, the agglomeration would also promote the development of Malaysian electrical and electronic industries. Such a cumulative development process is known to have large linkage effects on several factors and leads to a significantly greater development of the local economy. Based on this consideration, Malaysia proceeded to create an FTZ to which the assembling sector were invited first and was encouraged to establish joint ventures with local Malaysian firms. The principal incentive offered to these assembling companies was the low labour cost. However, due to increasing wages, labour-intensive sectors, which localize in low-labour-cost countries, tended to again relocate to other countries that offered a more attractive labour cost. Furthermore, in order to maintain capital inflows even after the increase in wages, Malaysia was forced to offer more attractive conditions besides low labour cost and aimed to build a value chain in the electrical and electronic industries. It was a challenge to make such a departure from the *Fordism periphery*,[11] the low value-added production in the context of international division of labour.

---

[7] JETRO, http://www.jetro.go.jp/jpn/stats/fdi/data/jfdi1111_01.xls

[8] Tanaka, S. and Kenney, M. (1996), p. 67.

[9] *Ibid.*

[10] *Ibid.*

[11] This is a concept from a French *Regulation* School. Fordism periphery implies a

3-2 *Malaysian Strategy for Building a Much Higher Value Chain*

Malaysia is known to be a country that has long paid special attention to its small- and medium-sized companies in order to improve the economic standard of the Malay or the indigenous ethnic group called *Bumiputera.* In Malaysia, the Chinese, a minority ethnic group, control its economy and the economic conditions of the Bumiputera is fairly poor, although they comprise more than 50% of the population. In 1971, the New Economic Policy, was established in response to the racial riots that had been ongoing for the two preceding years with the objective of reducing inter-racial tensions by improving the income and economic conditions of the Bumiputera, without transferring income from the Chinese.

Under the Vendor Development Program (VDP) in 1988, the government formulated the policies for strengthening the linkage between large companies, including multinational firms (anchor companies), and local small- and medium-sized businesses (vendor companies). VDP refers to the arrangement wherein a large company promotes local vendor companies by acting as an anchor company. It was initiated with the objective of increasing the supply of intermediate materials from the firms of the Bumiputera to Proton, the national automobile company, which was started in 1983. As an anchor company, Proton was required to promote local small- and medium-sized companies in which at least 70% of the capital was invested by the Bumiputera and more than 55% of the employees were Bumiputera.[12] Under the VDP, small- and medium-sized companies were also entitled to receive several privileges as vendor companies. The anchor companies were required to purchase products from their vendor companies. Local vendor companies could access management resources from their anchor companies, including technology and product management, by supplying their products to them. While, even after ten years, the plan, which initially sought promote more than 800 small- and medium-sized businesses as vendor companies, remained unaccomplished due to insufficient development of the Bumiputera companies, 196 vendor companies received extensive support from 76 anchor companies, including 39 electrical and electronics companies in 1998.[13] This VDP could serve as a guide wherein few formal companies exist apart from the state owned and multinational companies.

---

low-level production sector that does not have any decision-making authority in the mass production system.

[12] Anazawa (2000), pp. 9-10.

[13] *Ibid.*, p. 10.

In the early 1990s, the VDP led to the next clusters promotion policy. The cluster, which is a concept proposed by Michel Porter, refers to the geographical concentration of industrial production units; in other words, it is an agglomeration of interlinked or related activities comprising several industries. The Silicon Valley is generally cited as a typical example of a cluster. Within a cluster, inter-firm cooperative relationship can be observed along the vertical structure. On the other hand, competition is highly intense along the horizontal structure. Such a cooperative and competitive relationship is considered to emerge as an engine of product innovation and improvement. The advantages of clusters are mainly external to firms; however, they have an indirect impact on internal productivity. This strategy seeks a collective efficiency among several firms through *flexible specialization* (Piore and Sabel 1984).

The Malaysian Second Outline Perspective Plan (1991-2000) and the Sixth Malaysia Plan (1991-1995) placed a strong emphasis on developing an integrated industrial structure. This does not imply the development of each individual firm, but refers to the promotion of a wider vendor network through a subcontracting system between small- and medium-sized companies and large foreign and domestic industries. At the second Industrial Master Plan (IMP2) in 1996, the cluster-based development concept was adopted as a guideline for the development because clusters were considered to serve as important driving forces in creating the competitive advantage of nations.[14]

In the era of globalization, Malaysia has offered not only attractive tax policies, infrastructure provision and easier bureaucratic procedures in order to attract large multinational companies, but also several policies

---

[14] Recently, the concept of *competitive advantage* has become a commonly encountered concept in the discussion of regional development strategy. However, it is so obscure that it is frequently confused with the concept of *comparative advantage* in international economics. Criticizing the principle of comparative advantage because of its failure in capturing the determinants of economic success in the modern world of economy, Porter conceptualized and proposed this new alternative concept of his own, namely, competitive advantage. His ambitious attempts at challenging the classical principle of comparative advantage provoked extensive criticism by economists because of his insufficient comprehension of the principles of international trade, which are exemplified by the Ricardo or Hechscher-Ohlin model. However in essence, the notion of competitive advantage by Porter is significantly different from that of comparative advantage in international economics. These two concepts tend to share a complementary rather than an opposing relationship. Warr, P.G. (1994) provides a sound description of the two concepts of competitive advantage and comparative advantage. According to him, competitive advantage deals with the determinants of the commercial performance of individual firms while comparative advantage deals with the efficient allocation of resources at the national level. He concluded that the former pertains to firms, whereas the latter pertains to countries.

to stimulate local firms and their networking with the objective of realizing their competitive advantage. Malaysia is one of the most important countries in the electrical and electronic equipment industries and is well known for utilizing a cluster-based development strategy in seeking to realize competitive advantage under the conditions offered by comparative advantage.

3-3 *Joint Ventures and Transfer of Technology*

FDI obviously offers an opportunity for developing countries to receive tangible as well as intangible assets such as technological, managerial or international marketing capabilities from developed countries. However, in contrast to traditional FDI, wherein foreign companies own either the entire or a majority equity of the subsidiaries in the recipient country, a new type of investment has emerged since the mid-1970s. Oman, C. (1989) defines it as New Form of Investment (NFI), wherein the entire or a majority of the equity in the local operation remains locally owned; for example, joint ventures in which foreign equity does not exceed 50%, licensing agreements, franchising, turnkey and product-in-hand contracts.[15] A joint venture refers to a partnership between companies that permits them to do business in foreign countries. This allows firms in developing countries to share not only technology but also several risks and rewards with firms in the developed countries. The size of equity ownership, in general, reflects the level of control. According to Oman, C. (1989), as a result of government regulations that restricted foreign ownership of investment, the number of NFIs increased during the 1970s and specific features are observed depending on the nationality or industry of investors. Oman indicates that in the mid-1980s, Japanese multinational companies were not reluctant to enter into NFI, whereas American multinational corporations preferred wholly owned subsidiaries; European companies occupied an intermediate stance.[16] In fact, as table 1 indicates, among countries that offered technical associations to Malaysian companies during 1975-1989, Japan was the most prominent.

NFI into Malaysia from Japan is considered to have contributed to training local workers, engineers and middle-level managers as well as to the transfer of technology. In general, in developing countries, subcontractors often start as low-cost producers of parts or low-cost assem-

---

[15] Oman, C. (1989), p. 9.

[16] He compares the types of investment of the three poles of the world, using the case of 116 European companies, 52 American companies and 138 Japanese companies. See Oman, C. (1989).

blers of foreign-designed products classified under the Original Equipment Manufacturing (OEM). However, they often subsequently acquire the capacity to develop their own products for the local as well as the export markets. According to Klaus North (1997), who focused on the transfer of know-how to the developing countries in global production, this pattern has been observed particularly in the electronics industry.[17]

According to Yamashita, S. (1996), with reference to a survey conducted by the Japanese Chamber of Trade and Industries Malaysia (JACTIM),[18] which was concluded in 1995, 28.8% (48 companies) of the 160 Japanese affiliated companies that participated in the survey have already started in-house R&D activities and 10% of them encourage the designing of new products.[19] JACTIM indicates that local vendors have business relationships with several Japanese companies and approximately 50% of their sales is due to the demand from these companies. Yamashita concluded that over 50% of local vendors had received management skills support from Japanese companies and hoped to expand their business with Japanese companies. According to his research, the vendors evaluate the business positively due to the following factors: (a) improved quality of the products, (b) better skills to produce parts of high value-added products, (c) expanded sales and (d) enhanced international competitiveness.[20]

Table 1. Technical association with Malaysian companies by country

	1975-1979	1980-1984	1985-89	Total	Percentage (%)
Japan	103	185	249	537	34.0
U.K.	44	73	90	207	13.1
U.S.A.	28	65	82	175	11.1
India	28	19	11	58	3.7
West Germany	22	34	21	77	4.9
Austria	10	28	33	71	4.5
Hong Kong	9	23	32	64	4.1
Singapore	10	27	16	53	3.4
Others	59	135	143	337	21.2
Total	313	589	677	1579	100.0

Source: The Malaysian Industrial Development Authority (MIDA)

[17] North K. (1997), p. 70.

[18] JACTIM, *A Survey on Technology Transfer of Japanese Affiliated Companies in Malaysia* (in Japanese), Dec. 1995.

[19] Yamashita, S. (1996), pp. 11-12.

[20] *Ibid.*, p. 13.

4. Development of Côte d'Ivoire and Foreign Firms

Côte d'Ivoire is one of the few African countries that registered a rapid economic growth of over 7% until the end of the 1970s. This growth is attributed to the agricultural sector, particularly the cultivation of coffee and cocoa. However, it faced budgetary and current account deficits since 1980 on account of the heavy investment during the economic boom in the 1970s and the subsequent decline in prices of primary products after 1980.

4-1 *Investment in Côte d'Ivoire and its Influence*

Unlike most African countries, Côte d'Ivoire was always keen on attracting FDI. Just prior to its independence, Côte d'Ivoire adopted its first investment law in 1959 in order to attract national as well as foreign enterprises to come in. It was viewed as extremely liberal by foreigners, who enjoyed complete exemption from this law for a certain period.[21] Since independence, the government encouraged the import-substitute industrialization of consumer products as well as the processing of local agricultural raw materials for export. The sufficiently-protected market for final goods was also attractive to foreign investors. For example, in 1984, a joint ventures, named NELCI, was established as a subsidiary of the Japanese electrical company, Matsushita Electric Industrial Co., Ltd.[22] According to the President, who was interviewed by the author in 1997 at Abidjan, unlike the case of Malaysia, NELCI produced electrical appliances such as colour televisions (7,200 units annually), air conditioners (4,200) and radios (28,000), aimed primarily at the domestic market. However, 98.5% of intermediary goods, with certain exceptions such as cartons, were imported from Asia due to a lack of local suppliers and ability. Compared to the developed countries where they faced fierce competition, the African market usually guaranteed the manufacturing companies a high margin, which NELCI had also benefited from until 2001, the year in which it had to face closure due to political crisis.

According to research by Mytelka (1984), at the beginning of the 1970s in Côte d'Ivoire, 71% of the capital was invested in the food industry, 86% in the wood industry, 92% in the textiles, shoes and clothing industry, 81% in the chemical industry and 89% of the metal-working indus-

[21] Bamba, B.M. (1987), p. 130.

[22] The company was established with 500 million CFAF in capital and 60% of its shares were held by Matsushita. The remaining capital was invested by several local individuals (in a telephone interview with the Headquarters of Matsushita in Osaka, Japan) in April 2005.

try was foreign-owned.[23] While this bias was corrected with the concept of Ivoirisation and the engagement of the government sector since the early 1970s, its political stability under President Houphouet-Boigny, who ruled the country for over 30 years, the pegged currency and positive relations with France enabled it to receive a substantial amount of money, particularly from France, since the colonial days. However, in Côte d'Ivoire, due to the small domestic market for import-substitute products, most of the money had been invested in agriculture, resource-processing industries like coffee, cocoa and palm oil processing and in construction & public works as indicated in table 2.

Table 2. Top Industrial Firms in Côte d'Ivoire and their Ownership (1979-1980)

		Turnover in Million CFAF	Government share %	Private share %	Foreign share %	Principal Foreign Shareholders
SIR	Refining	61,300	47.5	0.0	52.5	Elf Union, Mobil, Shell, Texaco, Esso, BP.CCP
EECI	electricity	40,868*	86.0	0.0	14.0	
UNICAFE	Agro-industry	na	0.0	0.0	100.0	
Blohorn	Soap, oils	na	0.0	20.0	80.0	Blohorn
UTPA	Agro-industry	na	0.0	0.0	100.0	
SODESCRE	Agro-industry	na	100.0	0.0	0.0	
Palmindustrie	Agro-industry	26,000**	100.0	0.0	0.0	
CIDT	Agro-industry	35,000	55.0	0.0	45.0	
SITAB	Cigarettes	18,900	19.0	21.0	60.0	Bastos-Job, Groupe Suisse, Régie Française des Tabacs
Gonfreville	Textiles	16,000	33.0	22.0	60.0	
SOLIBRA	Beer	15,875	0.0	20.0	80.0	
SACO (cocoa)	Agro-industry	11,200	35.0	0.0	45.0	Groupe Français
BRACODI	Beer	9,398	0.0	22.0	78.0	SOGEPAL
SODECI	Water	na	52.4	45.0	2.6	
GMA (milling)	Agro-industry	11,500	0.0	25.0	75.0	Jacques MIMRAN, GMA Dakar, Emile MIMRAN, Sometra
CAPRAL (Coffee)	Agro-Industry	11,053	24.0	9.0	67.0	NESTLE
Decorticaf	Agro-Industry	na	0.0	0.0	100.0	
COGEXIM	Agro-Industry	na	na	na	na	
SCA	Cement	6,200	40.0	0.0	60.0	
SMB	Petrochimie	4,265	93.0	0.0	7.0	

* 'sales' as opposed to turnover
** 'value of production' as opposed to turnover
Lynn Krieger Mytelka (1984), pp. 160-161.
Bamba, Moussa B. (1987), pp. 133-134.

[23] Mytelka (1984), p. 153.

Conditions such as a lack of sufficient infrastructure, skilled labor, strong political initiative and large market were not conducive to receiving investments in the assembling industries, although the government did attempt to promote it under its import-substitution policy. In fact, Côte d'Ivoire is noted for its high wage rate. The average wage in the manufacturing sector in 1997 was US$6159, even after the 50% devaluation in 1994, while its GNI per capita stood at a mere US$500 in that period. This phenomenon has also been widely observed in other African countries. Table 3 shows that labor wages in the manufacturing sector in some African countries tend to be considerably high as compared to their economic level. This fact is also one of the reasons for the promotion of resource-based industrialization in Africa.

However, the resource-processing industry is not expected to generate high inter-linkage effects in the local economy because it does not require a large number of local support industries in contrast to the assembling industries such as observed in Malaysia. In addition, as shown in table 2, the government of Côte d'Ivoire did not appear to take much interest in controlling the activities of foreign companies or their capital composition, apart from a few exceptions. In other words, it is difficult to observe private local enterprises and large foreign enterprises on an equal footing in case of joint ventures between the two. In general, resource-processing companies tended to refrain from forming joint ventures in order to prevent the outflow of technology. According to research by the United Nations Center on Transnational Corporations (UNCTC), industries such as alimentation or pharmacy whose brand images are important, tend to acquire 100% subsidiaries, while industries that require extensive skilled labor or tacit technology, due to their complexity, do not hesitate to offer licenses through the intermediary of NFI.[24] Consequently, the development of local labor skills or technological diffusion from a coffee processing company such as Nestlé, which is one of the most prominent companies in Côte d'Ivoire, cannot be sufficiently expected.

An additional drawback in this regard is that resource-based industries tend to be capital intensive. They do not create much employment and require a relatively higher level of educated labor such as engineers. The capital-labor ratio of this industry, which is an indicator of the level of labor wage, is relatively higher than that of labor-intensive industries such as assembling sectors in Malaysia. Although most African countries do not have large populations, they possess abundant resources. In this

[24] UNCTC (1987), 17-29.

Table 3. Average wage in the Manufacturing Sector and GNI per Capita of selected Asian and African Countries (US$)

Sector	Senegal 1997	Côte d'Ivoire 1997	Zimbabwe 1998*	Mauritius 1999*	South Africa 1999*	Philippines 1997*	Malaysia 1999*
Average wage in the manufacturing sector	3194	6159	1869	3805	7787	2966	4836
GNI per capita	500	670	530	3540	3170	1050	3390

Source: UNIDO and World Bank 'World Development Indicator', 1999
* including estimation.

circumstance, the resource-based industrialization strategy seems to be rather appropriate. However, since the capital-labor ratio in resource-processing industries is generally high, they are not necessarily the ideal comparative advantage industries for developing countries, which do not possess sufficient capital. Consequently, the development of these industries raises again the level of their labor wage in the manufacturing sector. This phenomenon was further accelerated by a lack of skilled and educated labor in Africa.[25]

4-2 *Some Factors Responsible for Poor Competitiveness of Côte d'Ivoire*

The price of raw primary goods is constantly fluctuating. The development of cash crops processing industries in developing countries is believed to stabilize the income of peasants. However, in Côte d'Ivoire, a strong marketing board called Caisse de Stabilisation et de Soutien des Prix des Productions Agricole (CSSPPA) that compensated for the difference between the domestic price and the price obtained in export markets was already in existence. This mechanism offered producers more stable incomes and also provided the government with substantial surpluses. However, it is indisputable that this arrangement also established an inefficient system under the pretext of stabilization of income.

For example, Barbier, J.P. (1989) compares the competitiveness of the palm oil sectors of Malaysia and Côte d'Ivoire in the latter half of the 1980s. According to his findings shown in table 4, the cost of crude

[25] For some concerns regarding resourced-based industrialization, see Roemer, M. (1978).

Table 4. Production cost of a ton of the crude palm oil (French francs)

	Malaysia 1987		Malaysia 1986	Côte d'Ivoire 1986	
	Enterprise A	Enterprise B	National Average	Industrial Plantations	Village Plantations
Agricultural Cost					
Maintenance	233	152	269	308	101
Harvest	161	293	212	193	–
Transportation	82	29	95	267	447
Purchase	–	–	–	–	1906
Total	476	474	576	768	2454
Industrial Cost					
Fabrication	52	10	84	348	385
Maintenance	92	99	122	–	–
Total	144	109	206	348	385
Amortization	232	232	78	355	46
Ordinary Expenses	229	438	299	885	937
FAB cost	1081	1253	1159	2356	3922

Source: Barbier, J.P. (1989), Marchés Tropicaux, le 29, Décembre, p. 3839

palm oil production (FAB cost) in Côte d'Ivoire was two to three times higher than in Malaysia. Barbier, J.P. (1989) indicates the following four points as the principal reasons for this high cost performance of Africa: high costs of factors of production such as fertilizers, energy, spare parts etc., which were often imported through French commercial companies in Côte d'Ivoire; high transportation costs due to heavy taxes and long distance; low operating rates of transformation plants; and the high cost of ordinary expenses due to the particularly high capital lending cost. Furthermore, in Côte d'Ivoire, the price of major cash crops was fixed by the governmental marketing board until the latter half of the 1990s, and the production of crude oil was almost monopolized by a governmental enterprise called *Palm Industrie.* In contrast, in Malaysia, where the palm oil was introduced in the 1960s from West Africa, the liberalized competition among refineries promoted the moderation of price and consequently, Malaysia is now the largest producer of palm oil in the world. Such overprotection of the African production system often becomes the most significant reason for its ineffectiveness.

Finally, the low competitiveness of Africa often results from appreciated exchange rates. The currency of Côte d'Ivoire, in particular, was pegged with the French franc, which underwent appreciation after the

Plaza Accord, while the Malaysian government devalued the Malaysian currency, the *ringgit* to the US dollar to a small extent in 1986 under the new exchange system introduced in 1984, which permitted much greater fluctuation in the Malaysian currency in contrast to the former strict basket peg system. According to research by the World Bank, between 1984 and 1988, the real effective exchange rate of Côte d'Ivoire was appreciated twice that of Malaysia.[26] Under these conditions, product manufacturing costs in Africa became higher than those in Asian countries. These developments obviously prevented foreign countries from investing in Côte d'Ivoire industries. Therefore, the Bretton Woods Institutions have often forced developing countries to accept the devaluation within the framework of structural adjustment. However, this prescription also stimulated an increase in the price of import at the local currency level and provoked other problems such as the growth in the number of urban poor and the widening income gap.

4-3 *Strong Dominance of European Commercial Firms in West Africa*

The other fact underlying the trend in West African countries facing difficulties in their industrialization is that this region has been to a large extent strongly monopolized by European commercial firms since the colonial era. In francophone Africa, this history can be traced back to the early 19th century just after the Grand Revolution or the independence of Saint Doming, the present day République of Haiti. The French traders – *negociants* – from the large ports of Métropole, who had lost a profitable place in the Caribbean, were encouraged to penetrate into the west coast of Africa, particularly, Sénégal. During the triangle trade era, Europeans had not yet settled on the Continent, but stayed off-shore because of the extreme African climate, tropical diseases and security problems. Consequently, their commerce was not approved without the expanded network of local African merchants. In other words, the development of this unfortunate trade ironically promoted the prosperity of certain Africans or African-Europeans referred to as *Mulatto*.

During the period between the arrival of the first French Governor *Schmaltz* at Saint-Louis in 1817 and the partition of Africa in the 1880s, French commercial establishments based on familial lineage that penetrated into the West Coast of Africa were interested in doing business in the Sénégal river, in particular, dealing in Arabia gum and peanuts

---

[26] Département de l'évaluation des opérations (1999), *Côte d'Ivoire, Revue de l'aide de la Banque mondiale au pays*, Banque mondiale, p. xxiii.

in exchange for European goods or Indian cotton, called *Guinée*, which was used as a means of exchange or currency. In this context, the French traders – notably the Maurel et Prom company, which originated in Bordeaux settled in French West Africa are well known – are considered to have had the greatest influence on the subsequent French colonization and the weakening of wealthy local merchants. Initially, France had contrived to convert Sénégal into a second Saint Doming. However, faced with several tribes who were hostile to the newcomers, France gave up this ambition as early as the 1830s and decided to preserve African kingdoms and maintain a good relationship with them by offering them customs because the French government believed that dominance through military power would not yield returns that justified the cost. In fact, the French local government desired the stability of the Sénégal society and brought the gum trade under control, in favour of local African merchants; however, traders from the ports of Métropole, who were inspired by liberalism, may not have accepted this interventionism. For example, Barrows, L.C. (1974) indicates that the merchants, referred to as *Bordelais* in Saint Louis, under the leadership of Marc Maurel, had been lobbying for liberalization of gum trade in the Sénégal river by exploiting connections with influential government politicians originally from Bordeaux and sent petitions for the removal of the governor who did not attempt to dominate African rulers and demanded later that Faidherbe be appointed. Subsequently, Faidherbe became the driving force behind the French colonialization in West Africa as the next Governor. Pasquier, R. (1983), Harding, L. (1992) and Assidone, E. (1988) also describe the emergence of European merchants at the expense of local Africans in those days.

Roughly around the period of the partitioning of Africa, trade firms based on relatively modern organizations such as CFAO, SCOA, Optorg and John Holt in French Africa as well as Royal Niger Co., United Africa Company and UNILEVER in British Africa, emerged. Unlike the previous organizations that were based on familial lineages, these were supported by large shipping companies and banks such as Banque de l'Afrique Occidentale and Banks of British West Africa[27] and repeatedly underwent several reorganizations through mergers and acquisitions (M&A). These trading firms played an important role when Europe began to import primary goods from Africa in exchange for their industrial goods through the expansion of the network of allocation/distribution even in the interiors of Africa. They often affiliated with several European

[27] Hopkins, A.G. (1976b), p. 275.

companies and established joint ventures for wholesale, retail, after maintenance of their products and manufacturing in the African market as well as for the production and processing of primary products for export to Europe. Most importantly, CFAO and SCOA were strongly dominant in the distribution sector of automobile, electric machines, pharmacy and materials for public works in francophone West Africa and competed with each other, until the former absorbed the later in 1996. Such strong dominance of these trade companies in Africa undoubtedly prevented it from real industrialization because the companies were primarily interested in establishing a distribution/maintenance network rather than the fabrication of final goods in Africa.

Incidentally, based on the analysis of import unit values for 1962-87, Yeats, A.J. (1990) indicates that the 20 former African French colonies paid an average price premium of 20-30% over other importers for iron and steel imports from France due to lack of sufficient competition in Africa.[28] The reasons surmised by Yeats for this include the concentration of import supply, institutional arrangements such as the Lomé convention, transnational firm linkages, factors limiting access to international markets and financial risk differences.[29] The entry barrier into the African market was relatively high and a few commercial companies of the former colonial powers enjoyed such a monopoly over the market.

5. Lessons for Africa

In this paper, one aspect of the economic development in less developed countries has been compared in light of the experiences of Malaysia and Côte d'Ivoire. While some comparative analyses between Asian and African countries have been made in the past,[30] the paper has focused on the different types of industries and their relationship with foreign companies in the age of globalization. Malaysia succeeded in developing through investments from Japan and NIES (New Industrializing Economies). This was a typical case of the flying geese growth model.

---

[28] Yeats, A.J. (1991), pp. 198-205.

[29] Yeats, A.J. (1991), p. 205.

[30] Since the second half of the 1980s, there have been various empirical analyses for this purpose. For example, Harrold, P., Jayawickrama, M. and Bhattasali, D. (1996) focus on the difference in industrialization and trade policy of three groups, namely, Indonesia and Nigeria, Malaysia and Côte d'Ivoire, and Taiwan and Tanzania. In the French Journal, Afrique Contemporaine published in Oct-Dec, 1995, comparative analyses between Indonesia and Nigeria (Collange, G.), Côte d'Ivoire and Thailand (Mongenet, L. and Simon J.-C.) and the differences in each regional integration in each case (Hugon, P.) are discussed.

Some African countries also began to show an embryonic movement of change. For example, South Africa, which accounts for approximately half the economic power of Sub-Saharan Africa, showed a stable annual economic growth through investments in both the resource and industrial sectors. Mauritius, Tunisia, Morocco and Egypt are known to have succeeded in the industrialization of the textile and clothing sector a long time ago. These countries are attempting to transform their industries into value-added enterprises similar to the cases of NIES and Malaysia. Further, Nigeria, which has a large population, is constantly in a state of chaos, but it may have latent potential for import-substitute industrialization similar to Brazil or India. These African countries, which are relatively developed and have abundant skilled labour as compared to other African countries, may have the potential to follow the East Asian flying geese pattern if they succeed in drawing forth a good linkage from the location of multinational firms.

As a matter of course, the preconditions of African countries are very different from those of East Asian countries in terms of history, culture, distance from Europe and population density. For example, apart from the aforementioned countries, the economic levels of some African countries such as Gabon or Botswana are relatively high. In addition, countries such as Equatorial Guinea or Angola have shown rapid economic growth in recent times due to their abundant precious natural resources. However, since the population density of these countries is very low, the East Asian development model, which is based on the preconditions of a large population and fewer natural resources, does not appear to be feasible for them.

The analysis in this paper is not meant to imply that Côte d'Ivoire could have necessarily developed sufficiently had it attempted to introduce the electrical and electronic equipment industries instead of resource-based industries and had switched to the export-oriented industrialization in the latter half of the 1980s. In fact, faced with the appreciation of its currency, the CFA franc, which was linked to the French franc after the Plaza Accord, in addition to the conditions of the scarcity of skilled labor, poor infrastructure and public leadership, this strategy might not have been sustainable even if Côte d'Ivoire had decided to adopt the Asian growth model in the 1980's.

The lessons from a comparative analysis between Malaysia and Côte d'Ivoire in the 1980s include the following. Firstly, they highlight the importance of adjusting to the global economy as opposed to maintaining a closed economy. This also suggests the opening up of the African markets to foreign companies other than those of former colonial powers, which have thus far enjoyed monopolistic markets in Africa. Myrdal expressed a concern that globalization may involve the risk of uneven development. However, at the same time, he indicates that spread effects from the developed to the underdeveloped regions are generated through the transfer of technology. Furthermore, modern international economics assumes that the localization of firms from developed countries into the periphery may also afford an opportunity for development to the latter through international factor-price equalization. In such circumstances, governmental initiatives become more important than ever. After the devaluation of 1994, Côte d'Ivoire has also been keen on attracting FDI. To this effect, several forums, known as *Investir en Côte d'Ivoire*, organized by UNIDO and Centre de promotion des investments en Côte d'Ivoire (CEPICI), have been established. CEPICI was founded as a one-stop window with the objective of investment promotion in 1994 under the strong initiative of the Prime Minister, Daniel Kablan Duncan, and after 1995 succeeded in receiving FDI of more than three times the amount that was received in 1994.[31] However, this trend was unfortunately halted because of the coup d'etat at the end of 1999. The cause of this political crisis has not yet been fully examined. However, dissatisfaction towards the widening disparity might be considered as one of the reasons. Political stability under a competent government is an absolute must in order to attract investment. Also, simple laissez faire policy could result in further widening of the disparity of incomes. Adjusting to globalization does not necessitate that a country unconditionally adopt a laissez faire policy.

Secondly, when the periphery attempts to profit from the implantation of foreign firms, regardless of the industry, local networking of economic participants becomes crucial. Even if a country succeeds in attracting FDI in the high-technology sector, in the absence of internal networks, the benefits may not be adequately widespread. At the same time, the location of foreign firms could also offer an important opportunity for involving local networks. In addition, governmental ownership and support will also become increasingly important for the purpose of stimulating effective inter-linkages between local participants and external firms. In Africa, the state is often considered to be dishonest by the people. The government is expected to make efforts to restore the public trust and build multilayered regional systems, wherein the linkage between small- and medium-sized firms or economic participants, i.e. the formation of *clusters*, would ensure the creation of high value chains. Compared

[31] The total FDI in Côte d'Ivoire: US$78.0 million in 1994, US$211.5 million in 1995, US$269.2 million in 1996, US$413.5 million in 1997, US$379.9 million in 1998 and US$323.7 million in 1999. Source: IMF, *International Financial Statistics Yearbook*.

to hierarchical systems, the networking of economic participants or firms, even if each of them is small or powerless, must be more flexible and resistant to external shocks as opposed to surviving at the disposition of large foreign companies or the international community. In this respect, the World Bank, international organizations and NGOs have recently been focusing on the development of small- and medium-sized companies even in Africa.

Thirdly, the promotion of labour-intensive industries, including service industries, is necessary in order to ensure an even distribution throughout the population. Theoretically, it is the investors who gain profits from capital-intensive industries. If investors do not reinvest a part of these returns in the country, the probability of the domestic population benefiting from capital-intensive industries becomes small. In order to develop the labour-intensive industries, an adequate amount of educated labour is required. In East Asian countries, under the strong influence of Confucianism, which is widely regarded as Protestantism in the Orient, education has been valued higher than anything else. However, in Africa, there is a large disparity in both education and income. A few individuals belonging to the elite class are well educated, often in foreign countries; however, a large section of the population does not even get a sufficient opportunity to be trained. Therefore, achieving an equal opportunity for basic education for the population is an issue that needs to be addressed at large.

Finally, a rational exchange policy is required. Sturdy exchange policies such as a soft pegged policy with US dollars under the basket peg regime, a dual exchange rate system, a currency board etc. have been recognized to be the reasons for the rapid East Asian economic growth until the financial crisis of 1997. It is difficult to identify the most appropriate regime because this depends on several macroeconomic fundamentals like inflation or foreign reserves as well as the global economic situation. However, following the Plaza Accord in 1985, as compared to Malaysia, which survived the appreciation of the ringgit under the dirty floating system introduced after 1984-1985, Côte d'Ivoire was directly faced with the dual problems of appreciation of its currency and deterioration of terms of trade due to the collapse of the prices of primary products. In such circumstances, devaluation is sometimes needed in order to prevent the deterioration of balance of trade, which is a consequence of the second problem. However, Côte d'Ivoire, under the rigorous currency board system pegged with the French franc, also shares its currency with six other countries[32] in francophone West Africa under

[32] Gunia Bissau became a member in 1997. Actually, this monetary integration –

a unique central bank, BCEAO. Under this monetary integration system, Côte d'Ivoire had to subsequently abandon its independent monetary policy in exchange for the following guarantees: unlimited convertibility from the operating account held in the French treasury, fixed parities and free transferability with the French franc.[33] However, this system prevented Côte d'Ivoire from adjusting flexibly to the global economic environment. Incidentally, during the overvaluation crisis, several French commercial companies that shared an underlying interest in a fixed, high exchange rate resisted the devaluation conducted by Bretton Woods institutions in the 1980s.[34] This is in sharp contrast to the Malaysian case, which attracted Japanese investment following the depreciation of its currency on the mid-1980s.

References

Anazawa, M.
2000 "Strengthening Linkages between Foreign and Local firms: The case of Malaysia (in Japanese)." Maruya, T. ed., *Restructuring International Division of Labor and the Role of FDI*, Institute of Developing Economics.

Aoki, M.
2000 *Information, Corporate Governance, and Institutional Diversity-Competitiveness in Japan, the USA and the Transitional Economies.* Oxford University Press.

Ariff, M.
"The competitiveness of Malaysian Exports: Policy Perspectives," *Asia-Pacific Development Journal* 1, no. 1 (June 1994), UN.

Assidon, Elsa
1988 *Le commerce Captif, Les sociétés commerciales françaises de l'Afrique noire.* L'Harmattan.

Balassa, B.
1977 "A stage approach to comparative advantage." World Bank Staff Working Paper, no. 256, May.

Bamba, B. Moussa
1987 The Impact of the Foreign Private Sector (including Banks and Multinationals) on the developing countries: A case study related to the Ivory Coast. Baer, W. and Due, J.E. ed., *Brazil and the Ivory Coast: The Impact of International Lending, Investment and Aid.* JAI Press Inc.

Barrows, Leland Conley
1974 "General Faidherbe, The Maurel et Prom Company, and French Expansion in Senegal." Ph.D. diss., University of California, L.A.

Franc Zone – comprised of eight countries (UEMOA): Sénégal, Côte d'Ivoire, Bénin, Burkina Faso, Mali, Togo and Gunia Bissau.

33 After the introduction of the Euro, the peg was shifted from the French franc to the European currency for CFA and Comorian francs, but the monetary cooperation mechanisms in the region were not affected.

34 However, the large conglomerates did not share their interest because they did not deal in the local currency or because their Franc Zone activities comprised an insignificant part of their total operations. See David Stasavage (2003), pp. 89-95. According to the author, however, after the emergence of the socialist government in the 1980s, commercial firms lost their hold on African politics.

BARBIER, J.-P.
"La Compétitivité africaine." *Marché Tropicaux Méditerranéen* (le 29 Décembre): 3837-3844

BERTHÉLEMY, J.C. AND BOURGUIGNON, F.
1996 *Growth and Crisis in Côte d'Ivoire*, World Bank.

HARROLD, P. JAYAWICKRAMA, M. AND BHATTASALI, D.
1996 "Practical lessons for Africa from East Asia in industrial and trade policies," World Bank Discussion Paper, no. 310.

HARDING, L.
1992 "Les Grands Commerçants Africains en Afrique de L'Ouest: Le cas du Sénégal et de la Côte d'Ivoire: Essai de synthèse," *Commerce et Commerçants en Afrique de L'Ouest: La Côte d'Ivoire*, L'Harmattan.

HOPKINS, A.G.
1976a "Imperial Business in Africa Part I: Sources," *Journal of African History* 29-48.
1976b "Imperial Business in Africa Part II: interpretations," *Journal of African History*, 267-290.

JETRO
2000 *Jetro white paper on foreign direct investment*, Tokyo, JETRO.

KOUMOUE KOFFI
1994 *M. Politique Economique et Ajustement structurel en Côte d'Ivoire*, Paris, L'Harmattan.

KRUGMAN, P. AND VENABLES, A.J.
1995 "Globalization and the Inequality of Nations." *The Quarterly Journal of Economics*, CX, no. 4.

KOSAI AND TRAN VAN THO
1994 "Japan and Industrialisation in Asia – An Essay in Memory of Dr. Saburo Okita." *Journal of Asian Economics*, 5, no. 2.

LAY, P.Y.
1991 "Electoronics and Information Industry." *MIER 1991 National Outlook Conference Papers.*

MYTELKA, LYNN KRIEGER
1984 Foreign Business and Economic Development, in Zartman, William I. and Delgado, Christopher ed., *The Political Economy of Ivory Coast*, PRAEGER.

MARCHAND, Y.
1996 *Une urgence: l'afro-réalisme; Pour une nouvelle politique de l'entreprise en Afrique subsaharienne*, La documentation Française.

MASAKI, T.
1997 Politique gouvernementale et Activites des firmes multinationales face à la mondialisation: "Une analyse comparative de la Malaisie et de la Cote d'Ivoire dans le cadre de l'industrialisation, DEA memoire." Université de Bordeaux IV.

MASINI, J. ET AL.
1979 *Les multinationales et le développement, trois entreprises et la Côte d'Ivoire*, PUF.

MYRDAL, G.
1957 *Economic Theory and Under-Developed Regions*, Gerald Duckworth.

NELSON, P.R.
1996 "The evolution of Comparative or Competitive Advantage: A preliminary Report on a Study." *Industrial and Corporate Change* 5, no. 2.

NORTH, K.
1997 *Localizing Global Production: Know-how Transfer in International Manufacturing*, ILO.

NYTAKOTEY, N.
1990 "Technology transfer regulation in Ghana," *Joint ventures as a channel for the transfer of technology*, United Nations.

OMAN, C.
1989 New form of investment in developing country industries: Mining, petrochemicals, automobiles, textiles, food, Development center, OECD, Paris.

Pasquier, Roger
1983 "Les traitants des comptoirs du Sénégal au milieu du XIXe siècle", *Entreprise et Entrepreneurs en Afrique XIXe et XXe siècle*, Tome 1, Harmattan.

Peemans, J.-P.
1987 "The social impact of food and energy technologies: Evaluation and perspective." *Paper prepared for the Food-Energy Nexus Programme of the United Nations University*.

Piore, J.M. and Sabel, C.F.
1984 *The Second Industrial Divide*. Basic Books.

Porter, M.E.
1990 *The competitive advantage of nations*. The Free Press.

République de Côte d'Ivoire et al.
1993 "Facilitation des exportations agricoles en Côte d'Ivoire", Juillet.

Roemer, M.
1979 "Resource-based industrialization in the developing countries." *Journal of Development Economics*, no. 6.

Samudram, M.
1996 "Cluster Based development: Macroeconomic Framework," MIER (Malaysian Institute of Economic Research), National Outlook Conference Papers.

Stasavage David
2003 *The Political Economy of a common currency: The CFA Franc Zone since 1945*, ASHGATE.

Tanaka, S., and Kenney, M.
1996 "U.S. and Japanese Electronics Industries in Malaysia: A comparative Analysis." *Journal of International Cooperation Studies* 4, no. 1.

UNCTAC
1987 *Transnational Corporations in World Development*, N.Y.

Warr, G.P.
1994 "Comparative and Competitive Advantage." *Asian-Pacific Economic Literature* 8, no. 2.

Williamson, J.G.
1965 "Regional inequality and the process of national development." *Economic Development and Cultural Change* 7, no. 4: 3-84.

Yamashita, S.
1996 "Technology Transfer for Upgrading the National Capabilities of Technology Absorption," IDEC Research Papers Series No. 1, Hiroshima University.

Yeats, A.J.
1991 "Do African Countries pay more for imports? Yes," Chhibber, A. and Fischer, S. *Economic Reform in Sub-Saharan Africa*, World Bank, 198-210.

"Perversion de l'Histoire": George Balandier, his disciples, and African History in Japan*

JOHN EDWARD PHILIPS**

It is only today that it has become possible for the first time even to imagine a whole world consisting of peoples who have in the fullest sense entered into history and become the concern, no longer of the colonial administrator or of the anthropologist, but of the historian.

Edward Hallett Carr, 1961[1]

Nobody in his right mind would argue any more that African history does not exist.

Henk Wesseling, 1992[2]

ABSTRACT

Japan's quest for a permanent United Nations Security Council seat could be expected to lead to an increased importance for foreign language and area studies in Japan, as it did in the United States. This is particularly the case with Japan, an insular nation proud of its homogeneity with little history

* Parts of this paper were included as parts of "Why Africa has no History: The Future of Japanese African Studies" presented at the conference *Pathways to Africa's Past* (University of Texas, Austin) March 30, 2001; other parts are from "What is African History?" chapter 1 in John Edward Philips (editor) *Writing African History* (Rochester: University of Rochester Press, 2005).

** Much research for this paper was carried out at the National Museum of Ethnology, Osaka, where I was invited by Professor Paul Eguchi to investigate the attitude of Japanese anthropologists to African history, under a domestic research grant [naichi kenkyuu] from the Japanese Ministry of Education. All responsibility for the conclusions contained herein rests with the author alone, especially in this case, where the grant might never have been given had the grantors known what I would find.

[1] *What is History?* (New York: Vintage Books, 1961 p. 199).

[2] "Overseas History," in Peter Burke (ed.) *New Perspectives on Historical Writing* (University Park, Pa., 1992), p. 75.

of immigration. Despite the inherently greater difficulties for Japan in trying to understand the outside world, there has been little increase in attempts to understand the outside world when compared to the efforts made by the United States, which started with several advantages over Japan. The example of African history is a case study of Japan's failure to interact with the wider world of international scholarship and its perpetuation of discredited ideas.

Introduction: Japan and area studies

This article is not concerned with the general quality of Japan's studies of the world beyond its shores, but rather with a particular case, African history – or more precisely, with its absence. At present, the only exception to this absence is African economic history, which to the Japanese Ministry of Education is structurally a sub-category of economics. Even casual observers of Japan can easily see that Japan is so serious about economics that it is sometimes referred to as "Japan, Inc." Japan's Foreign Ministry pioneered economic diplomacy, and various private and public entities in Japan spare little effort to understand and analyze the economies of other countries. When the leading minds in Japan exert themselves they can do very well in any field; when Japan's conventional wisdom is certain of a premise that is false, the strong cultural tendency to conformity and consensus make it difficult for an outside, or even inside, dissident to have any influence. To determine possible causes of this phenomenon would involve social psychology beyond the scope of this article, but the conclusion is that once Japan's mind has been made up it will not be changed by mere facts is not an uncommon one among Japanologists, or any with experience in Japan.[3]

[3] This article does not intend to reprise the vast literature about Japanese tertiary education except to note that few commentators have much good to say about it. Works that praise Japan, such as Ezra Vogel's *Japan as Number One* (Cambridge: Harvard University Press, 1979) are silent about universities.

For the most recent academic study of Japanese universities see Brian McVeigh, *Japanese Higher Education as Myth* (New York: M.E. Sharpe, 2002). For a more general study of the mechanisms that perpetuate Japan's intellectual isolation from the rest of the world see Ivan Hall, *Cartels of the Mind* (New York: W.W. Norton, 1998).

To get an idea for how little most Japanese realize how dysfunctional their universities are, especially in studying the world outside Japan, one need only consider that the main character of Nobel prize winner Yasunari Kawabata's *Snow Country* (Tokyo, 1968) is a university professor of western dance who has never actually seen a performance of western dance. Not only do most Japanese not get the joke, I have even been informed that Kawabata is considered a rather humorless author, even by Japanese standards. The fact that Japanese professors have been treated with unquestioned, and in some cases unearned, respect, is relevant to understanding the unquestioned acceptance his

This article describes Japan's record in my own field, African history, to see why it failed to develop in Japan. Understanding this failure is important for understanding relations between Japan and Africa, but the failure also raises serious questions about Japanese academia, and especially about Japanese area studies, in general.

Japan is, of course, not the only country that needs to understand other countries. The United States, when it accepted a permanent seat on the United Nations Security Council after World War II, began a careful and deliberate expansion of foreign language and area studies, including setting up the Fulbright exchange programs and a network of Foreign Language and Area Studies (FLAS) Centers. This was despite the fact that the United States is a nation of immigrants from throughout the world, many of whom maintain strong ties to their homelands. The United States had a head start over perhaps every other nation on earth, but nonetheless (or perhaps therefore), opinion leaders in the U.S. recognized that it would have to apply itself to really understand the rest of the world. They took seriously their nation's responsibility to do so.

Japan, by contrast, is a nation that prides itself on its ethnic homogeneity and which for approximately two hundred years was almost entirely sealed off from the outside world. There are few immigrants, Koreans whose families have lived in Japan for generations are "foreigners" and even refugees recognized by the United Nations have been expelled. Despite (or perhaps because of) Japan's history and tradition of isolation, and therefore greater need to apply itself to understanding the outside world, the government of Japan has never created the equivalent of a Fulbright program, much less the equivalent of a network of Foreign Language and Area Studies Centers. The entire country has only one small Japan Center for Area Studies, at the National Museum of Ethnology in Osaka. Less commonly studied languages are mainly taught at only two universities in Japan, the Tokyo University of Foreign Studies and the Osaka University of Foreign Studies. Indeed, the level of instruction of compulsory English is nothing to be proud of. Surely Japan must take action to improve its study of the rest of the world if it is really serious about meeting its international responsibilities.

The intellectual isolation of Japan is particularly dangerous as Japan seeks to take a more active role in world affairs, for example lobbying for a permanent United Nations Security Council seat to replace the permanent League of Nations Council seat Japan walked out on in 1932.

Japanese students have given Georges Balandier. They have simply never challenged even his weakest positions, but have been content to reproduce them faithfully.

Japan is still trying to recover diplomatically from its defeat in World War II, but if Japan does not learn to look more objectively at the world that lies outside its archipelago, and to understand that world as it is and as it has developed, Japan will inevitably come into needless conflict with it again. Japan's increasing role in organizing African development projects such as the TICAD (Tokyo International Conference on African Development) series of conferences, and in UNESCO, an organization of the utmost importance to both Africa and African history, requires that Japan make a sincere, deliberate and massive effort to understand the histories, and not just the economies, of the African continent's varied societies.[4]

Japan is the largest single contributor to UNESCO, the UN Development Programme (UNDP), and the UN Population Fund (UNFPA). Japan is not only UNESCO's single largest source of funds but also one of its greatest supporters in other ways as well. Japan's major role in UNESCO is growing, especially since the election of a Japanese Director-General of UNESCO, Mr. Koichiro Matsuura. His election was marred by allegations of vote-buying on the part of the Japanese government, an activity that, if Japan were actually guilty of, would suggest not only the general importance this government attaches to UNESCO but also the possible failure of other forms of persuasion. Local UNESCO Associations are found in every Japanese prefecture, organized into a federation by the Ministry of Education and part of the Ministry bureaucracy. Support for UNESCO is a major part of the Japanese government's United Nations strategy, organized around the acquisition of a permanent UN Security Council seat. Nonetheless, the assertion has been made that Japan had to resort to crude bribery to convince other countries to choose one of its diplomats to head UNESCO.

Despite the great importance the Japanese government attaches to UNESCO, Japanese support for African history at UNESCO is so conspicuously absent that one Africanist historian working on an African history project supported by UNESCO contacted me to try to get Japanese support. He was unaware that Japan was even a member of UNESCO, much less that it provided the lion's share of the funding. Once it gains the UN Security Council seat it has been working toward, Japan will have even less reason to tolerate African history at UNESCO, an African history that has not been attacked only because Japan needed African

[4] In the context of TICAD I made a case for studying African history in "Making the most of TICAD II: Africa and Japan are still worlds apart" *The Japan Times* December 28, 1998 but the article generated little response, none from Japanese.

votes at the United Nations. Once the Japanese government no longer needs those votes, it will have no incentive to even tolerate UNESCO funding of African history projects by nationals of other countries. Until the Japanese attitude toward African history changes, it is useless to expect Japan to begin to participate in, or even support, UNESCO activities related to African history.

African countries are in no position to confront Japan about this. It is a matter that should concern all scholars in the field, no matter where they are employed, as well as Africans and people of African descent around the world, especially in the light of the history of disparaging Japanese comments about African-Americans that so damaged U.S.-Japan relations in the 1980s. At least there have been no explicitly racist statements coming out of UNESCO, in contrast to the infamous remarks about Africans and their language abilities made by Hiroshji Nakajima, whose tenure at the World Health Organization seems to have been a public relations disaster for Japan. When I spoke to an American diplomat at the Tokyo embassy about another subject the Nakajima affair came up. The American diplomat informed me that the American government, despite (or perhaps because of) its close relations with Japan, was willing to confront the Japanese about this, but that the Japanese government had called in all the African ambassadors and told them that there would be no more foreign aid from Japan if they insisted on pressing this issue. Why the Japanese Ministry of Foreign Affairs thinks African criticism, rather than Dr. Nakajima's remarks themselves, is the problem is beyond me, but I am not the only one who thinks it must be related to the assumption that the "information" they are getting from their African experts is accurate.

> Japan's self-centered and materialistic approach to Africa has derived in part, from the largely distorted and unwholesome image of Africa among the Japanese. The apparently faulty prisms through which Africa is viewed in Tokyo, is an important supportive factor when searching for the raison d'etre of a policy geared towards vigorous economic exploitation of the continent rather than the promotion of genuine interdependence between the economies and peoples of both sides.[5]

It is useless to expect serious cultural exchange between Japan and Africa when Japanese experts teach their people that Africans have never been part of human history, and the study of the African past is confined to anthropology, not even to archaeology, let alone history. Those who are

[5] Jide Owoeye, *Japan's Policy in Africa* (Ibadan, 1995) p. 143.

interested in the future of African history can no longer afford to ignore Japan, and the distortions of African history still prevalent there. Those who are interested in the future of Japan-Africa relations should note that, unlike the slow and deliberate expansion which has been taking place in Middle Eastern studies in Japan for nearly 20 years, African studies in Japan is nearly stagnant.[6] As long as Africa is economically insignificant, and as long as enough African leaders' votes in the UN appear to be for sale, Japan has no incentive to take the study of Africa seriously enough to bring it up to date, much less to add history to the repertoire of disciplines involved in the Japanese study of Africa.

How did Japan come to have this distorted image of Africa and the past that has produced the Africa of today?

Background: the struggle for African history[7]

Our story begins in France. In 1951 the influential anthropologist Georges Balandier wrote an article in which he argued for the importance to anthropologists of an understanding of history.[8] He did not, however, argue that colonized peoples, the traditional subjects of European anthropology, had histories of their own. He rather argued that history, in the form of European colonialism, had affected these societies and that anthropologists should be aware of the effects of this externally imposed history on these societies. The only case he mentioned where an attempt had been made to write a history of a colonized people (Madagascar) he referred to as a "perversion de l'histoire." History was a discipline that studied only the European colonizers. It only concerned the Africans, whom anthropologists studied, by way of colonialism, by means of which the Africans entered history.

Lest this be misunderstood, let me emphasize here that this paper is not an attack on anthropology, however popular such an attack might be with many Africans who suffered under colonial governments that made the assumption that anthropology was only a discipline for studying supposedly inferior and primitive societies. Anthropology is an important subject that should be used to study all societies, not only so-called "primitive" ones. Although it lies beyond the scope of this paper, Japan

---

[6] "African Studies in Japan" (African Forum: H-Africa African studies discussion list) <http://www.h-net.org/~africa/africaforum/Philips.html> (14 August 2001).

[7] For my understanding of the early development of African history in France I am indebted to conversations I have had with Jan Vansina and Catherine Coquery-Vidrovitch. There are of course, in no way responsible for any misunderstandings I may have had, and the sole blame for any errors in this paper rests with the author alone.

[8] "La situation coloniale: approche theorique" *Cahiers international de sociologie* 11:44-79 (1951).

could increase its understanding of the United States by means of anthropology. In particular, the folklore of the United States is rarely studied in Japan, despite the many American folksongs whose tunes are commonly heard in Japan.

Although anthropology is an important discipline, if it is the only social science by means of which a society is studied an inevitable distortion occurs. As an undergraduate I took a course on the anthropology of Europe in which one of the textbooks was a study of rural France written by an American researcher who had lived in a French village for a year.[9] In that class I learned that the French people spent most of their money on food but ate mostly French bread and onion soup. They bowled without pins, never heated their houses in the winter, blamed everything on the Algerians and weren't even circumcised. All of this may well be true, but surely other, equally valid disciplines can be used in studying the French. Certainly our understanding of France would be distorted if we looked at them only anthropologically without also looking at their history, art, literature, music and philosophy. The same is true of Africans, Americans, Japanese and every other people who share this planet.

I do not intend to do a complete study of the development of Professor Balandier's thought, which would take at least a volume, but simply to note that as the debate about African history began in earnest in France his thoughts on the subject continued to evolve. Balandier came to think that, although Africans might have had history, the history of Africa could be written only by anthropologists, not historians.[10] He seems not to have considered seriously the idea that disciplinary training in history could have validity for the study of African history. It is important to remember, however, that unlike his fellow anthropologist Claude Levi-Strauss he was not opposed to history *per se*, only to historians studying Africa.

To say this in another way, the idea was plainly absurd if applied to any other discipline. Could anyone study African earthquakes *except* a seismologist? Could anyone study African apes *except* a primatologist? Could anyone study African folklore *except* a folklorist? Could anyone study African economies except an economist? Obviously, if Africa had history then those who studied it were historians. The absurdity of arguing otherwise was so obvious, and the importance of Africa for France so great, that this position was abandoned there in the 1960s. Yet this same absurdity prevails in Japan today, speaking volumes not only about

[9] Laurence Wylie, *Village in the Vaucluse* (Cambridge, MA, 1957, 1964, 1974).
[10] Jan Vansina, *Living With Africa* (Madison, 1994) p. 120.

Japanese intellectual isolation from the rest of humanity, but about the contempt for Africans which is common in Japan even among some Africanists. No other part of the world is denied its participation in human history, with the possible exception of Amerindians. This is simply another instance of Japan as a cultural cul-de-sac, in which are to be found ideas which have been discarded in the rest of the world, but which have never been seriously questioned in Japan because of the power of those who hold them. If it is true that "Modern scholarship is a highly competitive activity and the intellectual dominance of any writer never goes unchallenged for long."[11] then Japanese scholarship seems to remain pre-modern.

The obvious absurdity of Professor Balandier's argument suggested to many that his actual interest was the preservation of anthropology's dominance in an African studies that was not growing in France, and in which any increased focus on history as a profession in African studies inevitably became a loss for anthropology. In the United States, meanwhile, African studies was growing rapidly, and such opposition from one discipline to growth in any other discipline occurred rarely, if at all.

Balandier's first Japanese disciple: Junzo Kawada

Professor Balandier exercised great influence over African studies in France at that time and delayed the development of African history there for several years. He trained three Japanese graduate students, who have gone on to make his ideas influential in Japan. His first such student, Junzo Kawada, has similarly dominated African studies in Japan and has blocked the development of African history there. Kawada wrote a dissertation on the Mossi of contemporary Burkina Faso in which he used oral traditions as data on the Mossi past.[12] In Japan he went on to publish his dissertation on the history of the Mossi, both as the original dissertation in French and as a highly revised version in Japanese, *Mumoji Shakai no Rekishi*, (the history of a letterless society).[13] This became his most famous book, and the basis of his reputation in Japan, as well as the confirmation for Japanese of his argument that only ethnologists, not historians, should write the history of Africa.

[11] Keith Thomas, "Politics: Looking for Liberty" *The New York Review of Books* LII(9) May 26, 2005, p. 53.

[12] Junzo Kawada, "Genèse et évolution du système politique des Mosi méridionaux (Haute-Volta)," Thèse pour le Doctorat de l'Université de Paris V (1971). This was published in a slightly revised version by the Institute for the Study of the Languages and Cultures of Asia and Africa (ILCAA) at the Tokyo University of Foreign Studies as Study of Languages and Cultures of Asia and Africa Monograph series no. 12, 1979.

[13] Tokyo, Iwanami Shoten 1976. It is only fair to mention that *mumoji* is not the usual pejorative Japanese term for illiterate, *monmo*.

I do not mean to suggest that Professor Kawada is not a scholar or is not of note outside Japan. While most Africanists outside Japan will not be familiar with his name, his dissertation did make an important contribution and is in fact cited in the UNESCO *History of Africa*, for being one of the first to work on the political structures of southern Mossi kingdoms.[14] He seems to have concluded from the fact that another author cited his work in an important publication that he had no need to read publications of historians. His recent theoretical statement in French about oral history cited no historians at all, and cited no recent studies by anthropologists other than himself.[15] This innocence of the work of historians is apparently a problem with students of Balandier, many of whom seem to assume that historians have nothing significant to say about Africa and therefore neglect to read or cite historians. At best they can reinvent the wheel. At worst they embarrass themselves.

Junzo Kawada's first theoretical approach to African history was presented in "African History: a Tentative Sketch".[16] Here he spoke about what he considered to be the difficulties of trying to research African history, specifically (1) not enough prehistorical (i.e. archaeological) studies, especially in Western and Central Africa, (2) almost no written documentation outside of Egypt and North Africa, (3) many migrations, so that the correlation of archaeological and ethnographic evidence is difficult.

Kawada went on to say that he considered it important to study the history of Africa. Whereas in Europe civilization spread widely and rapidly, coming to colonize the coast of Africa after the great age of exploration in the 15th and 16th centuries, Africa's history was a matter of contact with outside civilizations, such as Mediterranean, Arabian, Indian, Southeast Asian, Chinese, and Islamic. Africa then suffered under slave trades from various directions only to have the interior colonized after the 19th century. Now African societies were trying to reconstruct themselves as "early modern" (kindai) states.[17]

Kawada went on to briefly discuss what was then known about the African past. He argued that ethnology and linguistics could reveal the

---

[14] M. Izard, "The Peoples and Kingdoms of the Niger Bend and the Volta Basin from the 12th to the 16th Century" in *General History of Africa (IV) Africa from the Twelfth to the Sixteenth Century* (Paris; UNESCO, 1984) pp. 225-26.

[15] "Histoire orale et imaginaire du passé: Le cas d'un discourse 'historique' africain" *Annales ESC*, juillet-août 1993, no. 4, pp. 1087-1105.

[16] "Afurikashi e no kokoromi" (more literally "an experiment towards African history") *Toyo Bunka* 33 (1962) 37-70.

[17] Japanese "kindaishi" is the rough equivalent of "early modern history" in western usage. The next period of history in Japan is "gendaishi" which begins in Western (which in Japan means mostly European) history with World War I, in Eastern (which in Japan

most about Africa's history, and that history as a discipline had no role to play in the reconstruction of Africa's past. He based this curious conclusion on the argument, which he claimed to have derived from the founder of modern scientific history, Professor Leopold von Ranke, that historians could only use written records.

This is a most strange attribution, which Kawada made without citation and which many historians would contest. Ranke's revolution in the writing of history did not consist in limiting historians to written evidence, but in relying mostly on primary documents and in trusting those written documents that preserved the past accidentally rather than documents that were written as narratives for some specific purpose. The latter tend to be very disingenuous and biased, whereas the former were less so. Thus Ranke's revolution in the treatment of written documents foreshadowed Vansina's revolution in the treatment of oral traditions, both scholars being skeptical and more sophisticated in their treatment of such material than their predecessors had been.[18]

The assumption that historians only work with written documents is a strange idea to most historians, but common among people who are not historians. Where it originated is hard to discover. In his history of the concept of objectivity in history Peter Novick[19] credited the idea to Langlois and Seignobos, methodologists who wrote around the end of the nineteenth century and who specialized in written documents. He quoted their maxim "Pas de documents, pas d'histoire," mistranslating or misunderstanding what these historians were saying. In the context of their book they defined "documents" as any survivals of the past in the present, not merely as written materials.[20] Moreover, they explicitly included not only oral testimonies taken down in written form but also oral traditions themselves among historical sources:

> . . . when the events to be related were ancient, so that no man then living could have witnessed them, and no account of them had been preserved

---

means mostly Chinese) History with the Chinese Republican revolution and which in Japanese history coincides with post World War II or more broadly post-Meiji history. (プログレッシブ和英中辞典「第2版」小学館) 1993.

[18] "The introduction of a critical approach to the sources into mainstream history-writing was Ranke's most important achievement." John Tosh, *The Pursuit of History*, 2nd ed. (New York, 1991), 56.

[19] Novick, *That Noble Dream*, 39.

[20] "Les documents sont les traces qu'ont laissées les pensées et les actes des hommes d'autrefois," Langlois and Ch. Seignobos, *Introduction aux études historiques*, chap. 5 (Paris 1898, 1992). The English translation reads: "Documents are the traces which have been left by the thoughts and actions of men of former times" (G.G. Berry, trans., *Introduction to the Study of History* (New York, 1898).

> by oral tradition, what then? Nothing was left but to collect documents of every kind, principally written ones, relating to the distant past which was to be studied.[21]

This seems to suggest that oral traditions are to be preferred to purely documentary history. It certainly makes clear that historians are not forbidden by the rules of their craft from using oral traditions. In fact historians have used such traditions from the days of Herodotus, the father of history, although the methodology of oral tradition has advanced enormously since the days of ancient Greece.

Where Kawada got the idea that historians were not allowed to use non-written evidence is a mystery. I certainly doubt that it was in any history class. History is a detective story, in which we try to reconstruct the past, in Ranke's most famous phrase, "as it actually happened." Imagine if detectives were only allowed to introduce written documents in court, and were forbidden to use either physical evidence or oral testimonies!

The argument that historians can only use written documents is even stranger coming from a Japanese scholar, and published originally in Japanese. Archaeology is classified as part of history in Japan, not anthropology. Archaeologists work in Eastern, Western and Japanese history, the three great divisions of the discipline of history in Japan. Kawada himself had complained about the relative absence of archaeological studies of Africa. Ironically, one result of Kawada's campaign against historians working in African studies has been that Japanese archaeologists have been almost entirely unable to work in Africa and Japanese funding for archaeological excavation and preservation in Africa has been almost nil. The exception has been primatologists working on human evolution, where there is little alternative to digging in Africa. One wonders what Kawada could have been thinking, or why other Japanese scholars took him seriously at the time, the contradictions in his thought are so obvious and many.

The usual argument against African history was the Hegelian argument that history studies the political evolution of humanity and that Africa represents the baseline of human political evolution, the primitive beginnings from which the rest of humanity evolved. Although beyond the scope of this paper, Hegel's confusion of the African kingdoms of his time, the

---

[21] Berry, *Introduction to the Study of History*, 20. The original reads "Mais s'agissait-il dévénements ancien, qu'aucun homme vivant n'aivait pu voir et don't la tradition orale n'avait gardé aucun souvenir? Il n'y a avait pas d'autre moyen que de réunir des documents de toute sorte, principalement des écrits relatifs au passé lointain dont on s'occupait" (Langlois and Seignobos, *Introduction aux études historiques*, 31).

end of the slave trade era, with non-evolved primitive human society not only misrepresented Africa, it seriously distorted his understanding of human political evolution. What Hegel thought was primitive human nature was actually the effect of centuries of slave raiding, plunder and intercontinental slave dealing. Hegel's refusal to see that these states had not only evolved, but also had in fact devolved, blinded him to other aspects of human history. But the Hegelian argument, implied in Hugh Trevor-Roper's notorious phrase, "unedifying gyrations of barbarous tribes," was unknown to Kawada, who had not studied Africa under a historian, but only under an anthropologist.

Kawada's argument that historians should not study the history of Africa was absurd on its face. If Africa has history – that is, if change there were not the "unedifying gyrations of barbarous tribes," but instead had direction and made sense – then of course it should be written by historians; more correctly, those who wrote it were historians, and if they wanted to be good historians and make serious contributions to historical literature they would have to learn the methods and theories of history that had developed over the thousands of years during which history had been written. It seems obvious to me that Professor Kawada simply did not understand what history was, and could not be bothered finding out. His mentor had told him what to think and he thought it.

Would it be possible, theoretically, for an anthropologist, or at least someone employed as an anthropologist but who was familiar with historical methodology, to write history of Africa? Certainly, and there is no doubt at all that anthropologists have made important contributions to the study of African history, both theoretically and practically. M.G. Smith's *Government in Kano, 1350-1950*[22] is a good example of a historically oriented anthropological work that has made important contributions to African history. An important guide to writing African history, Daniel McCall's *Africa in Time Perspective: A Discussion of Historical Reconstruction from Unwritten Sources*, was published in 1964 and was written by an anthropologist, albeit one who had also had substantial training in the discipline of history. *The Historian in Tropical Africa*[23] also included several important contributions by anthropologists. The argument here is not for the exclusion of anthropology but for dialogue between anthropology and history. Two disciplines cannot have a dialogue if one of them is silenced.

The problem here is with an anthropologist who even denies that historians can make any contributions to their own discipline. In fact

[22] (Boulder, 1997, edited by Shula Marks and Paul E. Lovejoy).
[23] (London: O.U.P. for the International African Institute, 1964).

Professor Kawada's own record with simple facts leaves much to be desired. In a brief article he wrote for a popular world history published by the Asahi Shimbun company he identified the famous West African jihadist and Sufi leader al-Hajj Umar as the son-in-law of another jihadist and Sufi leader, Usuman Danfodio.[24] In fact al-Hajj Umar was the son-in-law of Usuman Danfodio's son, Muhammad Bello, and the claim that al-Hajj Umar converted Bello to the Tijaniyya order of Sufis is a claim of much controversy and political importance in Nigeria today, where it plays a role in rivalries between Danfodio's Qadiriyya order and the Tijaniyya.[25] Consulting written documents, primary or secondary, would have made this clear to Professor Kawada.

Balandier's other Japanese disciples: Shimada and Takezawa

Two other Japanese scholars have studied to the doctorate level under the supervision of Professor Balandier, Yoshihito Shimada and Soichiro Takezawa. It is particularly strange that both of them specialize in Islamic Africa. One European anthropologist even sought me out, because I was from Japan, to confront me about the things they were writing, and pointed out that there was something very strange about the situation, because, as he claimed, in the French system Balandier should not have been the professor to supervise their topics. At the very least it should be obvious that no Islamic society could be considered "letterless".

Yoshihito Shimada was one of the first Japanese scholars who followed Kawada to study under Balandier in Paris. He is another scholar who insists that written documents (and therefore history) have no role to play in our understanding of African societies. Professor Shimada wrote his dissertation for his *doctorat du troisième siecle* (actually equivalent to a master's degree, and only offered to foreign students at French universities) on the Lamidat of Rey Bouba, a sub-emirate of Adamawa in the Sokoto Caliphate, in what is now Cameroon. He seems to have been unaware of the existence of such written documents as the *Tarihi Rai-Buba* in the Yaounde Cultural Centre. One manuscript dealing with the history of the area has even been published.[26]

---

[24] In (世界の歴史) (*World History*) no. 101 – 19 (世紀の歴史) {19th Century History [1]}). (Tokyo: Asahi Shimbunsha; November 4, 1990) p. A-655. In the interest of full disclosure I should note that a photograph of mine accompanied the article, otherwise I might never have even known about the article. I was only asked to provide a photograph, and was not asked or even informed about the text of the article before it was published.

[25] John N. Paden, *Religion and Political Culture in Kano* (1973; Berkeley, UC Press) pp. 76 et seq.

[26] H. Bassoro, "Un manuscrit Peul sur l'histoire de Garua" *Revue Culturelle Camerounaise*

Even if the argument is accepted that history only involved written records, another inconsistency, found in the Takezawa-Shimada debate over J.S. Trimingham's writings about Islamic Africa, exposes the basic flaw of the whole argument. This debate took place in the pages of the official journal of the Japan Association for African Studies, *Afrika Kenkyu*, and therefore may be taken as meeting with the scholarly approval of the Association, though not necessarily representing its official policy. Although this debate involved African history, the two authors who engaged in it disagreed not over what kind of history Africa had, or even whether Africa had history, but over why historians shouldn't study Africa.

The opening article in this debate was a criticism of the perspective of J.S. Trimingham's *A History of Islam in West Africa*. Publishing a review essay about a book that was already over 25 years old speaks volumes about the importance of original thought in Japanese culture, a point that becomes relevant when we consider the failure of other Japanese scholars to counter the attack on African history. The author of this criticism of Trimingham cited more than one more recent survey of Islam in West Africa in the references, but rather than write a review essay about those works, he appropriated some of their insights, along with those of more recent articles, to come to the not-so-startling conclusion that Trimingham's work was out of date, had been superceded, and had overestimated the role of violence in contrast to that of peaceful conversion in explaining the spread of Islam in West Africa.[27]

Professor Takezawa made another criticism of Professor Trimingham's study, that was in fact his basic criticism. According to Takezawa, Trimingham's perspective had been that of a historian. The historical perspective, again according to Takezawa's interpretation, was only concerned with great political or economic events, unlike that of anthropologists, who are interested in studying cultural change among the masses of the people. As all good disciples of Georges Balandier know, historians have no business studying Africa, the reserved domain of anthropologists.

In fact, on page eight of *A History of Islam in West Africa*, however, Trimingham himself had pointed out that the perspectives of other disciplines, "especially cultural anthropology" are indispensable to the his-

(Feb/Mars 1965, p. 55), cited in S. Abubakar "The Establishment of Fulbe Authority in the Upper Benue Basin, 1809-47" *Savanna*, v. 1, no. 1, June 1972.

[27] Shoichiro Takezawa, "Essai sure l'islamization en Afrique occidental: critique de la perspective historique de Trimingham" *African Studies (Afrika Kenkyu)* 32 (March 1988) pages 19-43.

torian of tropical Africa. Those who have read Trimingham have often criticized him for this[28] (although I would not). From his citations it is clear that Mr. Takezawa cannot read Arabic, but he also demonstrates, to all familiar with the historiography of Islam in Africa, that he cannot read English either.

But Professor Takezawa's lack of training in the discipline of history is even more striking than is his ignorance of Trimingham's works. The so-called "new social history" is already decades older than either he or I, and the fact that his abstract was written in the language of Marc Bloch, Fernand Braudel and the journal *Annales* adds a note of surrealism to his article. This article demonstrated how dangerous it is to allow scholars in one discipline to exercise a veto over what scholars in another discipline are allowed to research.

Such a weak discussion of Trimingham's work could not go unchallenged, of course, even in Japan. Dr. Yoshihito Shimada, then of Shizuoka University, wrote a response in the very next issue of the same journal.[29] Shimada pointed out that Trimingham had in fact written one book, *Islam in West Africa* (Oxford, 1959), which was not at all historical and which therefore could not be accused of having had a (shudder) historical perspective. Like Takezawa before him, Shimada also neglected Trimingham's use of an anthropological perspective. His own objection to Trimingham's analysis was to allege that Trimingham had neglected the Fulani ethnic factor in the "Fulani" jihads.

Once again a Japanese academic advertised his failure to read even the secondary sources in English, thus basing the central thesis of his article on a major factual error. If I were to photocopy every page on which Trimingham mentioned the Fulani ethnic factor in the West African jihads I would have a hefty pile of paper. One example of Trimingham's over-reliance on the ethnic factor as an explanation of the jihads is where he said that "from 1786 [Usuman Danfodiyo] preached the jihad in such a way that it became a racial as well as a religious war."[30]

Neither Takezawa nor Shimada commented on Trimingham's Orientalism, or his "explicitly Social Darwinist and racist" perspective.[31] Indeed,

---

[28] E.g. I.U.A. Musa, "On the Nature of Islamization and Islamic Reform in Bilad al-Sudan up to Sokoto Jihad" *Dirasat: a Research Journal Published by the University of Jordan* VI (1) 7-34, especially pages 10-11.

[29] "Le jihad peul et trois types d'Islamisation en Afrique occidental: reconsideration de la typologie de S. Trimingham" *Afrika Kenkyu* 33 (December 1988) 1-18.

[30] *A History of Islam in West Africa* (Oxford, 1962) 162.

[31] J. Spaulding, "The Old Shaiqi Language in Historical Perspective" *History in Africa* 17 (1990) 283.

Takezawa and Shimada share those perspectives with Trimingham and other scholars from the colonial period, no matter how discredited other scholars (probably including even Trimingham himself by now) consider those perspectives today. The disciples of Balandier in Japan have been most interested in reproducing the anthropology of the colonial era, not in understanding the reality of African societies and their development.

The Takezawa-Shimada debate continued for several more issues of *Afrika Kenkyu* and was never questioned by other Japanese Africanists. The opinions of these two, and their contempt for the discipline of history in African studies, are in fact typical of many in Japan. Takezawa and Shimada have both been promoted since the time of the debate. One is now esconced in a former Imperial university, the elite of Japan's higher education system. The other is at the National Museum of Ethnology in Osaka. Their own disciples can be expected to dominate the field for decades, perhaps generations, unless something is done to allow other perspectives.

One of the most extreme examples of the absence of African history in Japan occurred a few years ago, when Professor Shimada presented a commissioned research paper about cities in the Islamic zone of West Africa at a major international conference on urbanism in Islam.[32] This conference was the culmination of a major, three-year project sponsored by the Ministry of Education, which involved dozens of Japanese researchers and their counterparts from around the world. As one of the most august bodies of Islamic and Middle East experts ever assembled watched in shock, the head of the committee working on Islamic West Africa gave a paper that contained neither factual (or even fictional) data, nor any coherent method of analysis.[33] The paper established the author's lack of training in either history or Islamic studies, and left foreign observers so stunned that at least three of them independently came to the same conclusion: the paper was so bad it did not bear discussion, and the conference should please go on to something else. Although the paper was published in the Japanese conference proceedings, it was neither translated for the English-language book that emerged from the research

[32] The final meeting of the International Conference on Urbanism in Islam (ICUIT) was held at the Middle East Cultural Center in Mitaka in December, 1990. The complete proceedings of the conference on were published in Japanese in Tokyo in 1991 as *Isuramu no Toushisei* by Daisan Shokan. An English volume, excluding the contribution of Professor Shimada, was published as Masashi Haneda and Toru Miura (editors) *Islamic Urban Studies: Historical Review and Perspectives* (London and New York, 1995).

[33] Professor Shimada's paper and a discussion of it are found in the Japanese proceeedings, pages 408-416, 432-448 and 450-453.

project,[34] nor did the author participate in the Japanese public lecture series [koukai kouza] that emerged from the conference. Here was a failure that Japanese scholars did not wish to make very public, even in their own country. It showed the dismal results to be obtained when one tries to study Islamic societies in Africa on the assumption they are not Islamic, but "black African" only, and that "black African" means illiterate.

More recent studies

Japan has also been conspicuously absent in the international campaign to save the Arabic and Arabic script manuscripts of Timbuktu. The reasons are obvious when one considers the kind of work Professor Kawada and his colleagues have done in the bend of the Niger, one of the most literate regions of Africa and one that has been heavily Islamized for centuries. From 1988 to 1992 the Institute for the Study of the Languages and Cultures of Asia and Africa, then Professor Kawada's home institution, published three interdisciplinary volumes on the bend of the Niger, under the direction of Professor Kawada and reporting the results of group research projects he carried out. None of these three volumes included the contributions of any historians or Islamic studies specialists. Essentially, these volumes give the lie to Professor Kawada's supposed concern with the study of "letterless societies," for in fact the societies in question have centuries of literacy behind them and were the sites of some of the most important centers of learning in the medieval Islamic world. It is simply impossible to study Islamic societies without considering the role of scholarship and literacy in them. Why these disciples of Balandier insist on confining their attention to the savanna zone of West Africa, where even the non-Muslims have been heavily affected by contact with Islamic literacy, is a mystery, but it shows the basic weakness of their position. Had they really been concerned with studying "letterless" societies they could easily have done so elsewhere in Africa.

Even well to the south of the bend of the Niger and even south of the Mossi whom Professor Kawada first studied, Islamic manuscripts and literacy are common and have affected the society. As Professor John Hunwick noted recently: "The historical writing tradition of what is now the north of the Republic of Ghana is very rich. As Bradford Martin wrote: 'If this material could be used for research it would contribute very greatly to a rewriting of the history of this region, which is so badly

[34] Haneda and Miura, *Islamic Urban Studies*.

needed.'"[35] At present there is little possibility of Japanese participation in the study of such manuscripts, as long as the disciples of Balandier exercise a veto over African studies.

That the case against African history in Japan is made by anthropologists who work almost exclusively in Islamic areas of Africa thus exposes a serious contradiction in the argument. While it is certain that writing was unknown in many areas of the African continent before colonialism, illiterate Islam is a contradiction in terms. That Kawada's anti-history argument is applied by his disciples even to Muslim societies, makes clear that his argument that historians should not be involved in writing the history of a people has nothing to do with the presence or absence of written documents in the society, it has to do with the color of the people in that society. This is especially the case in Japan, where archaeology is part of history, and where Japanese history textbooks commonly begin with the Jomon period, centuries before literacy was introduced to Japan from China and Korea. The presence or absence of history in a society, in the view of Balandier's disciples in Japan, is purely a matter of race. Black Africans have no history, whether they write or not. Other peoples do have history, whether they write or not.

This is not to say that Kawada is necessarily a racist. No one can look into another's heart and see what is really there. In his defense it must be pointed out that his animus towards history seems to extend beyond Africa, although his power to influence Japanese academia does not. Kawada is well known in Japan for having invited Professor Claude Levi-Strauss to Japan and for having interviewed him on national television during his visit.[36] Professor Levi-Strauss's antipathy to history is well known, and is often reciprocated by historians.[37] That Professor Kawada sees him as such an important scholar suggests that he is really interested in attacking history, but that African history, other than African economic history, is the only history he has the power to prevent in Japan. Whether or not he is racist is irrelevant. He is wrong about Africa and wrong about history and he has no business deciding things for scholars in another discipline that he refuses to engage in dialogue with.

Professor Kawada is still propounding these same ideas and they are still powerful and influential in Japan. His edited volume *Afrika Nyumon*

---

[35] John Hunwick, *Arabic Literature of Africa* vol. 4, *The Writings of Western Sudanic Africa* (Leiden: E.J. Brill, 2003) pp. 3-4.

[36] The interview is available from NHK in Japan as 2 volumes of 45 minute videotape (1994).

[37] For example the ancient historian M.I. Finley in *The Use and Abuse of History* (New York, 1975). An example from an Africanist is Jan Vansina, *Oral Tradition as History* (Madison, 1985) pp. 162-5.

(introduction to Africa) was quite popular and influential, and was the only volume sold at the registration table of the Japan Association for Africa Studies annual meeting in Kyoto in 1999. While the volume contained important explanations of the contributions of various disciplines to African studies, Professor Kawada chose to write the chapter on history himself. Had his ideas changed in the 30 years since he first attempted to write history of Africa? Unfortunately, they had not.

His chapter again began discussion of African history by pointing to the lack of written documentation. Here he specifically contrasted Ethiopia with "so-called" Black Africa (kokujin Afurika). He did acknowledge that some local areas of Black Africa had written documents, but only considered the major chronicles worth considering. Ranke's idea that history should be based as far as possible on primary sources, rather than on previously written discursive, narrative texts, had still not entered his consciousness, although he dropped the reference to Ranke.

His next point about the absence of history in Africa seemed related to the concept that archaeology, in Japan, was part of history. He complained of the near lack of great stone ruins in sub-Saharan Africa except for Zimbabwe. Here is someone who is not only out of touch with the "new" archaeology, but to whom the methods and principles of the old archaeology are still unknown. If he is ignorant of Ranke's method and significance, he is equally ignorant of Schliemann and Flinders-Petrie.

He goes on to point out two basic problems with the application of the discipline of history to Africa. The first is the difficulty of assigning absolute dates in the absence of written evidence. The fact that archaeologists rarely use absolute dates, again, seems not to have occurred to him. Dates are important to historians not because historians need absolute dates in order to call their products history (an error Claude Levi-Strauss seems guilty of falling into)[38] but rather because dates (whether relative or absolute) are important for determining causation. The past caused the present will cause the future, and thus relative chronology is important if that is the only kind that can be ascertained. Past events may (but don't necessarily) cause future events, but the future cannot cause the past, at least in this universe.

Professor Kawada's next point is especially revealing of the attitude of many in Japan towards history. He argues that because the currently existing nation-states of Africa were mostly created in the last 40 years,

[38] "It is thus not only fallacious but contradictory to conceive of the historical process as a continuous development" *The Savage Mind* (Chicago, 1966) translation of the French original *La Pensée sauvage* (Paris, 1962) p. 260.

and since history is the story of nation-states, that African history can at most go back only a few decades. One's amazement can best be tempered here if one remembers that to many (but by no means all) Japanese the school subject "history" is and ought to be a class in nationalist propaganda, rather than the truth of how the past developed to turn into the present.[39] Many (but by no means all) Japanese honestly object to attempts to teach the truth about World War II to Japanese school children because they assume that "history" consists in praise-singing the virtues of a nation-state; they do not expect a history classroom to be a production point not for informed citizens.[40] The history of a stateless society is impossible to imagine, especially since such societies lack specialized oral historians and throne histories, according to Professor Kawada. But, according to such an analysis, neither would the history of non-political aspects of state societies, such as intellectual history, social history, women's history, the history of emotions, or any of the other varieties of history that have become popular in recent decades, be possible.

To sum up the argument, there are no written records, they didn't have nation states or stone buildings, Ethiopians are white people, . . . stop me if you've heard this.

Everyone who remembers or has studied about the fight to create African history has heard this. These are the discredited arguments the colonialists gave for not allowing historians to work in Africa, arguments that were really meant to slander Africans, not to find the truth about how their societies had evolved or devolved. The failures of independence in Africa make it all the more necessary to reject these arguments, rather than go back to them. If Africa is to get out of the mess it is in, it must figure out how it got there, which means studying the relevant history. While Africanists and Africans must study the past, they should not try to live in that past, particularly not the colonial past.

More recently Professor Takezawa, perhaps reacting to the criticism of the absence of the lack of archaeology in Japanese African studies,

---

[39] A brief history of Japanese historians' obsession with the nation, and their confusion of nation with ethnic group (minzoku) can be read in Stefan Tanaka's "Objectivism and the Eradication of Critique in Japanese History" in *Learning Places* edited by Masao Miyoshi and H.D. Harootunian (Durham: Duke University Press, 2002) pp. 80-102.

[40] I once asked a Japanese history professor, who had actually done research in the United States, for his opinion about this perennial Japanese textbook problem. He hesitated, and asked why should Japan be the only . . . He stopped. I could have finished it "only democracy to deny any dark side to its past" but his hesitation told me that that wasn't what he meant. I asked if he meant the only country to admit atrocities in its history. He nodded yes. I took him down the hall to my office, and pulled a popular U.S. history textbook off the shelf. I had no trouble finding information about colonial atrocities committed during the "Philippine Insurrection" not to mention slavery, the "Trail of Tears" and many other less than exemplary episodes of American history.

has undertaken the excavation of archaeological sites in West Africa.[41] While this is better than the outright looting of sites that has become so common in Africa, given his lack of archaeological training it is not a great improvement, and could prove potentially dangerous to the development of African history in Japan.

Conclusion

Thus we see how ideas that have been tried and found wanting outside of Japan are still unquestioned in Japan. Several years ago, when I first attended an annual meeting of the Historical Society of Japan and asked prominent historians there why there was no African history in Japan, other than colonial and economic history, I was told that I needed to take up the matter with Professor Kawada, that historians wanted to study Africa but that he was powerful enough to prevent them. I was later told by an important scholar, who was neither a historian nor an Africanist, that since I had never heard of Professor Kawada before coming to Japan I obviously knew nothing of African history because Professor Kawada was the most important scholar of African history in the world, and was shown great deference by all Africanist historians in France. This comment generated some amusement when I later spoke to a graduate seminar at Oxford because Professor Anthony Kirk-Greene had never heard of Professor Kawada either. It well illustrates the extent to which some Japanese scholars live in their own little world. Japanese professors have, in fact, been compared to Japanese rice farmers in that they are protected from foreign competition by the Japanese bureaucracy. Rice farmers, however, are at least aware that they are so protected. Some Japanese professors seem to be completely unaware that they benefit from government protectionism.

Even so, Japanese scholarship is capable of making important studies of foreign societies, and of making theoretical contributions which could be significant for others understanding of those societies. For example, the influential Professor Yuzo Itagaki has come up with an idea he calls "area x." As I understand this idea, it means that one should define the area of one's study by the characteristic one is studying, rather than trying to define the characteristics of the area one wants to study by preconceived qualities of the area. Thus if one wants to study societies without traditions of literacy one should study such societies, rather than

---

[41] Shoichiro Takezawa, Mamadou Cisse and Hirotaka Oda, "Mema in the History of West Africa: Economic Bases of Ancient Ghana and Mali" (Japanese with English summary) *Africa Kenkyuu* no. 66 (March 2005) pp. 31-46.

decreeing that all societies in the African area have no literate tradition and studying them under that assumption, whether it is true or not. This stands in direct contrast with Professor Kawada's idea. At the very least the Japanese Ministry of Education should allow the funding of research from different perspectives, especially in the Islamic areas of Africa.

In fact the growth of funding for Middle Eastern and Islamic studies in Japan stands in conflict with the Balandier school's dominance of the study of Islamic Africa in Japan, which hinders that expansion into Islamic Africa, as explained above. At the very least, as Japan expands its area studies, it should try not only to come up to an international standard by instituting blind peer review of publications, but it should also try to avoid the mistakes of area studies in the U.S. by not bureaucratically dividing areas in the strict way that has been done in the United States, where it has not always been easy to study Islamic Africa, either. I generally prefer to present papers on Islamic Africa to the Japan Association for Middle East Studies because I don't have to explain what Islam is and I don't have to explain what history is. At an African studies meeting the persons who don't understand, and who sometimes even want to argue about it, are likely to be involved in study of Islamic societies in Africa.

Because I advocate not only a reform but also an expansion of area studies in Japan, I suppose that my criticism of Japanese African studies could be compared to a joke Woody Allen told in *Annie Hall*. Two old women were talking over a meal at a Catskills resort, when one complained about the poor quality of the food. "Yes," the other responded, "and such small portions."

Yet, it is not only the small quantity and uneven quality I am objecting to, it is the lack of variety on the menu. Thirty two flavors of ecological anthropology at the Kyoto University African studies center does not make for a balanced diet of African studies, any more than do thirty two flavors of economics at another institute. There needs to be not only more African studies, but also a real variety of work in different disciplines and more disciplines working together, as well as more different disciplines.

For example, a recent major interdisciplinary conference on African problems held in Japan included no historians except an economic historian from Japan itself, despite the fact that scholars were invited from Europe, Africa and the United States.[42] It should no longer be possible

[42] The conference proceedings were published as *Rewriting Africa: Toward Renaissance or Collapse* edited by Kurimoto Eisei (Osaka: Japan Center for Area Studies, National Museum of Ethnology, 2001).

to study Africa in a comprehensive way without including input from historians, but in Japan only economic historians are considered to have input worthy of inclusion. It is indeed fortunate that Japanese economic history is of high quality. Even Japanese anthropology, except for the disciples of Balandier, is often of high quality. The tradition of ecological anthropology in Japan has particularly come in for international praise.

This article will inevitably attract charges of Japan-bashing, of having been created out of hatred of Japan. In fact it is written more in sorrow than in anger, a creation of frustration, of long years of difficulty in being heard. I consider the dominance of the Balandier school of anti-African history in Japan to be a kind of fraud carried out on Japanese scholarship and, ultimately, the Japanese taxpayer.

Unfortunately, as with many cases of fraud, the victim refuses to admit that they have been cheated. I tried to bring some of these problems to the attention of Japanese scholars at a workshop on U.S.-Japan cooperation in African studies to which I was invited by the American side. I did not originally intend my paper[43] to be for publication but rather for the information of the scholars present at the workshop. I was encouraged by both Japanese and American participants to publish the paper in the proceedings, and was privately assured by some of the Japanese participants in the workshop that something would be done about the problem. Little happened, and in fact the situation got even worse. Now an African, who was directed to me by another African, has asked me to write this paper. I hope it will finally bring some attention to this long festering problem in Japan's study of the outside world. More importantly, I hope it will finally do some good. I would have settled for the good without the attention, but if I have to get attention to do some good I will do so. I can only agree with that famous abolitionist of the 19th century, William Lloyd Garrison:

> I am aware, that many object to the severity of my language; but is there not cause for severity? I will be as harsh as truth, and as uncompromising as justice. On this subject, I do not wish to think, or speak, or write, with moderation. No! no! . . . urge me not to use moderation in a cause like the present. I am in earnest – I will not equivocate – I will not excuse – I will not retreat a single inch – AND I WILL BE HEARD.[44]

[43] "African History in Japan: Problems and Prospects" pages 225-238 in *Proceedings: Japanese/American Workshop for Cooperation in Africa* edited by Merrick Posnansky (Los Angeles: UCLA James S. Coleman African Studies Center, 1994) – a source for this paper.

[44] "To the Public" from *The Liberator* January 1, 1831.

While I do not intend this article to be an attack on Japan, or even on Japanese higher education, in general, I cannot help noting that the problems discussed here inevitably reflect on Japan more broadly, if only because they are now unique to Japan. Every other country that I know of, if it has African studies, includes history among the disciplines that study Africa. In part the problem is with the structure of history in Japan. Since the Meiji Period (1868-1912) history in Japan has been divided into Eastern, Western and Japanese, rather as history in the US has been divided into American, Western, and non-Western, but more rigidly. Western historians in Japan do in fact study Africa, or more accurately they study European colonialism in Africa. Historians may have thought it was simpler to leave African history to anthropologists, especially if one of those anthropologists was highly respected overseas. This would fit in with the general absence of the Socratic method in Japanese education and the reluctance to question other scholars.

This is an inadequate explanation, though. The fact that historians in Japan do study the history of Africa (though not the history of Africans) suggests that Eastern historians could easily extend their field to study the history of Africans, since they already study the Middle East and other Islamic areas. They should certainly be encouraged to work in Islamic Africa and on Islamic documents. That they do not is indicative of problems with Japanese research. The lack of originality of Japanese, such an unfortunate stereotype, is not any innate characteristic of the Japanese people, it is something drilled into them by an educational system that rewards blind obedience. At the university level it is reinforced by an incestuous appointment system that rewards blind adherence to the ideas of one's mentor, and a rigid hierarchy of universities that provides no reward for novel, creative scholarship but instead works to ensure the promotion of mediocrity.[45] I do not know what it will take to bring real reforms, I only know that it is beyond my powers.

When the relevant powers in Japan have decided a question, discussion of the subject is closed. For example, in Japan the debate about whether ethnic conflict is natural and primordial, or whether it is con-

---

[45] Chie Nakane, probably the greatest Japanese expert on Japan, wrote in her classic *Japanese Society* (New York: Penguin, 1973) p. 122 "Applications for vacancies caused by retirement are normally only considered from graduates of the university in question and, as the selection of candidates is at departmental level, the voices of a narrow group at the top become very influential. Unless a professor or head of department is distinguished and broad-minded, he is most unlikely to select someone stronger (academically as well as in personality) than himself.

"So departments or institutes within the topranked universities do not necessarily possess the best available scholars; in fact, the competent scholars often fail to reach the best posts."

tingent and politically provoked, is not a debate. The existence of a debate is not even acknowledged. Thus when some of my Japanese students wanted to debate the old question from U.S. history of which came first in the Chesapeake Bay colonies, racism or slavery, those students taking the position that slavery had come first and caused racism complained that they were at a disadvantage because Japanese sources universally held that racism had caused slavery, and ignored even the existence of a controversy. This is the way ethnic conflict is conceptualized in Japan, as natural and primordial.

The result of accepting only such perspectives, and of unquestioned obedience to Professor Kawada's line (actually Georges Balandier's line, now discredited even in France) is apparent if we look carefully at a recent publication in English from Japan that praises Professor Kawada's perspective. Chizuko Tominaga wrote that

> What makes up history for people in an unlettered society is an accumulation of memories, an oral history that is indispensable to their perpetuation as a people. Each ethnic group has its own accumulation of memories, which is a representation of their culture and the source of their identity. Independent states in Africa are busy forcing ethnic groups to abandon their memories, considering them to be insignificant for the construction of a modern society, and to be interfering with modernization by preserving a tribal mentality.[46]

Here we see compounded several different, unquestioned Japanese assumptions that have made it so hard for Japanese to understand the outside world. These are the assumptions that history is the official propaganda of nation states, that nations are, or should be, synonymous with ethnic groups, and that memories and traditions can never be held in common across ethnic boundaries, which assumptions are axiomatic in Japan. The ideas that oral traditions are somehow collective memories (instead of individual memories – there really being no such thing as a group mind) and that contemporary African nation states are trying to erase ethnicity (as opposed to tribalism) are flatly at odds with reality, as is her statement in the same article that the societies of hunter-gatherer groups "had not changed for thousands of years." Her conclusion that area studies in Africa should involve the recording of ethnic histories, for the purpose of destroying African countries and replacing them with ethnically defined states shows how potentially dangerous the Balandier school, as practiced in Japan, could be for Africa:

---

[46] Chizuko Tominaga, "Perspective: The Significance of African Area Studies" *JCAS News* no. 5 (The Japan Center for Area Studies; National Museum of Ethnology, Osaka, Summer 1999) p. 10.

> Setting up areas free of the frameworks of the state becomes possible after a recompilation of oral histories. Area studies necessarily involve setting up such areas, and recording these unlettered histories – thereby reforming the standard history – may provide guidelines for setting up such areas. This may be done with relative ease in Africa.

Africa needs to unite, and if Japan has still not learned, even 60 years after defeat and occupation by a multi-ethnic United States of America that Japanese leaders thought could never unite in face of an attack by Japan, that multi-ethnic and even multi-racial societies are possible,[47] then Japan ought at least not use its influence to interfere with the creation of a United States of Africa, or even the very limited African Union. It especially should not be allowed to subvert the existing African states with the goal of replacing them with ethnically defined states.

While this article of mine may seem to be a sudden explosion to many who read it, it is instead a final, desperate attempt to get someone in Japan to understand how bad this situation is. I have long been trying to deal with this in private. Scholars in Islamic studies could readily see that there were manuscripts in West Africa, but could not interfere with African studies, or even influence it. The same goes for history, where most scholars realize that the presence or absence of writing is not what defines the field. Every lead I tracked down trying to find the causes of the lack of African history in Japan ended behind Professor Kawada's door, but he was never there. He never responded to letters or e-mails, or the entreaties of go-betweens. I once even tried speaking him directly at an annual meeting of the Japan Association of African Studies, but he would not speak to me. There is no other Africanist, or historian, anywhere in the world that I have had such trouble trying to meet. I can only bring to the attention of the world, especially the black and African world, the power this man and his fellow disciples of Georges Balandier hold in Japan and the results of their wielding that power. I can do no more than that.

[47] John W. Dower, *War without Mercy* (New York: Pantheon, 1987) is a comparative study of Japanese and American racism during World War II that examines how the Japanese underestimated American ability to unite against an outside attack, because of the Japanese assumption that national unity can only be based on ethnic homogeneity.

Is Japan's Cultural Experience Relevant for Africa's Development?

SEIFUDEIN ADEM

ABSTRACT

Japan broke a new path of modernization when it became the first successfully-industrialized nation in the non-Western world. Therefore Japan's modernization experience has a wider relevance for Africa and beyond. The objective of this paper is, however, to single out and discuss only the role of cultural factors in the process and then consider the implications for Africa's development. A conclusion is then drawn – that is, Japan's historical experience strongly suggests that Africa's own cultures have a greater relevance for Africa's development. What does this mean, and why is it so? The paper addresses these questions.

1. Introduction

Does Japan's modernization experience, and in particular the role of culture in it, have any relevance for Africa's renaissance? It is argued in this paper that Japan's experience is rich in suggestions and that therefore it does have relevance for Africa. On the other hand, Japan's culture is irrelevant for Africa as an object of emulation. Based on the contention that the mainstream discourse marginalizes the role of culture and indigenous values in Japan's modernization, I shall first attempt to recast the modern history of the nation and re-interpret it from an African point of view, and then examine, as a punctuated case study, the evolution and contemporary features of modern education in Japan in order to underscore that Japan was able to modernize not in spite of its culture but because of it. It is argued further that Africa's renaissance could come closer to realization if the effort is geared toward linking the new to the old, and re-modeling past or existing institutions and modernizing them, rather than merely transforming or dismantling the old. I conclude with a brief review of a new genre of culturally-deterministic explanations of development which has been proliferating in recent years.

A cultural route to modernity is one of the few areas which have not been sufficiently explored in relation to Africa's renaissance. But an African renaissance which is based on African culture is possible. It is also more sustainable, once realized, since such a renaissance would not be rooted in the shallow soils of imported ideologies. The idea that Africa should mobilize its cultural resources in its modernization effort is, of course, hardly new. What is rare is the intellectual endeavor to marshal supportive evidence for or against the validity of the idea from the modernization experience of other non-Western societies such as Japan.

Let me begin by clarifying the main precepts on which the argument in this paper is predicated. As a rule, the problems which confront all societies at different stages are limited in scope. This is our first key assumption. And secondly, the range of solutions is also of finite variability, even though the collective actions and reactions of all societies to internal and external stimuli are always mediated by particular set of beliefs, assumptions and worldviews. Thirdly, the potential for resolving these common problems exist in all cultures in a variety of forms (see Caudill and Scarr 1974: 39). As a fusion of different cultural entities, Africa's dispositions present no exception in regard to the above assumptions in spite of the multitude of challenges the continent faces today. In this paper, I seek to substantiate the relationships between culture and modernization suggested above partly by re-interpreting Japan's historical experience. Then I shall try to offer one perspective on what this means for Africa's renaissance.

In comparing the experience of Japan and Africa, one cannot overstate the difference in the specific features of the two societies such as the varied historical time and space and related internal and external factors which were intertwined to influence the trajectories of their respective modernization efforts. Fundamental as they are, such differences do not nevertheless undermine the central argument of the paper or the assumptions on which it is based. On the contrary, they reinforce them by suggesting that a society which seeks to indigenize modernity is more likely to succeed than one which tries to transform its indigenous values to accommodate the putative requisites of modernity.

But how can one compare Japan – a wealthy, generally homogeneous, ancient nation-state in the Far East, with Africa – a continent with more than fifty weak, multi-ethnic, post-colonial states? First and foremost, interesting and useful insights could be gained sometimes from comparing the seemingly incomparable, not in spite of the high level of arguability of the comparison, at least on the face of it, but even because of this very fact. Granted, comparing one state, on the one hand, and a conglomerate of diverse states on the other, has its own intellectual hazards particularly in relation to units of analysis. But for all the variations between one and another African state, it can be also argued that all of them find themselves at a more or less similar stage of development (or underdevelopment). The challenges these countries face and the experiences they passed through are also generalizable to a significant degree. The difference between one African country and another is too negligible in this sense to render our generalization inaccurate, and more so in a study which uses no raw data for measuring variables. Secondly, Japan and Africa are compared with one another as much to highlight that there are different similarities as there are similar differences between the two. And such a perspective not only adequately accommodates but even calls for a comparison of seemingly incomparable cases.

Another related question also arises: when I write about Africa and African cultures, have I studied all African cultures, or am I simply extrapolating my observation about my country onto the whole of Africa? My answer is twofold. Of course, I have not studied Africa as a whole, but in order to generalize about Africa, I need not necessarily conduct field studies in every country. The discipline of comparative politics, a field with which I am affiliated, does allow generalization of this nature. I do not have to be an expert on Nigeria to say that corruption is widespread in that country, or that there is discordance between the cultural and political boundaries of Nigeria, or that post colonial Nigeria has failed to modernize, etc. I am not also trying to systematically extrapolate my observations in and about my own country onto the continent as a whole even though my lived experience does indeed influence my perspective. And yet, even if I do consciously extrapolate, the discipline of comparative politics does also permit usage of evidence from one part of Africa as a potential material for formulating Africa-wide hypothesis.

With regard to our key concept, culture, sometimes used interchangeably with the concept tradition, the paper borrows Ali A. Mazrui's (1990: 7-8) functional definition in which he maintained that culture serves seven major functions – namely, as lenses of perception and cognition, motives for human behavior, criteria of evaluation, a basis of identity, a mode of communication, a basis of stratification, and a system of production and consumption. This definition is chosen for our purpose primarily because of its breadth, as it encompasses the cognitive, affective and evaluative aspects of culture. The definition is also less abstract. Another key concept used is modernization which I simply define as an incremental improvement in human condition that is consistent with the level of scientific and technological progress achieved in the world.

I should also like to point out in passing that until very recently political scientists have been generally reluctant to explain behavior in cultural terms, which, in my view, also explains why the role of cultural values in the discourses about Japan's modernization has been marginalized. But why did scholars generally shy away from culture? The first reason is that cultural variables are not easy to operationalize. Secondly, cultural explanation of behavior is, by definition, a sensitive subject because of the unavoidable racial overtones in it. This has contributed to the lack of enthusiasm to using the cultural approach. But the perception regarding the relevance of culture to social theory has been changing in recent years even though it is not clear whether to celebrate or to lament the return of culture in view of its contemporary expressions, which are anchored in a rigid notion of cultural hierarchy. I shall return to this issue in the concluding section.

More specifically, the paper is organized as follows. The next section critically looks at one element of the dominant discourse about the modernization of Japan which revolves around the notion of the 'best of two worlds'. In seeking to interrogate this idea, the purpose is not so much to revise Japanese history, much less to re-write it, but is to lay down the requisite parameters of the discussion which ensues. I suppose that such re-interpretation would also be useful to stimulate further discussion of the subject.

Broad considerations, and some reconstructed formulations, of the discourses about Japan's modernity will be followed, in section three, by a brief but thick description of the history of modern education in Japan. At this juncture a reader may ask: Why education sector? Three major reasons may be given. Firstly, education in Japan clearly demonstrates, perhaps more than any other sector, the links between tradition and modernity. Even as it has maintained continuity with the past, education was also a sector which had been subjected to a series of conspicuous reforms and changes. Secondly, a look at this sector lucidly illustrates the occasional tension between culture and modernization by virtue of the fact that education is the most modern in so far as new ideas are often transmitted through it, and, at the same time, the most traditional in so far as the unbroken link with the cultural past has been maintained. Last, but not least, education has always played a vital role in all modernizing and modernized societies, and Japan is no exception in this regard. Section four synthesizes the modernization experience of Japan and draws some generalizations as to what this implies for Africa's renaissance. The last section closes the discussions by raising a question about the steadily-proliferating, culturally-deterministic explanations of modernization, from which this paper wishes to distance itself.

2. Narratives of Japan's Modernization: A Critical Appraisal

That Japan borrowed ideas and institutions from the West as part of the effort to transform its society is a point which many scholars often make a note of in the discourse about the nation's modernity. What this mode of discourse also does, advertently or inadvertently, is marginalize the role of indigenous values in the process. True, Japan's rise to the ranks of industrialized nations after the Second World War brought the nation maximum respect and admiration of many around the world. It is also true that scholars had followed suit and labored to explain how Japan succeeded, with many of them attributing the phenomenon to such factors as hard work, high saving rate, successful introduction of technology, effective state intervention and/or favorable external environment. The contribution of one or another factor or combination of factors was highlighted in the multitude of studies dealing with the modernization of Japan. But even the richness in the variety of theories about Japan's modernization does not obscure the marginalization of the contribution of culture and traditional values to Japan's success.

In its modernization effort following the Meiji restoration in 1868, the way the master narrative goes, Japan borrowed from the West and used what it thought were instrumental for its purpose, and this propelled her to the path of successful modernization. This notion of the 'best of two worlds' was perhaps best captured in English in the title of Michio Morishima's 1982 book, *Why Japan Succeeded? Western Technology and the Japanese Ethos*. This slogan for sure reflects a deeply naturalized conception, which had been accepted even by many of those who acknowledge the complexity of the phenomenon of Japan's modernization. And there is still sufficient interest in the concept to inspire young Japanese scholars to 'theorize' it from a post-structuralist perspective (Oga 2003: 21-37). But how valid is such a conception? I argue that this way of looking at Japan's modernization is neither entirely accurate nor free from bias. For one thing, such conception wrongly connotes a considerable measure of freedom of choice Japan's early modernizers had enjoyed, as it downplays the degree of confusion which accompanied the initial phases of Japan's transformation.

The slogan also creates the wrong impression that Japan readily adopted Western science after the Meiji Restoration. The period after the Meiji Restoration was indeed characterized by the emergence in Japan of a widespread perception of the felt need to catch up with the West. But the process itself was neither smooth nor uncontroversial – instead it took place against the background of crises and conflicts, contradictions and confusions, compromises and concessions among the main actors. As it is incorrect to view Japan's adoption of Western science after the Meiji Restoration as smooth and linear process, it is also inaccurate to see Japan's interest in Western science and technology as a totally post-Meiji phenomenon. It was less widespread, but persistent interest for certain Western things was clearly visible even before the motto for modernization was said to have become 'Western Technology, Japanese Spirit'.

Moreover, by inevitably exaggerating the transformation in the Japanese culture, the 'best of two worlds' approach masks the interdependence and remarkable continuity between Japan's indigenous values and its modernization process. Here is where it would be perhaps profitable to briefly remark in passing also on a related (but equally misleading) metaphor: the 'Japanese Miracle'. Even though useful in some respects, the representation of Japan's postwar rapid industrialization as miracle is, at least in one sense, highly misleading. If a miracle is to be understood as something that happens without a comprehensible reason, postwar industrialization of Japan fails to meet the criterion of a miracle. The transformation, specially the swiftness of the changes, was for sure truly remarkable, as the nation accomplished "within some thirty years what had taken European countries two hundred years" (Okamoto 1992: 10). But it is sometimes overlooked that for this to happen, and long before the so called the miracle occurred, there had been in place a solid foundation.

The material and cultural foundation of modern Japan was laid during the Edo period (1639-1867), when the country closed off itself from the outside world, and not after the Meiji Restoration (1868). And the modernization process in Japan did not certainly start after the Second World War. In the late Edo period, Edo, as today's Tokyo was then known, had the largest population in the world (Sims 2001: 4). T. Morris-Suzuki (1994: 43) has also claimed that Japan experienced a 'minor technological revolution' in the 16th century which made it in the early Edo period one of the largest exporters of precious metals in the world. But such stories are rarely mentioned in the discourse about Japan's modernity. "In the pre-contact years of the early nineteenth-century," writes also Preston (2000: 114), "Japan had a better educated people than the USA and Europe." There were others, too, (such as Passin 1965; Yamamoto 1992; Holloran 1972; Robertson 1992) who have voiced a similar view about the dearth of long-range perspectives in the discourses about Japan's modernity. Such dissident voices are rather rare, as stated above, and are therefore exceptions in the discursive domain which only prove the rule.

The foundation which had been laid during the Edo period was thus solid when the country was fully opened to the outside world after the Meiji Restoration in 1868. With persistent threat from the great powers of the time, and with the country open to see and interact with the external world, Japan realized that it was lagging behind these powers in some areas and that it must catch up with the West if it was to safeguard its national security. At this historical juncture, as Jansen (1965: 65) put it, "[t]he notions that improvement of the nation was possible through determined effort, and that the times required this if Japan was to maintain its independence [became] universal." One administrative regulation promulgated in 1869 plainly stated: "Intellect and learning shall be sought for throughout the world, in order to establish the foundations of the Empire" (McLaren 1979: 8). And only two years later, in 1871, Japan sent its government – fifty high officials – accompanied by as many students and tourists in a journey, known as the Iwakura mission, which encompassed twelve countries, with a view to making a first-hand, comparative studies of governmental organizations, industrial development, trade and education (Jansen 2002: 355). It was with such a clear sense of purpose and with full awareness of the opportunities and the challenges that Japan mobilized its cultural resources and began its modernization process.

Thus, postwar Japanese industrialization did not start from the scratch or begin with the introduction of 'Western capitalism' after the Meiji Restoration. In fact, as Preston (2000: 106) suggests, the reference to the contemporary system in Japan as capitalism may itself be a misnomer. And if it was capitalism, it may be more accurate to refer to it, like Andrew Barshay (2004: 72) has done, as "noncapitalist capitalism, a capitalism in which non-, or precapitalist values and practices are held to remain salient, indeed decisive in shaping institutional as well as personal behavior in the economic sphere." True, in the early post-War period, Japan was indeed left with a ravaged economy, but even then the driving force of rapid industrialization, in the form of a highly disciplined and educated manpower as well as the cultural infrastructure of it, was left almost untouched.

The point that the 'best of two worlds' approach to Japan's modernization could be somewhat misleading has been made. The question thus becomes if the approach is inaccurate and misleading, at least viewed retrospectively, why does it persist? One reason for this would perhaps relate to the fact that Japanese modernizers had been engaged in large-scale socio-political experiments which gave the impression that they were trying to transplant new, foreign systems of ideas. Again as Barshay (2004: 39) has noted, "Japanese of the Meiji era did not speak of 'modernization' (*kindaika*), but of 'Westernization' or 'Europeanization' (*oka*)". This was so, simply, because at the time the concept of modernity was unknown. But when one closely examines the ideas which had been successfully 'transplanted' in Japan, it becomes clear that there is a nexus between them and aspects of Japan's own culture and institutions.

As we shall see in the next section, both prewar and postwar systems of Japan's education had, for instance, a firm cultural basis and, in important respects, exhibit essential continuity between them. When a foreign idea or institution is considered to be incompatible with Japan's own culture or values – or if there is no way of 'inventing' some kind of link between the two – the Japanese system had been adamantly rejective regardless of whether that particular idea or institution was known to have had a well-proven record of usefulness in other societies. In spite of the relevance and centrality of individualism to the process of modernization in the West, for example, it never took root in the Japanese system because of its obvious incongruence with the group-oriented value system of the Japanese.

The bias in the concept of the 'best of the two worlds' is evident in its implicit premise that non-Western cultures are incompatible with technical modernization without the adoption of Western ideas and institutions, or that the former lack what it takes to modernize without substantial input from the latter. John Hall (1965: 8) had thus observed: "Most Westerners have assumed without much questions that the standards of modernization against which Japan should be measured should be taken from the values inherent in the West's own experience of modernization." It was suggested above that such (mis)conception might have led to the erasure of Japan's own 'mini-industrialization' in the 16th century from the discourses about the nation's modernization. But the fact remains that Japan's 'pre-industrial' culture was in a way not any more incompatible with its modernization than medieval Europe's culture was incompatible with what was later called the industrial revolution. Herbert Passin (1965: 448) long ago made this point clear when he noted: "It is possible to exaggerate both the continuity in the Western world and the discontinuity in the non-Western world. From a certain point of view, the Western world of today is as different from the Western world of, say, the year 1600, as the modernizing non-Western society is from its own immediate past, and in much the same way. The Western past was also a traditional society with its domination of sacred over secular elements, its low mobility and hierarchy, its preference for stability and order rather than change. To the pre-Cartesian Western world, the notion of 'progress' could have been no less alien than it first appeared to the people of the Far East." Japanese historian Tadao Yanaihara (1966: 7) had expressed a similar view even earlier: ". . . some Westerners thought rashly and imprudently that Japan had been a barbarian country with no culture and no education until the Western peoples visited her around the time of the Meiji Restoration."

And yet it is incorrect to suggest that Westerners were alone in deploying and consequently reifying the Euro-centric idea of the 'best of two worlds', as it is incorrect to say that Japanese had single-mindedly promoted ideas which challenged the notion. The picture is more complex than that. As indicated above, some Westerners had, in fact, sought to challenge the idea. Another example in this regard may be B.I. Schwartz who went as far as arguing that it was possible that the so called 'feudal mentality' might have been a springboard which made possible the rapid modernization of Japan (mentioned in Maruyama 1965: 492-493). On the other hand, it may be useful to remember that the idea of 'Western Technique, Japanese Spirit' was first used in the 1880s by the great Japanese educator and thinker Yukichi Fukuzawa (Nathan 2004: 8). Natsume Soseki, another renowned Meiji Japan intellectual, had maintained: "There are those who gloat over this civilization of ours as if it was internally motivated, but they are wrong. They may think they represent the highest fashions, but they are wrong" (Quoted in Nathan 2004: 11). And for Michio Nagai (1971: 35): "The transformation of Meiji Japan which began in 1868 is the first and most striking example of Westernization in the non-Western world." In a similar vein, Hiroshi Watanabe (1996: 122) insisted: ". . . one can argue that the Japanese 'succeeded' not because they kept on being Japanese, but because they became, in a sense, 120 per cent Western. I am inclined to argue that the modernization of Japan is basically nothing but Westernization."

As suggested above, there have also been Japanese intellectuals, though few in number, who have sought to systematically debunk the notion of the 'best of two worlds'. One such voice, and an articulate voice at that, was Chie Nakane (1998: viii-ix), who had compellingly argued that modernity should not deprive Japan of its subjectivity. In his own words, ". . . it is their thesis that any phenomena which seem peculiar to Japan, not having been found in Western society, can be labeled as 'feudal' or 'premodern' elements, and are to be regarded as contradictory or obstructive to modernization." And such an approach, according to Nakane (*Ibid.*), is based on the view that ". . . when it is completely modernized, Japanese society will or should become the same as that of the West . . ." "In my view," Nakane added, "the 'traditional' is one aspect (not element) of the same social body which also has 'modern' features." Similarly,

Yoshihiko Uchida had asserted: "[i]t is precisely the survival of modernity itself that has permitted such a rapid development of supermodernity in Japan" (Quoted in Barshay: 2004: 69). But it should be noted that the influence of foreign ideas and institutions was also there for sure even though these ideas and institutions themselves often had to be blended with Japanese traditional values ingeniously before they were put in use (Shively 1971: 85). The contribution of the West in this way is a widely documented subject, and appropriately so (for examples see Pedlar 1990; Muramatsu 1995). But it can be still argued, for instance, that what the Japanese borrowed was technology as a means to an end; technology as a human activity is a home-grown phenomenon.

The conclusion that the techniques of modern Japan are Western and the spirit Japanese should not therefore necessarily follow. As far as foreign contribution to Japanese civilization, and in a subtle way to its modernity, is concerned, the Chinese civilization is also relevant (see for instance, Buruma 2003: 20). But such contribution is barely mentioned in the dominant discourse. And yet the fact remains, as Passin (1965: 42) observed in his study of Japan's intellectual history, "[modern Japanese intellectuals] did not spring into existence full formed from the brow of Zeus but rather evolved from antecedent structures and situations that were highly elaborate. It was men educated in the traditional society who led the way across the vital gap of modernity." The point is not that the Japanese did not learn from the West, but that they could not have done that so effectively and so selectively without the decisive support of the home-grown culture.

Let me turn now to the issues relating to the manner in which Japan's culture influenced how the society organized itself particularly in the context of the role indigenous values play in the modern system of education. But first a brief historical survey of the system before the Second World War.

3. Modern Education in Japan

A. *Education in Japan before the Second World War*

The educational foundation of modern Japan was laid in the Edo period (1600-1868). The mode of learning and the nature of schools in this period were, of course, markedly different from the system which was to emerge after the Meiji Restoration in 1868. The Meiji Restoration, a kind of revolution from above, which also brought about substantial social and economic reforms such as the unification of hitherto separate lands and abolition of class distinctions, marked a major watershed in the history of Japan's modernization. A national education master plan was also formulated right after the Restoration. Most important feature of the pre-Meiji education system was that class considerations determined who gets what education, where, when and how. The system during this period was, as R.P. Dore (1965: 99) put it, "class-ridden, formalistic, backward-looking, out-of-date." But this changed after 1868. Let it be noted in passing that the suggestion here is not that the whole system of education changed after the Meiji Restoration or that the "modern" system is better in every way than the "pre-modern" system. First, the very hypothesis of this paper is based on the claim that not all had changed. On the latter point, it need to be noted that there are some Japanese intellectuals who are presently making a plausible and strong "scientific" case for a return to the "pre-modern" system of education, at least as far as teaching methods are concerned (for example see, Kawashima 2005).

In any case for the first time in the history of the nation, everyone was free after 1868 to join any school regardless of where they reside or what their place was in the social hierarchy. Education was also narrowly defined at this time in materialistic and utilitarian terms in direct contrast to what was the case before the Meiji restoration when education had emphasized the learning of moral and Confucian values.

Behind almost all major social innovations are usually some personalities. In the early post-Meiji Japan, such personalities include, first and foremost, Yukichi Fukuzawa, also known as the father of Japanese enlightenment. Fukuzawa lived in a crucial juncture in his country's history, in the second half of the 19th century, and his life reflects the social and political upheaval of Japan during this period. He was a pioneer of Western, specifically American, education in the country, as well as a genuine Japanese-internationalist. I shall make intermittent references to Fukuzawa's own life and ideas in this section to support some of the principal hypotheses of this paper, as they offer important clues about the driving forces behind the changes and continuities in the history of education in Japan as well as the enduring and endurance aspect of Japan's culture. His observations and experience point to the waning of Confucian influence on Japan's system of learning, the beginning of American influence instead, and Japan's determination to change gears to adapt to the new system.

Born into a lower-rank samurai family and trained in Chinese and later in Dutch studies, Fukuzawa had already reached maturity when Commodore Perry came to Japan in 1853 with his famous black ships, and forced the country to open its ports to the outside world. Following the growing influence of the US after the Perry mission, Fukuzawa was soon to realize that his previous studies were becoming irrelevant. "It was a bitter disappointment," Fukuzawa (1966: 98) reflected later, "but I knew it was no time to be downhearted."

The first master plan of education in Japan in the context of the nation's overall modernization strategy was drawn up in 1872. This development came about, of course, only three years after the Meiji Restoration. The master plan was drawn also just one year after the Japanese Ministry of Education, Science and Culture was established. Among other things, the education master plan promulgated that a) children were to receive eight years of compulsory education b) success in life and enlightenment were to be the goals of education c) practical studies such as medicine and engineering were to be emphasized and d) the cost of education was to be left to individuals (Okano and Tsuchiya 1999: 15). In this way the Meiji administration sought to bring to an end the fragmented schooling system of the earlier era which was characterized by strong emphasis on ethics and morality and excessive differentiation based on geographic and class background.

Believing that Japan was far behind the West and that there should be changes in the education system if the nation was to survive and succeed, the Japanese began to ask themselves what was to be done. Fukuzawa (1966: 215-216) thus shares what went on in his own mind at the time: "Granted that a nation's destiny depends upon the education of its people . . . I reasoned that Chinese philosophy as the root of education was responsible for our shortcomings." Shortly thereafter, Fukuzawa (1966: 214) drew up what he called the new principles of education: 'number and reason'. And with that, the nation started a disciplined search for the most appropriate model of 'scientific' education.

All in all, in the 19th century three major educational reforms were adopted in Japan – in 1872, 1879 and 1890, with some revisions in between. The second reform changed the system of education which was highly centralized, after the French system, to a decentralized one, after the US model, and the last one introduced a Prussian model, based on the differentiation of the elite and the masses (Nagai 1978: 38-39). The 1890 reform also brought to an end the major controversial issues in education until the middle of the 20th century, as it synthesized "elements of Confucian ethics and Shinto statism – as well as a modern orientation toward learning – into the imperial frame of the state" (Shimahara 1979: 55). The first three major educational reforms were testimony not only to the relentless effort of adaptation but also to the prevailing state of confusion.

As indicated above, the modern system of education in Japan exhibited certain characteristics right from the beginning. Firstly, there was the emphasis on elementary education rather than secondary or tertiary education. The philosophy behind this was that "the improvement of the general educational standard of people was more important for the economic and technological development in the future" (Yamazumi 2003: 21). There was also the emphasis on technical training. In 1899 the government passed a legislation designed to promote the training of medium and lower level technicians in industry – vocational subjects were made compulsory at upper primary schools. Both academic and vocational schools at all levels were consolidated. Government subsidies were also allocated for the purpose. By the turn of the 20th century, a modern education system which sufficiently accommodated traditional values and science was thus firmly in place, and the 'hardware' of Japanese culture was ready to be integrated into the 'software' of science to accelerate the modernization of Japan.

B. *The Indigenous Roots of Modern Education in Japan*

What are the indigenous values in the Japanese system of education? How are they expressed in the education process? What are the consequences and implications? I shall here concentrate on the first question and attempt to address the last two in the next section. Depending on the level of abstraction, several core values relating to Japan's 'education culture' can be identified, including those relating to: 1) social attitude towards children; 2) group orientation; 3) the normative place and nature of the concepts of study, imitation and hard work and the relationships among them; and 4) the notion of cultural flexibility.

In some societies, when children misbehave, it is usually the stick which follows. But in Japan, it seems, the stick is almost never even a means of the last resort at all levels, from kindergarten and nursery schools to elementary schools. Several studies have shown (for instance, Singleton 1993; Lewis 1996; White 1987) that relatively more concern is shown to children in Japan. Underlying such social attitude is the firm belief that children are basically good, and that when they misbehave, it is only because of 'misunderstanding,' not because of any inherent proclivity to misbehave.

On the other hand, one cultural idiom in Ethiopia, for example, maintains that children are to be instantly rewarded for good behavior and punished for bad behavior, in accordance with the weight of each. On the punitive side, a typical old proverb declares, *yemaimetut lij sikotut yaleksal* (a child without the experience of the stick would weep even when reprimanded). And this, according to the oral tradition, is something to be avoided by all means. In Japan, disciplinary approaches for dealing with misbehavior are emotional, not mechanical. When a child or a student misbehaves, indirect emotional appeals are made to induce correct behavior, since saving the face of a misbehaving student is considered to be of greater importance. "In the Japanese system," Singleton (1993: 14) has observed, "positive self-image is encouraged by parents, grandmothers, and kindergarten and elementary school teachers who would never accuse a child of willful mischief. The child just 'doesn't understand' what is proper."

Another distinguishing characteristic of Japanese school system is its group orientation. From pre-school to the last level of education, this social value is systematically inculcated in the minds of the Japanese. Even the US occupation, which had attempted to modify some of the school cultures, could not alter this social value. Deeply embedded as 'groupism' is in the Japanese social psyche, no changes in school curriculum were able to bring about a radical shift. While the formal curriculum is only a means to an end, the cultural curriculum anchored in 'groupism' is an end in itself (Singleton 1993: 11).

Even though such instinctive 'groupism' pervades Japanese society, it is one without rigid structure of identity and interest. In place of rigid structures, what one finds is flexibly defined boundaries and constitutive elements, reflecting the social acceptability of corresponding shifts in loyalty at various levels of commitment. At the same time, the Japanese experience demonstrates that 'groupism' is not necessarily an undesirable attribute and that modernity and groupism are not always natural enemies.

The Japanese school system in any case transmits and reinforces this primordial feeling of 'we-ness' through curriculum but, above all, through extracurricular activities, beginning sometimes with the assignment of elementary school students into small *ad hoc* groups called *han*. And group orientation of the Japanese is an area that has been least affected, if at all, by the forces of modernity. Iwama (1993: 73) noted on this: "[t]he basic motivation in Japanese society seems to be 'social needs' or needs for belonging, and for acceptance by fellow members . . . Japan's school system is not an exception."

Further discussion of indigenous values of modern Japan can be organized around two enduring concepts – study and hard work, as well as their meaning and the complex relationships between them. The Japanese equivalent of the term study, *benkyoo*, has the connotation of hard work and perseverance; *benkyoo* is seen not as a burden but as "an opportunity to commit great amount of effort to a task" (White 1987: 52). If the process of learning is regarded highly in Japan, so also is the related task of teaching. In fact, such attitude predates the 'modernization' of

Japan. To quote Herbert Passin (1965: 465): "Since teaching had always been looked upon as *tenshoku* (heavenly calling), it ranked . . . as honorable modern occupation. . . . During the Edo period even commoner teachers in the *terakoya* had been treated as samurai, and this attitude continued into the early years of Meiji."

The act of studying, with all the challenges accompanying it, is thus regarded at least as important as the end result. Closely related to such philosophy of education is the principle of *gambaru*. Singleton (1993: 10) has maintained that this principle distinguishes the contemporary Japanese theory of learning: "Literally, *gambaru* is a verb that means 'to persist, hang on or do one's best.' In its imperative form, *gambare*, it is used among members of a group to encourage each other in cooperative activities." Similarly, B.L. De Mente (1994: 94) has observed: ". . . [a] word everyone in Japan hears over and over is *gambatte*, from the word *gambaru*, meaning to 'persevere, never give up . . .' One might say that that *gambaru*-ism is the primary philosophy of the Japanese. *Gambarimasu* 'I will do my best,' or '*gambatte*,' 'do your best,' are constantly on the lips of the Japanese in virtually every situation imaginable. The term is used as encouragement, as a promise, as a dedication, almost as a prayer, and as a battle cry."

It also appears that in Japan engaged effort is valued over ability. The systematic articulation of the philosophy of effort and persistence in its original form can be probably traced to the ideas of Baigan Ishida, a merchant and thinker who lived in 18th century Japan (Sakaiya 2003: 143). Reflecting on his own experience in the heydays of 'modern' education in Japan, Yukichi Fukuzawa (1966: 91) had also said: "[i]n hardship we found pleasure, and the hardship was pleasure." Such understanding of incentive may account, at least partially, for the institutional and intrinsic quality of Japanese education.

It is widely recognized that Japanese also attach more value to imitation (adaptation or domestication, as some would prefer to put it) than to invention. Japanese love of imitation is summarized in a somewhat dramatic form by J. Tobin (1992: 3): "The genius of the Japanese lies not in invention but in adaptation – of Korean pottery, tombs and textiles, Chinese script and scripture; Dutch science and medicine; French education; English colonialism; German militarism; and American egalitarianism, corporate efficiency and popular culture." To suggest that representation such as this commit the sins of oversimplification and exaggeration is not to deny that Japanese love imitation and that they are also good at it. What is more, they are adept in blending imported ideas and are excellent modifiers of what has been imitated, making a borrowed technical device or philosophical idea fit for the need of their society. Tadao Yanaihara's (1966: 11-12) statement about this phenomenon in the context of Meiji Japan is both elaborate and philosophical in which he outlined how Japan adopted from France the systems of army, education and law, and the Republicanism of Montesquieu and Rousseau, and how the French system was then eliminated from the army, the educational system and the legal codes and was replaced by the German model; and how the ideal state which the Meiji government aimed to create was made to approximate the German spirit of state centralism. But Yanaihara (1966: 7) was also careful to add: "Our study and imitation of Europe have been what Socrates used to call the maieutic method, by which our own minds have been helped to deliver their contents, to give birth their own fruits." Honna and Hoffer (1989: 48) also looked at the general attitude towards imitation in Japan, though from slightly different angle, and concluded: "At the core of the Japanese culture lies the idea that imitation is an important process of basic education. The word *manabu* (to learn) and *maneru* (to imitate) are said to have derived from the same origin, *manaberu*, and students and apprentices are often told to follow their masters' models before they acquire their own ideas and skills." Would the etymological history of the Japanese word "*oshieru*", which literally means "to teach", as well as "to tell" also be reflective of a similar conceptual link between the two notions? Perhaps.

Not all societies, of course, view imitation in the same way. Some encourage it; others are indifferent to it; and still others actively discourage or proscribe it. In its attitude towards imitation, Japanese culture clearly falls into the first category. On the other hand, the dominant culture in Ethiopia, for instance, seems to fit in the third category. One time-honored expression in the Amharic language is: *sew inde betu inji inde gorebetu ayadrim*, which is roughly translatable into: an individual is supposed to live as he/she is destined to live and not like his (more successful) neighbor. It is clear that the message behind the expression borders between complacency and fatalism. Granted, expressions such as the above have only a very limited value for explaining social behavior. But they also sum up important aspects of truth about philosophy of life in one segment of the society.

A related point is the speed with which new ideas, once they are believed to be useful, spread across a land. Recollecting his impression just before sailing to the United States with a newly built steamship in 1860, Fukuzawa (1966: 110) had observed: ". . . about seven years after the first sight of steamship, after only about five years of practice, the Japanese people made a trans-Pacific crossing without help from foreign experts." George Basalla (1988: 78) also shared the following story about what happened in the 16th century after Portuguese adventurers brought to Japan two handguns made in Europe, objects which were at the time generally unknown in the country: "The Japanese were so impressed by these primitive firearms that they purchased them on the spot and set their swordsmiths to work duplicating them. Within a decade, gunsmiths all over Japan were turning out firearms in quantity." On the other hand, in a place far from Japan, the same foreigners, the Portuguese, introduced the same type of guns at almost exactly the same period to people at roughly the same stage of development as the Japanese were. In addition, the new weapon had also a similar utilitarian appeal to the two peoples. The idea of making gun proliferated rapidly in one society (Japan), as indicated above; in the other, however, it did not gain any ground. For succeeding generations, the spear continued to play its traditional role in the latter. The place I have in mind is the 16th century Ethiopia, a Northeast African Christian kingdom, located in the Northern part of present-day Ethiopia. What, then, explains the difference? One of the crucial differences between the two societies perhaps relates to one observation which R.P. Dore (1956: 101-103) had made, that is, the relatively widespread nature of basic education and the diffusion of the notion of the possibility of individual and national 'self-improvement' in contemporary Japan. It may be argued that this combination of factors was absent in Ethiopia. Another factor would perhaps pertain, as pointed out above, to the attitude towards learning, particularly towards imitation, as well as adeptness in the art of imitating, which is in turn itself a function of cumulative experience.

Cultural flexibility is also another relevant factor, cultural flexibility understood simply, as, in the words of Takeo Kuwabara (1983: 80), "the proclivity and the versatility to change in response to the needs of the times, rather than stubbornly clinging on." The disposition to cultural flexibility in Japan is a well-documented subject by other observers too (for instance, see Vogel 1988; Benedict 1996). It is this type of flexibility which had allowed the Japanese system of education to re-invent itself at different stages. It has been already indicated that three radical changes took place in Japan's system of education in the 19th century. Although the changes were sometimes referred to as reforms, they were no less than revolutionary in substance. The constant process of change and adjustment in Japan's system of education continues to this date. I shall now turn to the evolution and principal features of the current system.

C. *Education in Postwar Japan and Contemporary Features*

At the end of the Second World War, Japan was defeated and was placed under US occupation between 1945-1952. Subsequently, significant changes were introduced in the system of education, as in other areas, first during what Trainor (1983: 29) has called the 'punitive' phase of occupation. This phase focused on cleansing the education system from 'militarism and ultra-nationalism.' One of the measures taken to this effect was the official dissolution of high schools in 1949 (Roden 1980: 232).

More broadly, the task during this phase involved wide-ranging educational reforms including decentralization of the education system, curricular revisions and issuing of new text books. In 1945, directions were given for the elimination of materials stressing national defense and armament that promote warlike spirit or obstruct international amity (Education in Japan 1952: 35). And for a while, even Japanese history and geography courses were suspended (White 1987: 63). Moral education was also removed from school curriculum because it was thought to have inculcated unhealthy nationalism in the minds of young people.

Then came the 'reconstruction' phase of the occupation which was geared more towards positively transforming the education system. Outstanding among the measures taken at this stage were the extension of compulsory education to nine years (in place of the six-years system introduced in 1907) and the adoption of the 6-3-3-4 division of the schooling system. In place of moral education, the new system emphasized a curriculum designed to justify the postwar democratic society.

In the meantime, there was deliberate attempt on the part of the Japanese education planners to link the new system to Japan's own long-standing indigenous values. As Merry White (1983: 64) noted: "Japanese educators, in an attempt to see the postwar democratization of education as an extension of indigenous values and practices, stressed the 'egalitarian' relationship of teacher and student. This they saw as consonant with Japanese tradition, which values the warmth and affection in the bond." White (1983: 64) also added, "In the traditional relationship it is said that the love between teacher and student (*kyoiku-ai*) is accompanied by and exhibited in discipline and morality. The combination makes the relationship one of respect but not of distance. In other words, traditional 'vertical' relationships could be seen as primarily benevolent rather than authoritarian or exploitative, and 'democracy' could be seen as consonant with the spirit, if not the structure, of relationships of the past."

Needless to say, education is a resource which replenishes a workforce. Changes in emphasis in the educational system in the postwar Japan, therefore, also reflected the changing needs of the society. Prior to the 1970s, the nation was pre-occupied with and excelled in manufacturing-led growth. But in the 1980s, there emerged the felt-need for a new type of workforce that is trained in the areas of highly complex information industry. It was in light of this imperative, among others, that the government showed solid commitment to reforming the education system by establishing the National Council on Educational Reform (NCER). The reform proposals under NCER's consideration were thus regarded by some as "a political response to Japanese industry's call for developing the human resources it expects to be crucial in the future" (Shimahara 1993: 272). The changing educational needs are not, however, dealt with merely on an *ad hoc* basis. There is a system in place which became operational in 1947 and calls for a major national educational review once every ten years. The 1989 revisions of the education guidelines stressed, among other things, computer and foreign language literacy for the new age of information and internationalization. The 1998 revisions prepared for the change to a five day school week which took effect throughout Japan in April 2002 (Nihon Jiten 2003: 203).

The current system of education in Japan, like the systems in other places, is designed to perform four tasks: transmission of knowledge, socialization and acculturation of students, selection and differentiation of young people for their future respective role in the society and legitimating of knowledge, tasks which are systematically performed at different levels in the schooling system. The whole process starts with preschool where 3-6 years old children, as well as those less than 3 years, are 'socialized' into group activities, followed by a six year elementary schooling.

Then comes junior high school or middle school, a transitional phase between elementary and secondary schools. At this stage students make preparation to join their favorite upper senior high schools; the next phase, the secondary school, is based on ability and ranking, unlike all the preceding levels of the schooling system. In terms of ownership, in 2003, 95 percent of elementary and middle schools were public; however, private schools play a larger role at the secondary school level – 24 percent of Japanese secondary schools were private institutions in 2003 (Nihon Jiten 2003). Also in 2003, there were 14,174 preschools; 23,633 elementary schools; 11,134 junior high schools and 5,450 senior high schools (Asahi Shimbun 2004: 221). Some of the salient features of each of these levels are briefly described below.

Two types of pre-elementary schools operate in Japan: *yochien* which comes under the jurisdiction and guidance of Ministry of Education and *hoikuen* which operate under the umbrella of the Ministry of Health and Welfare. Both *yochien* and *hoikuen* receive government curriculum guidance and their main function is to cater for children who are less than six years old. As a nursery school for children whose parents are unable to look after them mainly due to work-related reasons, *hoikuen* accepts a child less than six years of age and school fees vary depending on the level of income of the parents. In principle, a child is supposed to attend *hoikuen* for a minimum of five days a week and eight hours a day. On the other hand, *yoichien* is educational school for children between ages three and six. A child is required to spend in it an average of four hours a day and thirty-nine weeks a year.

The process of instilling values in the minds of children begins with the pre-school years, usually at the age of three. At this stage, the child is introduced to 'home curriculum' by his/her mother and is taught 'the right way of doing things.' In Japan, perhaps more than in many other countries, it seems, how something is done is as important as, or perhaps even more important than, what is done, whether it is the manner of eating, sleeping, bowing or the holding of chopsticks. One of the things which continued to puzzle me after I came to Japan and began to learn writing Kanji (Japanese characters of Chinese origin) was why it was so important when writing an ideograph, for instance one with a rectangular shape, to begin from the left or right side, from top or bottom, and I kept wondering why it was not more appropriate to judge the writing by the end result. The puzzle of the so-called stroke order has yet to be fully resolved. It is said that the principle of 'the right way of doing things' is strictly observed, in any case, mainly for three reasons: sense of propriety, comfort of uniformity and avoidance of responsibility (Taichi 2003: 151-153). Such basic and initial training prepares the child for future social interaction. *Kyoiku mama*, or education-obsessed mother, as the Japanese mother is often called, also prepares the child in the areas of basic skills so as to familiarize him/her with some of the challenges the child is about to face in early schooling. Such is the case in spite of the fact that "schools prefer to regard the child as a blank slate, trainable in the specific behavior and skills seen as appropriate to specific educational environment" (White 1987: 102).

Experts on elementary level education in Japan (for instance Lewis 1996: 82-83; Tsuchiya 1999: 58-59) agree that the Japanese system at this level differs from those in many other countries in that the former adopts an egalitarian approach in which all students are considered equal and receive equal attention from teachers regardless of variations in their academic potential. Consequently, cooperation rather than competition is encouraged at this level, and both the social and emotional needs of children are carefully looked after, in addition to their intellectual needs. "Japanese elementary schools" Lewis (1996: 82-83) observed, "refuse to privilege intellectual development over social development."

Furthermore, students are divided into smaller groups and periodically assume different responsibilities for the class, in areas ranging from athletic activities to school excursions. What is also worth noting is that the 'whole development' approach which places emphasis on the social and intellectual enrichment of the student is reflected not only in the contents of the curriculum but also in how it is taught. For example, the goals of first-grade science lessons, in the words of one teacher as paraphrased in Lewis (1996: 84-85), were to "find out which bottle holds more and explain to your classmates how you found out" and "to share water without grabbing, so it won't get spilled, and if we do have water spills, to help each other clean up without saying things like 'It's not my fault' or 'You did it'."

Japanese elementary schools instill values in the minds of students at least in two ways. One is through the omni-present banners. As to the forms and contents of these banners, Lewis (1996: 92-93) in one instance observed: ". . . all [are] written in hiragana (a simple phonetic script) so that the first graders could read them . . . . many goals emphasized friendship, cooperation and caring for one's belongings and oneself. Of the 94 goals, about half focused on friendship, cooperation, and other aspects of social and emotional development. The remaining half of the goals fell approximately equally into five categories: persistence, responsibility, enthusiasm, healthy habits and academic striving." Another way through which values are transmitted at this level is academic lessons such as moral and social studies which are based on standard curriculum across the nation.

Middle school (grades 7-9) enrolls children from ages 12-14, and is the transition stage between elementary and high school. The major objective of the middle school is to prepare students for high schools. The main features of middle school education include the following: students receive education from specialist teachers, lessons are more intense, it is more factually-oriented than in the elementary schools, and the egalitarian relationship of elementary school years is replaced by a hierarchical one. Yet academic instructions are based, like in elementary schools but unlike in high schools, on a nationally standardized curriculum.

Through curricular revisions, clear emphasis was also placed after the Second World War on training students in different vocations, or at least giving them the opportunity to explore them, beginning in the 7th Grade in the middle schools. But the attempt initially encountered two major setbacks. One was the inability of local schools to secure the necessary equipments to teach these programs. Another problem was that non-educational sectors offered more attractive pay to technical specialists and schools were not able to compete with them (Education in Japan 1952: 78-82). Needless to say, today's schools face none of these problems as there is no more shortage of training equipments. Due to the affluence of the nation, today schools can also pay, and do pay, competitive salaries to their teachers. In fact, on average, an elementary school teacher with an M.A. degree today gets roughly the same amount of monthly salary as a similarly trained teacher at a Japanese university. It is fair to assume that the same holds true at the level of middle schools.

The first formal organization of Japanese secondary schools took place in 1886. Historically, Japanese secondary schools had been under the scrutinizing eyes of the central government officials who were keen on making sure that the schools were well prepared to contribute to Japan's modernization effort. This was the case between 1890 and the First World War. After the First World War, however, schools were subjected to less central control. But the scrutiny re-emerged in the 1930s.

With the rise of unemployment specially among graduates of liberal education in the 1930s, it became necessary to restructure the system in such a way that secondary schools would concentrate on training students in vocational education. Japan thus entered the age of *vocationalization* even though, as I elaborate below, emphasis on vocational training in the country has indeed a long pedigree. But it was only many years later that the vocationalization of secondary school education acquired an institutional status. One American report (Education in Japan: 1952: 77) put the establishment in the Ministry of Education of a Vocational Education Section of the Bureau of Elementary and Secondary Education and a Technical Education Section of the Bureau of Higher Education and Science as "one of the most hopeful developments indicating recognition of the importance of vocational education."

It must be noted again that while institutionalization of vocational education in its 'modern' form may be a relatively new development, Japanese concern with and emphasis of vocational education itself is a longstanding one. "Japanese educators showed interest in vocational education early in the Meiji era," according to Trainor (1983: 243), "and the early Ministry of Education had in it a Bureau of Technical Education charged with providing agricultural, commercial, nautical fisheries and trade schools." In a related way, Herbert Passin (1965: 462) also noted: "It is a refreshing contrast with the intellectuals of many 'underdeveloped' countries today [in comparison to Japan] to see how many of them . . . devoted so much attention to practical matters, such as medicine, geography, economics, astronomy, zoology, national defense, armaments and ship design, as against genteel letters and moral commentary. Even orthodox Confucianism was willing to acknowledge – increasingly as we approach the Restoration itself – the importance of practical learning, however much it strained to confine it within permissible limits."

Contemporary Japan has a differentiated system of secondary schools which are divided into two main groups: academic high schools and vocational high schools. One important difference between middle schools (as well as elementary schools) and high schools (or upper secondary schools, as official documents refer to them) is that the former exhibits homogeneity in its school culture across the nation while the latter is marked with heterogeneous sub-cultures. This in part reflects both the differing hierarchies of various high schools and the variations in the contents of their curriculum.

Unlike for elementary and middle schools, there is no standard curriculum for high schools (although school textbooks at all levels have to be approved by the Ministry of Education, Culture, Sports and Technology experts). The absence of standardized curriculum and textbooks at this level is, at least in part, due to the constantly changing nature and the richness of the subject menu at this level. The entrance examination, administered by local governments or private high schools, determines who would and would not be admitted to these schools. On the other hand, the academic ranking of students at the end of compulsory education also largely influences the decision as to which student would choose to go to which high schools.

Academic high schools which are, in theory, designed to prepare students for further education, fall into two categories: elite and non-elite academic high schools. The official classification of upper secondary schools in terms of their content is into three types: general, specialized and integrated. General courses offer general education putting emphasis on academic subjects, while specialized courses are designed to provide vocational, technical or other education for students who have chosen a particular vocational area as their future career. These courses are further classified into several categories: agriculture, industry, business, fishery, home economics, nursing, science-mathematics etc. Integrated courses comprehensively offer general and specialized education (Outline of Education in Japan 1997: 1996: 4).

Elite high schools prepare their graduates for top universities and non-elite high schools for the less prestigious universities and junior colleges. The latter is the mainstream high school system in that the majority of students in academic high schools are included in this group. These students for the most part end up not in any university at all but rather in private specialist schools (*senshugakko*). Book-keeping, language and computer programming are some of the subjects offered in these schools (Okano and Tsuchiya 1999: 64-65). Yet the number of students who have opted to join universities and junior colleges has steadily increased over the last several decades from just 17.1% in 1965 to 49.1 per cent in 2000 (*Nihon Jiten* 2003: 201).

Vocational high schools, aimed at preparing students for immediate employment by training them in such areas as commerce, technical subjects, agriculture, home science, nursing and fishery, are easier to join than academic high schools. Following graduation, however, a great number of students proceed for further education in private specialist schools (*senshugakko*) and many others for 4-year universities. But the greatest majority still joins the workforce (Okano and Tsuchiya 1999: 65). In addition to the above types of secondary schools, there are evening high schools, correspondence high schools and schools for the handicapped.

In general Japan's system of modern education is firmly anchored in indigenous values, the essence of which has largely remained the same over the last several hundred years. In other words, despite the 'modernity' of contemporary education in Japan, it is not hard to see in it the resilient Japanese 'traditional' cultural values. Even the quintessential modern agents of socialization, such as schools, seem to be enforcing the Japanese culture. What this means is tradition and modernity are not as incompatible as they appear to be. Modernity can be traditionalized, and tradition can be modernized.

4. Relevance of Japan's Experience for Africa

To the question, "Is Japan's experience relevant for Africa's development?" the answer we suggested was that it depends on what is meant by relevance. According to standard definition, relevance could mean applicability; relevance could also mean usefulness. In the first sense, Japan's experience is not directly applicable to Africa's problems. On the other hand, if what is meant by relevance is the usefulness of the experience as a source of meaningful insight into Africa's own challenges and opportunities, then Japan's experience is indeed relevant for Africa's development. Africa could learn from Japan that Africa's own cultures are more useful for Africa's development. And this constituted the hypothesis of my paper as I sought to explain Japan's success in cultural terms with a view to highlighting the need for Africa also to pursue a similar approach.

Why did Japan succeed in modernization? Many theories purport to explain why Japan succeeded, ranging from those claiming Japan succeeded because it was completely westernized to those insisting Japan succeeded because the nation remained loyal to its core values and traditions. And there are perspectives which fall somewhere in between these two. More specifically, according to the first school Japan succeeded because it abandoned its culture. This school equates Japan's modernization with Westernization, arguing that Japan borrowed from the West not just scientific techniques but also the values and institutions which support them. Not surprisingly, such a view was most common in the period prior to the Second World War. Meiji Japan intellectuals also did not use the concept modernization (kindaika), simply because it didn't exist then, instead, they talked and wrote about Westernization (oka). Natsume Soseki is perhaps one of the more renowned Meiji Japan intellectuals who had held this type of view.

The second school held that Japan succeeded because it embraced its culture, Japan's modernization was internally driven and it was Japan's culture which provided the foundations for sustained economic growth and industrialization. This school rejects the Euro-centric notion that non-Western regions cannot modernize without substantial input from the West. Adherents of this school go further and argue that it was, in fact, Japan's pre-capitalistic, and even feudal, culture that prepared the necessary condition for Japan's modernization. This view was most fashionable in the postwar period. Masao Maruyama's views as well as that of Akio Morita, among others, seem to be of this brand.

According to the third school, Japan succeeded because Japanese spirit and Western techniques were synthesized. Chronologically, this perspective seems more trans-historical as it has persisted across different phases of the modernization of Japan. In fact, one can even say that this way of looking at Japan's modernization has naturalized. On the other hand, compared to the two perspectives above, this onc can be seen as a middle-ground approach whose proponents included the great Japanese educator Yukichi Fukuzawa.

Just as there are different theories which purport to explain why Japan successfully modernized, so also are there different perspectives when it comes to the question of why Africa failed to modernize. Broadly speaking, these theories can be classified into two: externally-oriented explanations and internally-oriented explanations. Theories such as "Europe underdeveloped Africa" or, in general, "the industrialized world underdeveloped Africa" are externally-oriented theories. Theories which attribute Africa's underdevelopment to the alleged fact that, to put it bluntly, "Africans are lazy" or that "African societies are low-trust societies" fall into the group of internally-oriented explanations of Africa's underdevelopment. Influential scholars such as Samuel Huntington, David Landes, and Francis Fukuyama have sometimes advanced views which neatly fit into this category.

It is a fact that as the new millennium opened, Africa stood face to face with seemingly insurmountable challenges. Disease, poverty and bad governance, and in some places, the vagaries of nature, often simultaneously operating, have robbed the continent of the vitality required for any meaningful progress. No other region of the world had faced so similar adverse forces at the same time. On the other hand, history also teaches, including Japanese history, that difficulties could strengthen the will power to succeed. It is believed that Japan was able to succeed, in part, because its people effectively mobilized their resources and worked harder when they realized that their survival hinged on success. It is also said that Japanese worked hard and became so successful partly because they were, in comparison with other peoples, so poorly-endowed in natural resources and that in order to survive, let alone succeed, they felt that they had no other choice. Indeed, it is a paradox of Japan that a country which is one of the least self-sufficient in the world in terms of producing its own basic needs at home is also, on the other hand, the second richest nation on the face of earth. If a challenge simultaneously creates an opportunity to overcome it, the enormity of the challenges Africa faces today should therefore greatly spur it to do the same.

In the process of modernization, the challenges Japan faced and the options available to it were of course vastly different from the situation in which Africa finds itself today. There is no way in which domestic and external factors prevalent when Japan initiated its modernization could be reproduced today elsewhere. But we should not jump from this premise to the conclusion that the experience of Japan is hence irrelevant for Africa. And this is perhaps the kind of error E. Alegere (1973: 52) was making when he argued: "The industrialization of Japan cannot be repeated in any other country since the cultural factors at work in Japan and those in other countries are quite dissimilar." But even if that was the case, as much lesson, if not more, could be learned when the object of comparison is dissimilar as when it is similar.

There may be a number of areas from which Africa could learn from Japan's experience, as a few studies have already suggested (for instance see Mazrui 1976; Mazrui 1984; Nafziger 1995). The role culture played in Japan's modernization is also one such area worth looking at. Japanese history demonstrates sustained modernization is possible when ones own cultural resources are used. Yet it is not Japan's culture *per se,* which Africans should focus on, but on how it has been used. What Africans should learn from Japan is how to learn. I have not seen any evidence which indicates that Japan's culture was conducive for modernization while other cultures are not.

Therefore, it is one important aspect of the lesson from Japan's modernization experience that Africans should not try to copy the culture of others in order to modernize. Even though some analysts have seen the need for a massive culture change in Africa, the Japanese experience demonstrates that such a project is neither feasible nor desirable.

I say it is not feasible, however, not to essentialize culture by reducing it to the realm of unchangeable; it is only to stress the incontestable fact that drastic change of culture takes a long period of time. Most importantly, there is no need for doing so since, as indicated above, all cultures are self-sufficient, and relying on one's own is more fruitful than relying on a borrowed one. For sure, there are elements in every culture which are resistant to modernization. But this is no truer of Africa than it was of Japan, or any other area for that matter. Rather than a massive culture change, what is required in this case is merely cultural flexibility – another area in which the Japanese have excelled so well.

As pointed out earlier, cultural flexibility denotes the versatility to change as circumstances require, rather than simply clinging to old ways of doing things. Japanese culture allows considerable degree of flexibility in this sense. Shifting gears is permissible, and is even encouraged, when an error is made in pursuing a course of action (Kuwabara 1983; Benedict 1996). The analysis in this paper has shown how cultural flexibility was put into use in the context of the historical evolution of modern education in Japan. It may be added here that during its modernization experiments Japan not only changed gears from one system or model to another from time to time, but also it was able to blend different models all at once. African modernizers in the post-independence period, on the other hand, seemed to have viewed such behavior as a sign of caprice and indetermination, and embraced wholeheartedly whichever system was in vogue. Binding commitment to an ideology continued to be the order of the day in Africa even when it was clear that the system was not working. Of course, the choices which were available to Japan were not as disharmonious as the ones with which post-colonial Africa was confronted. Japan had the comfort of choosing between the models of the American and the British, or the French and the Prussian, etc., and these models were not always mutually exclusive. And most importantly, the ultimate choice the Japanese made were never arbitrary, but was often a choice filtered through the cultural prism, as much as it was also conditioned by the felt-need of the society.

A related issue to cultural flexibility is modification, a craft for which the Japanese have also proved to be the undisputed masters. Whatever the Japanese borrowed from abroad, and there were indeed many such borrowings, they often skillfully integrated it into their own culture and made it fit for their specific social needs. The blending of a foreign idea with one's own, before it is put to use, also lends the idea legitimacy and ensures its wider acceptance. In Japan, the modern ideas and institutions which have taken root are precisely those which were also harmonized in this way with the indigenous culture. Tadao Yanaihara (1966:

7) was thus correct when he argued that "the intellectual capital we borrowed from the West was largely invested in opening our own existent resources . . ." When there are no precedents in Japanese culture to support an otherwise useful new idea, Japanese have also shown adeptness in inventing one. Despite its disapproving overtone, therefore, there is more than a kernel of truth in Buruma's (2003: 44) observation that ". . . [in modern Japan] some ancient or quasi-ancient customs were invented or revived to dress up modernization in a nativist garb . . ."

But the proclivity to modify applies not only to techniques and devices but to systems of ideas as well. Confucianism is one such foreign idea which constituted a core element of Japanese culture and which had undergone significant changes after it was imported from China. Whereas Confucianism in its original form emphasized the virtue of benevolence, the Japanese reformulated it, placing greater emphasis on loyalty instead (Morishima 1982: 3; Yoshino 1992: 160-162; Preston 2000: 27). Perhaps this is why it is sometimes said Japanese Confucianism is more Japanese than Confucian. The *Western Technique* in the slogan *Western Technique, Japanese Spirit*, too, can be understood in a similar sense, as more Japanese than Western.

To reiterate what has been already said above, Japan was able to modernize because of its culture, and not in spite of it; but this does not mean that there are not any elements in modern Japan which are simply not compatible with 'reason and number.' Japanese still observe some age-old Buddhist and Shinto practices which don't mesh well with science. Thus it does make sense for some to talk about 'high-tech healers and computerized cults' in Japan, and do so without a touch of irony (Picone 1998). A society does not have to completely wipe out traditional and unscientific practices to make use of modern science. Such observations also throw into doubt the argument (for instance, of Passin 1965: 484-487) that many past traditional practices and behaviors persist in Japan in modern times because of the modern conditions, or the practical necessity which sustain them in modern times. It may be more plausible instead to argue that Japanese mobilized their energy and resources to build a new, modern society when they were engaged in the modernization effort; they did not labor as much to abolish age-old practices, or completely cut themselves off from the past. In fact, the Japanese government had even made conscious efforts to preserve some of these very practices (Yoshihara 1994: 45), enabling traditional values to remain in place, specially those which were believed to be harmless to modernization even if they were not also positively contributory to it. It may be time for Africa to take these lessons to heart: the old system should not necessarily be completely obliterated in order to build a new and modern one. In fact, selectively linking the old and the well-established to the new and emerging system may be the best approach to modernization, as this would not only enhance the process, but, in time, it would even help to further consolidate it.

Africa's abortive modernization efforts were based on a plethora of imported ideas, and Africa's post-independence modernizers often sought to transform traditional culture in a fundamental way, with little attempt to incorporate the modern into the traditional or vice versa. In the end, the old was badly dismantled, and the new was not also in place. The effort itself was never ill-intended, of course, but the outcome almost always turned out to be disappointing. Japan's modernizers never sought a radical transformation of their culture in order to modernize. They saw to it that if there was a change, it was to be only incremental, often with some sort of a link between the old and the new. The case of Japan seems to demonstrate, therefore, that one can be modern and traditional at the same time, however oxymoronic such a notion sounds, and that Japan is what it is today in large measure because of its culture.

To sum up, Japan's culture did not change to fit the putative requirements of modernity; instead it was modernity which was made to serve the dictates of Japan's culture. And when there emerged a tension between the two, between what is sanctified by culture and what is presumably required by modernity, it became often the case that culture took the upper hand. Of course, Japanese had also to grapple with this issue and vigorously debate it right after they launched the modernization project. The choice made by some African modernizers, on the other hand, tended to emphasize that one could not build a new, modern society without destroying the old. And regrettably, the end result of such an effort had been a situation where the old gave way not to something new, but to nothing at all, based as the process was on the wrong assumption that the nearness to modernity was measured in terms of the distance from one's traditional values. The dominant discourse on modernity is also complicit in perpetuating such a conception.

The major lessons which could be extracted from Japan's experience include the imperatives to see culture as an asset rather than a liability in the process of modernization, to modify imported ideas and institutions and adapt them to the local conditions and to abandon imported ideas and institutions if they do not yield expected result. In other words, my reading of Japan's experience bears out that it is useful to be flexible; rely on cultural resources, link traditional values to modern ideas and vice versa, and if there is no tradition with which to link new ideas, to invent one; remember that there is no universal model of modernization; realize that society can be modern and traditional at the same time; understand that level of modernity is not measured in terms of social distance from tradition. The long overdue renaissance of Africa can be realizable therefore if we look inward to mobilize the cultural resources at our disposal even as we look also forward to chart a course of action most suitable under the prevailing circumstances. But culture should be summoned and not sidelined in the process.

5. Conclusion

Since the end of the Cold War, the relevance of culture for modernization has been widely recognized. But does this mean culture suddenly acquired a new significance after the fall of the Berlin Wall? The renewed interest comes from the change in our perception of culture, and in our capacity or willingness to express it. Increased quality and quantity of research have also contributed to the renaissance of culture. And yet, it can be argued, the change has not always been from cultural ignorance to knowledge, but it was also sometimes a shift from ignorance to prejudice, as is evident from the plethora of recent works which seek to explain the relationship between culture and development by legitimating cultural hierarchy. In light of this, it is sometimes befuddling indeed whether to celebrate or lament the return of culture. The works which pose this type of acute dilemma include Francis Fukuyama (1995), Joel Kotkin (1992) and Lawrence E. Harrison and Samuel Huntington (2000). On these specific works, I should like to remark briefly, if only to underline that there is no affinity shared between the analysis in this paper, which is also focused on culture, and the new genre of cultural explanations of development.

"[T]he most important lesson we can learn from an examination of economic life," wrote Francis Fukuyama (1995: 7), "is that a nation's well-being, as well as its ability to compete, is conditioned by a single, pervasive cultural characteristic: the level of trust inherent in one society." From this perspective, Africa's future is very dim indeed, because judging by the criteria set forth by Fukuyama, the continent represents an area where the lack of trust prevails. And there is little chance for this cultural trait to go away easily since "a strong and stable family structure cannot be legislated into existence as government can create a central bank or an army" (Fukuyama 1995: 91). Fukuyama's *post hoc* observation could be challenged in regard to issues of definition and measurement and, more crucially, on the grounds that it takes too much for granted about the direction and shape of the causal link between trust and the creations of wealth. In addition, Fukuyama does not also bother to answer the important question of why some are low-trust societies while others are not, even as he asserts that his theory of "cultural variations explain 20% of variations in human behavior" (1995: 13). It was Max Weber who reminded us how shallow in relative terms our knowledge is of the precise extent of the influence of culture on development. Weber said: "I saw no way of exactly or approximately measuring either the extent or the form of the influence of culture on development" (1958: 30). In his book *Tribes*, Joel Kotkin (1992: 4) also advanced a roughly similar argument to Fukuyama's: "[i]n the post-Cold War era, where ideology has faded and peoples seek definition from the collective past, dispersed groups such as global tribes seem particularly well adapted to succeed within today's progressively more integrated worldwide economic system." Kotkin (1992: 16) defined global tribes as "dispersed groups held together by a common culture." Like Fukuyama's, Kotkin's argument is also undermined by internal inadequacies and contradictions.

In a foreword to *Culture Matters*, another culturalist work edited by Lawrence Harrison and Samuel Huntington (2000), the latter makes a passing comparison of Ghana and South Korea in the 1960s and 1990s and asks why this pair of countries which had a roughly similar GDPs in the 1960s are so different today in their level of development. Huntington's own response to this question also reflects the substance and tone of many of the other chapters in the edited volume, as well as of the many recent works of this type: "South Koreans valued thrift, investment, hard work, education, organization, and discipline. Ghanaians had different values. In short, cultures count" (Huntington: 2000: xiii). Generally the same charges as the two works mentioned above could be leveled against this brand of argument. In relation to Huntington's more specific point about South Korea and Ghana, one obvious question which arises relates to the consistency of the impact of culture. Comparing South Korea and North Korea, one can surmise more plausibly that in this context ideas have had greater impact since both Koreas subscribe to the same culture. How else can one explain the difference between the two countries in the level of their development? Is it misguided policies or is it cultural disposition which explains the difference?

In addition to the questionable validity of their arguments, notwithstanding the scientific pretensions, another feature of the new genre of culturally-deterministic theories of development is the condescension with which societies that have not modernized are viewed, an attitude which even advance blanket apologies would do little to mute. Before opening his culturalist salvo, Francis Fukuyama, for instance, wrote: "To those who feel I have misunderstood their culture or, worse yet, said something slightening or belittling about it, I apologize in advance" (Fukuyama 1995: xiv).

In any case, Samuel Huntington has thus explained the development of South Korea (and would most probably say the same thing about Japan) and the underdevelopment of Ghana in terms of the hard work and discipline of the former and lack thereof of the latter. Even if we assume Huntington's explanation was at least partially valid in this specific case, his logic does not stand if we apply the same line of reasoning to account for the difference between South Korea and North Korea. Clearly, as indicated above, there is no corresponding cultural variation between the two countries. If cultural similarity between South Korea and North Korea could not produce similar outcomes, then how does the cultural difference between Ghana and South Korea explain the difference between their levels of development? But Huntington did not seem aware of the contradiction suggested by his statement.

The case of Ghana versus the two Koreas is interesting for yet another reason. In contrast to Huntington's hypothesis, the difference between North Korea and South Korea seems to support the hypothesis that no culture is intrinsically superior to or more congenial for modernity than another; that all cultures are good enough to accommodate and sustain modernity and vice versa; and that for positive potentials to be realized new ideas should not dismantle, but rather they should be systematically linked to the cultural givens of the society. In all of these, of course, enlightened leadership plays a crucial role. In the past, modernization theories had argued that, among other things, institution building could lead to democracy and development in non-Western societies. There was a consensus, more or less, that active involvement of the West in developing societies was needed for the latter's modernization effort to bear fruit. Unlike modernization theories, the new theories of cultural determinism do not share even this minimal optimism since "the degree to which the ability to create institutions and run them effectively is itself culture-bound" (Fukuyama 1995: 4). The question which arises, therefore, is this: are we coming full circle: from Social Darwinism, to modernization theories and back to Social Darwinism?

References

ALEGERE, E.
1973 "The Modernization of Japan and Its Limits," in *Japan and the Japanese*. Compiled by Mainichi Newspapers, Tokyo and San Francisco, Japan Publications, Inc., 52-57.

ASAHI SHIMBUN
2003 *Asahi Shimbun Japan Almanac 2004*. Tokyo: Asahi Shimbun.

BARSHAY, A.
2004 *The Social Sciences in Modern Japan: The Marxian and Modernist Traditions*. Berkeley: University of California Press.

BASALLA, G.
1988 *The Evolution of Technology*. Cambridge: Cambridge University Press.
BENEDICT, R.
1996 *The Chrysanthemum and the Sword: Patterns of Japanese Culture*. Tokyo: Charles Tuttle.
BURUMA, IAN
2003 *Inventing Japan 1853-1964*. New York: The Modern Library.
CAUDILL, W. AND H.A. SCARR
1974 "Japanese Value Orientation and Culture Change," in T.S. Lebra and W.P. Lebra (eds.), Japanese Culture and Behavior: Selected Readings. Honolulu: University of Hawaii Press, 37-89.
DE MENTE, B.L.
1994 *Dictionary of Japanese Cultural Code Words*. Lincolnwood, Illinois: NTC Publishing Group.
DORE, R.P.
1965 "The Legacy of Tokugawa Education," in Jansen, M.B. (ed.), *Changing Japanese Attitudes Toward Modernization*. Princeton, NJ: Princeton University Press, 99-131.
EDUCATION IN JAPAN
1952 *Post-War Developments in Japanese Education. Vol. I.* Tokyo: General Headquarters, Supreme Commander for the Allied Powers, Civil Information and Education Section, Education Division.
FUKUYAMA, F.
1995 *Trust: The Social Virtues and the Creation of Prosperity*. London: Hamish Hamilton.
FUKUZAWA, Y.
1966 *The Autobiography of Yukichi Fukuzawa*. Trans. by Eiichi Kiyooka. New York: Columbia University Press.
HALL, J.W.
1965 "Changing Conceptions of Modernization of Japan," in Jansen, M.B. (ed.), *Changing Japanese Attitudes Toward Modernization*. Princeton, NJ: Princeton University Press, 7-41.
HARRISON, L.E. AND S.P. HUNTINGTON. (EDS.)
2000 *Culture Matters: How Values Shape Human Progress*. New York: Basic Books.
HUNTINGTON, S.
2000 "Foreword," in Harrison, L.E. and Huntington, Samuel P. (eds.), *Culture Matters: How Values Shape Human Progress*. New York: Basic Books, xiii-xvi.
HOLLORAN, R.
1972 *Japan: Images and Reality*. New York: Knope.
HONNA, N. AND B. HOFFER
1989 *An English Dictionary of Japanese Way of Thinking*. Tokyo Yuhikaku.
IWAMA, F.H.
1993 "Japan's Group Orientation in Secondary Schools," in J.J. Shields, Jr. (ed.), *Japanese Schooling: Patterns of Socialization, Equality, and Political Control*. University Park: Pennsylvania State University Press, 73-84.
JANSEN, M.B.
1965 "Changing Japanese Attitudes Toward Modernization," in Jansen, M.B. (ed.), *Changing Japanese Attitudes Toward Modernization*. Princeton, NJ: Princeton University Press, 43-89.
2002 *The Making of Modern Japan*. Cambridge, Mass., London, England: Harvard University Press.
KAWASHIMA, R.
2005 "Edo Scholars Have Brainy Approach to Education," *Asahi*, 14 July 2005. Online Version. http://www.asahi.com/english/Herald-Asahi/TKY200507140172.htm (Accessed on 14 July 2005)
KOTKIN, J.
1992 *Tribes: How Race, Religion and Identity Determines Success in the New Global Economy*. New York: Random House.

Kuwabara, T.
1983 *Japan and Western Civilization: Essays on Comparative Culture.* Tokyo: The University of Tokyo Press.

Lewis, C.C.
1996 "Fostering Social and Intellectual Development: The Roots of Educational Success," in Rohlen, T.P. and LeTendre, G.K. (eds.), *Teaching and Learning in Japan.* New York: Cambridge University Press, 79-97.

Maruyama, M.
1965 "Patterns of Individuation and the Case of Japan: A Conceptual Scheme," in Jansen, M.B. (ed.), *Changing Japanese Attitudes Toward Modernization.* Princeton, NJ: Princeton University Press, 489-531.

Mazrui, A.
1976 "The Baganda and the Japanese: Comparative Response to Modernization," *Kenya Historical Review,* 4, 2, 167-186.
1984 *Africa between the Meiji Restoration and the Legacy of Attaturk: Comparative Dilemmas of Modernization.* Ankara: TISAMatabaacilikSanayl Ltd.
1990 *Cultural Forces in World Politics.* Oxford: James Currey, Nairobi: EAEP, Posrtsmouth: Heinemann.

McLaren, W.W.
1979 *Japanese Government Documents.* Tokyo: Asiatic Society of Japan.

Ministry of Education, Science, Sports and Culture
1996 *Outline of Education Japan 1997.* Tokyo: Japan.

Morris-Suzuki, T.
1994 *The Technological Transformation of Japan.* New York: Cambridge University Press, 1994.

Morishima, M.
1982 *Why Japan Succeeded? Western Technology and the Japanese Ethos.* Cambridge, UK: Cambridge University Press.

Muramatsu, T.
1995 *Westerners in the Modernization of Japan.* Tokyo: Hitachi Printing Co.

Nafziger, E.W.
1995 *Learning from the Japanese: Japan's Pre-war Development and the Third World.* Armond, London and New York: M.E. Sharpe.

Nagai, M.
1971 "Westernization and Japanization: The Early Meiji Transformation of Education," in Shively, D.H. (ed.), *Tradition and Modernization in Japanese Culture.* Princeton, NJ: Princeton University Press, 35-76.

Nakane, C.
1998 *Japanese Society.* Berkeley, Lost Angeles and London: University of California Press.

Nathan, John
2004 *Japan Unbound: A Volatile Nation's Quest for Pride and Purpose.* Boston and New York: Houghton Mifflin Co.

Nihon Jiten
2003 *A Kodansha Encyclopedia.* Tokyo, New York, London: Kodansha International.

Okamoto, K.
1992 *Education of the Rising Sun.* Tokyo (Unpublished Manuscript).

Oga, T.
2003 "Constructing Meiji Japan: Toward the Politics of Wakon Yosai," *Tsukuba Journal of International Political Economy.* no. 11, 21-37.

Okano, K. and M. Tsuchiya
1999 *Education in Contemporary Japan: Inequality and Diversity.* Cambridge: Cambridge University Press.

Passin, H.
1965 "Modernization and the Japanese Intellectual: Some Comparative Observations," in Jansen, M.B. (ed.), *Changing Japanese Attitudes Toward Modernization.* Princeton, NJ: Princeton University Press, 447-487.

PEDLAR, N.
1990 *The Imported Pioneers: Westerners Who Helped Build Modern Japan.* Sandgate, Follestone, Kent: Japan Library Ltd.
PICONE, M.
1998 "Science and Religious Movements in Japan: High-Tech Healers and Computerized Cults," in Hendry, J. (ed.), *Interpreting Japanese Society. Anthropological Approaches.* 2nd Edition. London and New York: Routledge, 222-228.
PRESTON, P.W.
2000 *Understanding Modern Japan: A Political Economy of Development, Culture and Global Power.* London, Thousand Oaks, New Delhi: Sage Publications.
ROBERTSON, R.
1992 *Globalization, Social Theory and Global Culture.* Sage: London.
RODEN, D.
1980 *Schooldays in Imperial Japan. A Study in the Culture of a Student Elite.* Berkeley, Los Angeles, London: University of California Press.
SAKAIYA, T.
2003 *The Twelve Men Who Made Japan.* Tokyo, New York, London: Kodansha International.
SCHOOLLAND, K.
1990 *Shogun's Ghost: The Dark Side of Japanese Education.* New York, Westport, Connecticut, London: Bergin & Garvey.
SHIMAHARA, N.K.
1993 "Japanese Education Reforms in the 1980s: A Political Commitment," in Shields, J.J. Jr., (ed.), *Japanese Schooling: Patterns of Socialization, Equality, and Political Control.* University Park: Pennsylvania State University Press, 270-281.
1979 *Adaptation and Education in Japan.* New York: Praeger Publishers.
SHIVELY, D.H.
1971 "The Japanization of the Middle Meiji," in Shively, D.H. (ed.), *Tradition and Modernization in Japanese Culture.* Princeton, NJ: Princeton University Press, 77-119.
SIMS, R.
2001 *Japanese Political History since the Meiji Renovation. 1868-2000.* New York: Palgrave.
SINGLETON, J.
1993 "*Gambaru*: A Japanese Cultural Theory of Learning," in Shields, J.J. Jr., (ed.), *Japanese Schooling: Patterns of Socialization, Equality, and Political Control.* University Park: Pennsylvania State University Press, 8-15.
TAYLOR, J.
1983 *Shadows of the Rising Sun. A Critical View of the 'Japanese Miracle'.* New York: William Morrow.
TOBIN, J. (ED.)
1992 *Re-made in Japan: Everyday Life and Consumer Taste in a Changing Society.* New Haven: Yale University Press.
TRAINOR, J.C.
1983 *Educational Reform in Occupied Japan: Trainor's Memoir.* Tokyo: Meisei University Press.
VOGEL, E.
1988 "A Non-Traditional View of Japanese Modernization," in G. Bernstein and H. Fukui (eds.), *Japan and the World: Essays on Japanese History and Politics in Honor of Ishida Takeshi.* London: Macmillan.
WATANABE, H.
1996 "'They Are Almost the Same as the Ancient Three Dynasties:' The West as Seen through Confucian Eyes in Nineteenth-Century Japan," in Tu Wei-Ming (ed.), *Confucian Traditions in East Asian Modernity: Moral Education*

and Economic Culture in Japan and the Four Mini-Dragons. Cambridge, Mass., London: Harvard University Press, 119-131.

WEBER, MAX
1958 *The Protestant Ethic and the Spirit of Capitalism*. Trans. by T. Parsons, New York: Charles Scribner's Sons.

WHITE, M.
1987 *The Japanese Educational Challenge: A Commitment to Children*. New York: The Free Press.

YAMAMOTO, S.
1992 *The Spirit of Japanese Capitalism and Selected Essays*. Trans. by L. Riggs and T. Manabu. Lanham: Madison Books.

YAMAZUMI, M.
2003 *Nihon Kyoiku Shoshi*. Tokyo: Iwanami Shissho.

YANAIHIRA, T.
1966 "A Short History of Modernization of Japan," in Seiichi, T. (ed.), *The Modernization of Japan*. Tokyo: The Institute of Asian Economic Affairs, 3-46.

YOSHIHARA, K.
1994 *Japanese Economic Development*. Third Edition. New York: Oxford University Press

YOSHINO, K.
1992 *Cultural Nationalism in Contemporary Japan. A Sociological Enquiry*. London: Routledge.

Notes on Contributors

SEIFUDEIN ADEM is a Foreign Professor in the Program of Area Studies, University of Tsukuba, Japan, and holds a Ph.D. in International Political Economy from the same university. His research interests are in the areas of comparative politics and international relations. Dr. Adem has published three books, the most recent of which is *Hegemony and Discourse: New Perspectives on International Relations* (University Press of America, 2005). His works have also appeared in edited books and academic journals such as *African Studies Quarterly, Millennium: Journal of International Studies, Journal of Modern African Studies, Journal of Contemporary African Studies, Review of International Affairs, Review of International Sociology*, and *International Journal of Organization Theory and Behavior.*

KWEKU AMPIAH is a lecturer at the Department of Asian Studies, University of Edinburgh. His publications include *The Dynamics of Japan's Relations with Africa: South Africa, Tanzania and Nigeria* (Routledge, 1997), and "Japan and the development of Africa: A preliminary evaluation of the Tokyo International Conference on African Development", *African Affairs*, 2005, vol. 104 (414). His article in this special issue benefits from interviews conducted in Tokyo in January 2004 with diplomats at the Nigerian Embassy.

GETACHEW FELLEKE holds a Ph.D. from the Graduate School of Public and International Affairs at the University of Pittsburgh. His research interests include problems of economic development and their interface with education, technology, and the environment. He is currently Associate Professor of Economics at Miyazaki International College in Miyazaki, Japan.

SHINSUKE HORIUCHI is currently President of the International Development Associates (Ltd). He was a career foreign service officer and had served as Japan's ambassador to Botswana, Burundi, Kenya, Malawi, Rwanda, Seychelles, Uganda, and Zambia in the 1990s. After his retirement from the foreign service, he served as the Special Assistant to the Minister of Foreign Affairs in charge of follow-up of TICAD II and as Adjunct

Research Fellow at the Japan Institute of International Affaires (JIIA). Dr. Horiuchi studied at the University of Texas where he received his MA and PhD in economics. He has published many papers in Japanese in the areas of African governance, NEPAD and aid to Africa. And his English publications include "Diversity, Stability, and Order in Asia," in *Social Capital and Social Cohesion in Asia*, N.T Colletta ed., World Bank publication, 2001; and "African Development and the TICADS Process," *Japan Review*, vol. 17, no. 4, 2003.

Toyomu Masaki received Ph.D. in Economics from Kobe University. Her research interests include French commercial companies in West Africa and EU-Africa economic relation. Dr. Masaki is currently Associate Professor in the Faculty of Economics, Kanazawa University, Japan.

Jun Morikawa is a Professor in the Department of Regional Environmental Studies at Rakuno Gakuen University on Japan's northern island of Hokkaido. He is the author of *Japan and Africa: Big Business and Diplomacy* (Hurst, London, 1997) and numerous articles including "Japanese Diplomacy, NGOs and the Ivory Issue" (in Japanese), Vol. 3 (2003), in the Japan Wildlife Conservation Society Research Journal. He recently presented a paper on "Japan and the Whaling Issue: The Reasoning and Power Structures behind Japan's Pro-Whaling Stance" at the 2005 conference of the Japanese Studies Association of Australia. Professor Morikawa is also a visiting research fellow at the University of Adelaide, South Australia.

E. Wayne Nafziger is University Distinguished Professor of Economics at Kansas State University, U.S.A. He is author of *The Debt Crisis in Africa* (Johns Hopkins University Press, 1993), which was nominated for the Political Economy Best Book Award given by the American Political Science Association; *Learning from the Japanese: Japan's Prewar Development and the Third World* (M.E. Sharpe, 1995); *Economic Development*, 4th edition (Cambridge University Press, 2005), and numerous other books and articles in development economics and causes of conflict.

John Edward Philips is a Professor in the Department of International Society, College of Humanities, Hirosaki University, Japan. He holds a Ph.D. in history from the University of California Los Angeles. He has taught at Tohoku University and many other universities since he came to Japan to accompany his wife in 1986. His writings on various aspects of African and American history have appeared in several edited volumes, as well as in *The Journal of African History*, *African Studies Review*, the

Middle East Studies Association Bulletin, and other journals, including several in Japan. Most recently he edited and helped write *Writing African History* (Rochester, 2005), an introduction to historical literature about Africa.

Index

www.ingramcontent.com/pod-product-compliance
Lightning Source LLC
LaVergne TN
LVHW011125300926
849160LV00008B/518
9789004152700